Pommie's Travels

By
Patricia E Sandys

The cover photograph shows Elaine Barton and Pat Sandys feeding the birds at the Bird Sanctuary, Gold Coast, Queensland, Australia.

ISBN: 978-1-9998463-9-8

Published 2019
By Phil Hadley Publishing.

CONTENTS

INTRODUCTION

In the 1950's and early 1960's I did my General Nursing Training followed by in the early Sixties with Midwifery Training. Although I enjoyed it all, Midwifery became my first love. I became a Christian, in the true sense, in 1964 and applied for missionary work in Africa but I was turned down at that stage.

After many home births I then applied to be a Senior Midwife in Southmead Hospital, Bristol. This was a training school for Midwifery and candidates had a choice of doing Part 1 for experience or completing Part 2 to do Midwifery practice.

It was at this stage I met students doing their Midwifery Training. We also had a lively Christian Fellowship so got to know many nurses. Two of these were Australians – Margaret Green and Ruth Lewis – who gave an invite to visit Australia. An English nurse Elaine Barton chose to accompany me on our trip to Australia in 1966. It was possible at that time to travel by sea to Australia for £10.00.

So let the adventure begin...

P. E. Sandys

AUSSIE DIARY

ALL ABOARD!

Wednesday 21ˢᵗ September 1966

Well! Here we are on our way sailing on the liner 'Fairsky' from Southampton. Elaine and I are in a four-berth cabin, about the size of a pocket handkerchief! We are, fortunately, both on the bottom bunks, which makes life a little easier. We are on the bottom deck, in the front of the ship, under sea level, no port hole, so we cannot tell when it is time to get up! Elaine is in the outer bunk and the waves crash against her head all night. She didn't sleep the first night but has been better since. I had very little trouble as usual! Our room mates are both married and are split up for sleeping as there are only a few double berth cabins, but they are very nice and easy going which is just as well in a confined space.

We have not had spaghetti yet! The food is good and not too greasy. Luncheon and dinner are both four course meals, so we do not bother about tea, etc. Going through the Bay of Biscay we had good weather and reasonably calm seas, for which we are both thankful, especially Elaine. We are now heading for the Rock of Gibraltar passing along the Spanish coast. We have not seen land since the Isle of Wight and what we thought were the Isles of Scilly. Today is very windy and we have already acquired tanned faces by the sea and super sunshine. Elaine has felt queasy and taken two sea-sick pills, but so far, she seems to be fine.

When we went on board at Southampton there was evidently a ship's photographer. Hundreds of photos appeared on the noticeboard and there is one of us going up the gangway. I will get a print and send one home as soon as I can. Elaine had a wonderful surprise soon after we sailed. The Steward delivered a lovely Cyclamen plant to her from all her workmates at Tadworth Court. I hope it lasts the trip – it is so beautiful – cheers out little match box cell up!

Friday 23rd September 1966

We are now in the Mediterranean Sea, as calm as a millpond. Brilliant sunshine, which is very hot, but we have fortunately got a breeze still with us to make the sunshine enjoyable and sunbathing comfortable. Our tan is progressing, but we are taking it slowly. We have been sitting on the top deck today watching the northern coast of Africa go by. The heat haze has prevented us taking photographs as we are probably a little too far off for it to look anything other than sea and mountains. Several schools of porpoises have passed us by and there is plenty of sea traffic. Gradually the clocks are being altered. We lost thirty minutes last night which was a little hard as we were very late to bed. The swimming pool is now in full use with pumped -in sea water. It is rather small and gets very crowded with the 1500 people on board, so we are withholding our energies for when it gets too hot and we need to chill off a little! We have about 400 children on board which makes life on deck extremely noisy, so we haven't slept much in the day. At night the deck is lit up with coloured lights and there are gaily coloured tables and chairs to sit by with drinks, etc. Last night it was beautifully warm, a clear night with clear waters and away in the distance we saw sheet lightning which lit up the sky brilliantly. We heard no thunder. We are going to the Pictures tonight to see 'Boeing Boeing'. I have seen it once before, I think, but never mind, it will be a laugh. On Monday night we reach Port Said. We are hoping to join a tour on land to Cairo to see the Pyramids, etc and then to motor down the Suez Canal to pick up our ship at the other end. We have just had lunch – consommé soup, Irish stew, biscuits and cheese, dessert, coffee and fresh fruit. It is funny eating cheese before dessert. Now all the food has gone down we are going to rest and sun-burn!

Monday 26th September 1966

We are now heading towards Port Said where we are hoping to dock late tonight. It is a glorious day and we have been sunbathing for most of the morning and then we played a game of Table Tennis. This afternoon we are going to sleep in the cool as tomorrow morning we have to be up for breakfast at 5am. We evidently go by coach to Cairo, then by camel ride to the Pyramids, and then back to the ship by coach sightseeing en route. I have written many letters and cards so feel I have done enough for a while. We will both have another session before we get off at Aden. Our luggage has evidently arrived on board ship as we had occasion to go to the luggage room and there it all was!

Yesterday was Sunday and it was a really peaceful day on board ship. We went to the morning service, with Communion, held in the Cinema and it was full. Most people rested quietly all day. We played Deck Quoits and Shuttle Board for most of the afternoon and saw some slides of Cairo in the evening. We have plenty of time to read and knit, but I cannot say we get a great deal done.

All the Italian Stewards etc. are very nice and always cheerful. Their standard of hygiene and cleanliness is good. We get clean bath towels every other day which is great. I have had my hair cut short which makes it much easier to manage and a lovely shampoo and set. It all took over three hours, but I didn't shrivel up! It looked good when it was finished. Even I am acquiring a brown face and arms. It is good to have some colour again. My legs do not take kindly to this type of heat and are inclined to swell, so I am keeping them well covered at the moment. Elaine's Cyclamen plant is continuing to flower beautifully. We have met some interesting people, but few going to Adelaide as yet.

Monday 10th October 1966

At present we are out on deck where the wind is whipping round, somewhere in the Indian Ocean. Elaine has been very sea sick for about eight days. I have been fortunate as one day of feeling very bad at the start is all I have had. This has given me time to help her. After leaving Aden we left calm seas behind us and struck out into storms and high seas. As there are no stabilisers on the ship the roll can be quite severe. Evidently the ship that left Southampton ahead of us, the Fairsea, is five days behind schedule in the middle of the storm. Fortunately, we have detoured slightly off course to miss the worst so we can count ourselves lucky. Poor Elaine has just wanted to die and has craved Bovril to drink and bread and butter. I have hunted everywhere but I have not been able to find any for her.

She is now surfacing again, being controlled by injections from the ship's doctor, which has produced bruises as well as reasonable results! She has eaten very little, if nothing. I am sure her weight must be going down. I feel so helpless to help her. I seem so rudely healthy beside her, but I have been able to fetch and carry and do little things like washing her face because her balance had gone completely and she could not remain upright for any length of time. Last night was a great occasion as I gave Elaine her first bath in a week and washed her hair, so she is beginning to feel a new person, clean and more comfortable again. She has two 'jelly baby' legs but is so patient and full of guts. Many people are in a similar situation, so she is not exactly alone. Praise God, she is much better now and, when we reach land, she should be fine. The weather has slowed us down a little in mileage, but we should reach the first part of Australia by Saturday.

We had about six hours ashore in Aden. The temperature was about 100° and, although we wore sun hats, it was rather too hot for us. A very barren country with little or no vegetation. The town was full of armed 'Tommies', both on foot and patrolling in jeeps. We wandered around the markets with all the Arabs trying to sell their wares. A colourful sight indeed, but you have to be quick and cute to successfully barter with them. We both bought small Iowa tape recorders, mains and battery, and I also had a small telephoto lens for my camera. We were very satisfied with our buys. We were met at the dock by Margaret Standish, a friend of mine working for S.S.A.F.A. She showed us all around the area in her Mini and then we went to her flat for something to eat and drink in the cool. That was Elaine's last meal, in fact, and she was obviously not feeling good by this time.

Our Cairo trip, a few days previously, was most exciting. We left the boat at Port Said at 7am. The ship was surrounded and invaded by little Merchant Barges displaying their wares to the people on deck, hoisting up things to sell by means of a rope and basket. We went by motor launch to the quay where we changed money and picked up our coaches – nine loads of us. We then had a three hour journey across the desert to Cairo.

The living conditions, sand huts, etc. of the little villages had to be seen to be believed. Tremendous poverty and malnutrition. We shouted out on espying our first camel and seeing children charging around on donkeys in their long robes. Indeed, it was just like the picture books of the Bible. The museum in Cairo was very interesting, plenty of mummies and historical personal belongings. Also, a mask of king Tutankhamen and all his wealth, jewels, etc. A very interesting legend surrounds him. What a laugh it was climbing on the flea-bitten camels. The ride up to the Pyramids was great fun but getting up and down on the camels was not so funny. They are very tall and rather smelly. We had snaps taken just for the record. Once at the Pyramids the heat was intense. We were taken inside one of them along dark musty passages clambering along almost on hands and knees – up and up and up wondering what was at the top. Perspiration pouring from us, we arrived exhausted to find an empty tomb in an otherwise empty room. Still, our curiosity was satisfied at least! Many women became claustrophobic and some nearly passed out and could not make the top. We all got out in one piece in the end.

We had dinner in a good restaurant by the Sphinx. Feeling more refreshed after a wash, we got back into the coach to return to Cairo. Here we did some sightseeing of the River Nile, Mosques, the Citadel and the Arabian Markets and Bazaars. It was enjoyable in a crowd, but not a place to wander alone, especially for a woman. About 6.30pm we began making our way across the desert to reach the Fairsky at the Port Suez end

Photo 1 – Elaine, David & Rosemary and me by a pyramid in Egypt.

of the canal. We were then beginning to feel rather weary as we had been up since 5am and the heat had been tiring. It was fascinating to see Arab tribesmen sitting around their camp fires in the middle of the desert land. We reached Port Suez at 9pm where we had dinner. Then we heard that our ship had been held up in the Canal and would not reach us until about 4am. We spent the night partly watching a night club cabaret where we happened to be, partly sleeping on the coach, otherwise we wandered in clusters of people along the sandy roads and beaches. I must say it was a long night. At 4am we were put on a convoy of motor launches and taken to the entrance of the Canal where we sat and waited for our ship to appear. The cheers and almost sighs of relief when Fairsky appeared. About 5am we clambered aboard where we were given a most welcome breakfast before falling into our bunks and a good sleep. An exciting day appreciated even more when we had recovered. Since leaving Aden we have not seen land. We had a ceremony put on by the younger adults as we crossed the Equator and we were all given certificates for having done so.

Wednesday 12th October 1966

The sun is shining, the wind has dropped, and we have calmer seas once again. Elaine's health is improving, and I am well. We expect to be in Freemantle, Western Australia, early Friday morning. We are looking forward very much to land, especially Elaine.

ADELAIDE

Friday 21st October 1966

We are here at last! We can hardly believe we have arrived in Australia, but it is a fact. Today is a very sunny day, not too hot but comfortable. It was lovely to be on land again. We were both thankful when we reached Perth. We had a whole morning free to go into the city. We joined a coach tour of all the sites. A small but beautiful place, clean and very friendly, and where we had our first experience of Australian life and currency. We were taken to various gardens, places of interest, and the panoramic views of the main River Swan, with the hills in the background, were wonderful. The colours of shrubs and wild flowers were fascinating; even the roses were at their best. As we had some free time in Perth we headed for a bookshop and found a guide book, which we perused to find places of interest to see.
An English corner of the city, called the London Court Arcade, was the main attraction. It was a typically Tudor arcade and good to see. Surprising how all the people off the boat found their way there! We got back on the boat about 1.30pm and once again we saw the land disappear. We found most of the passengers had spent their time eating in cafés, cups of tea and

fish and chips, but we were glad to have made the most of our visit as Perth is somewhat cut off from the other parts of Australia. We may not make it back again. The scenes have been magnificent. We continued our voyage across the Australian Bight, which has the reputation of being rough like the Bay of Biscay, but we were fairly lucky. We were late arriving at Melbourne and we thought we would not be able to see Ann McRobert, who had worked with Elaine in England, as people from Adelaide were not supposed to get off. As we docked, we saw Ann with her mother and father in the V.I.P. enclosure. Evidently her father is a top knob in nautical harbours, and he came aboard having got permission for us to get off for the night and day. Ann is working hard here in the Midwifery Department. The first thing Elaine had, with great thankfulness, on arrival at their house was a glass of milk! It was great to be in a bed that did not move! In the morning we went to the ship and collected our luggage, went through the Customs and de-contamination examination. Then Ann and her parents took us for a run about sixty miles outside Melbourne, where we had a picnic lunch in a wild animal sanctuary. We saw kangaroos, koalas, a platypus, plenty of coloured parakeets and cockatoos, and, of course, the nosy old emus who came looking for titbits. It rained and rained, a real downpour, and we had to borrow macs! Obviously, a special welcome!

After having supper with Ann, we went down to the station where we joined the other passengers for Adelaide. We were given pink badges to wear and felt like convicts. However, the immigration department have looked after us very well throughout. We then went by overnight train to Adelaide, having left Melbourne at 8.40pm and arrived in Adelaide at 9.40am. We did not sleep too well, but dozed, and the night didn't drag too much. The compartments were open and had seats like aeroplanes that moved into any position. There were quite a few children that cried. I don't think they thought much of the trip. We played Scrabble and read. We were provided with packed meals, fruit and drinks. In fact, we had no need to spend or do anything.

At Adelaide we were met by Mrs Green and daughter Margaret. We collected our cases, our heavy luggage is following in a few days, but we saw it all at Melbourne, so we know it was on the boat with us. Then we were taken for a brief drive around the town, saw Elaine's hospital, which looks very grand from the outside. She is commencing work on the 31st October, but she has to confirm it with them when we get sorted out a little. She will be a Staff Nurse for six months, then become a Sister automatically. Adelaide is beautifully set out with gardens, but we have only seen a little so far. Blackwood, where we are staying, is about ten miles outside the city, rather like a residential area of England, with plenty of garden and space between houses. We had a good long sleep and got up around 10am! We had brunch and then we were taken for a drive. This time of year, their spring, is obviously the prettiest time, as all is green, new and bright. In a few weeks it begins to dry up and go brown. We then went up to a place called Mount

Lofty, the highest hill surrounding Adelaide, which is mainly flat. We had a superb view over the city and out to sea. The fields are a mass of yellow dandelions, which look like large daisy flowers, and others a blue flower called 'Salvation Jane' – it looks similar to our Bluebell fields. We are going to have a slide show tonight. Margaret is on night duty but has nights off just now. The Greens attend a Methodist Church, were originally Baptists from London, and have close connections with the Church.

All our post was awaiting us on arrival. We have little time to get Christmas presents off for home, but we have been rushing around and have mainly finished now.

The temperature varies between 65° and 85° but it gets colder at night time. Elaine has had her interview; her Matron seems very nice and helpful. She will start work on November 7th, a week on Monday, on a Surgical ward, which she is thrilled about. Her uniform to start with is fawn with small white caps, brown shoes and stockings.

Our banks took a while to settle but are now fine. We are still awaiting our trunks, but they should come soon now. I am not having a successful time job-wise or in any other way! I lost my best ring on the train coming down, then my handbag was stolen in Woolworths with all the lovely new things I had given me in it. There are no Maternity vacancies going for me at the moment, but I know the good Lord must have something for me here. We have been good girls and had our chest X-rays done, as migrants to the country, and they are quite clear.

We are busy flat hunting, so we will be tramping around once more tomorrow. We played tennis all the afternoon. It was good fun and we enjoyed it, but we were jolly stiff afterwards. All the plays and films on in town are just the same as at home – Oliver, for example. People don't believe in walking anywhere, so we class ourselves big walkers. They wear out more tyres than shoe leather, I think! We are so thrilled being on land again, but I expect our seafaring days are not finished yet. We went to a slide show of Canada and Hong Kong yesterday, which made us realise just how much there is to see.

Saturday 5th November 1966

We have been rushing around this week. At first it was disappointing, frustrating and rather hard on the feet. I guess we must have covered miles with two days of trudging the streets. In the end we got so fed up getting nowhere. Elaine hired a car for two days – a Volkswagen. We both enjoyed being at the wheel again and trying to remember the rules of the road – such as giving way to all traffic on the right, very confusing at times. In the two days we clocked up 110 miles just around the city. Elaine is the only one legally able to drive, as my licence was stolen with my handbag. We went round many flats but nothing was suitable in the area; some the right price had double beds, but they would not be practical especially with different jobs and shifts! We found one we liked, no price given initially, but we took it. Nothing else compared favourably; a semi-detached bungalow at nine guineas a week. Two bedrooms, fitted carpets, sitting room, large kitchen, laundry and bathroom. We had the use of a lovely garden kept by the couple, Mr and Mrs Rowe, who live next door and own the property. We have our own entrance and a driveway of our own, overshadowed by an enormous palm tree. Here we are settled at 11, First Avenue, Forestville, Adelaide. We have now got all our luggage unpacked and it was intact except two of my mugs were broken. All necessary things are provided such as a washing machine, fridge, iron, toaster, electric frying pan, all cutlery, crockery and saucepans. In fact, sheets are about the only thing we have to provide.

Our next quest was second-hand car hunting. We spent an entertaining afternoon going round large dealers. We learned much about cars in that time! We considered all kinds but decided on a Simca 1963 model, in excellent condition in body and the engine sounds sweet. It's green in colour with a column gear change. The cost £335, but we got it reduced from £395, which wasn't too bad! Mini cars were too small for the bush travel and not enough boot room. It is difficult to acquire a fit second-hand bargain, but the Simca has a large boot and seats which can got back flat to make a double bed which we considered better than tenting.

We are at present 160 miles north of Adelaide for the weekend with Ruth Lewis, another girl who worked with me in Bristol, England, on her parents' farm, acres of wheat land being harvested. Last night we herded cattle and sheep by car –

Photo 2 – The flat in Adelaide.

Photo 3 – Donna, the car, second-hand but sturdy and strong.

rather bumpy! On the way here we called to see Jan Gibbs, one of Elaine's friends at Clare. She now has three children, curly redheads aged 2 years, 1 year and 7 weeks – quite a handful. We have been picking fresh oranges and lemons from the trees, which was great fun. We hadn't seen them growing in groves before. Tomorrow, Sunday, we return to Adelaide and Elaine starts work on Monday.

Friday 11th November 1966

Elaine has completed one week now in work and seems to be enjoying it very much. The uniforms are well made, and they have plenty of staff, much more than she had in England. Being on the 8th floor of the Children's Hospital she has a beautiful view over the city, especially with some of the sunsets we get and all the lights at night time. The Staff seem very friendly and she has met people from Great Ormond Street, the Doctors that is, and she has straight shifts with a 40 hour week, which is easy to cope with.

I have had a few days at the unmarried Mothers and Babies Home – the Kate Cox Babies Home. I sensed this was a clear leading from the Lord. After spending an evening at the Adelaide Bible Institute and mixing with the students, this Home was opened up to me and I knew it was for me. I am working with one other Midwife. We relieve each other, and sleep in approximately every other night. I love it, but it is a disadvantage sometimes having two homes, and having to leave Elaine alone at least three nights a week. As Senior Midwife I am in charge of the Hospital and being my own boss is simply wonderful. We wear white dresses and caps, nice and light for the hotter weather, and they look clean and fresh. The Staff are all very friendly. It's more like a home than a Hospital. The pregnant girls are a mixed bunch from different areas and cultures. They run the place completely, working very hard. The other part of the Home is used as a Children's Home and they are fairly permanent residents through one reason or another. The other Sister is a lovely girl, has only recently completed her Midwifery training, but she seems very competent. The Home is run by the Methodist Church and depends on voluntary contributions to keep it going. It is a wonderful Christian Centre and most of the staff are committed Christians. We have fifteen minutes of prayer every morning and we all have to attend. Each of the Sisters take it turns to lead the prayers, so my turn will be soon, which will be good for me, and a real challenge. We have named our car 'Donna' and she is running very well. We have mastered the gears pretty well now. We both have a day off on Wednesday and we plan to take a picnic to the beach. Today is Christmas Pageant Day in Adelaide – sunny periods with showers. Elaine went by coach with the kids from her Ward, while I went with Mrs Green and Margaret. I did not have such a good vantage point as she did, but I managed to get some good shots with my camera. It's Adelaide's big day of the year to herald the arrival of Father Christmas. Rather like our Carnival, only the theme is for children with nursery rhymes and animals etc. It was full of colour and very enjoyable with plenty of bands including the Scots bagpipes!

Tuesday 22nd November 1966

While I am busy working at the Girls' Home Elaine is basking in the sun at the flat. The weather is now very hot with temperatures up to 103° - therefore frequent changes of clothes and showers! Although it has been in the 90's all the week, it is a very dry heat, and the Hospitals are mostly air-conditioned. Ours isn't particularly, being only a Home. The car is burning hot when you get in and you can hardly bare to touch the handbrake or steering wheel. Walking across tarmac roads is a headache as you usually get stuck in the melting tar. Most days we go swimming in the sea near where I work and it really is wonderful. We spent our first days off together yesterday, and so began our sightseeing tour of Australia. We went about 100 miles south to Port Elliot, where there are lovely sandy beaches and surf breakers. We had a swim to cool off and picnicked on a lovely quiet beach. In the evening we walked across the headland and on the other side was a Cornish type rocky coast. Making our way back to Adelaide we saw a beautiful sunset across the waters. I forgot to mention our wildlife sanctuary where we spent some time watching the activity everywhere, Black swans, all sorts of Ducks, Storks, Pelicans and Herons, some of which had vivid colourings. This was Donna's first run for any distance, and she did very well indeed.

Everywhere is now beginning to look brown and dried up, and already bush fires are burning and sprinklers, in gardens and parks, are working overtime. Tomorrow night we are going out for supper and then give a slide show at a meeting.

Sunday 4th December 1966

The Christmas cake is now made ready to go in the oven and I am busy doing a Christmas pudding. It has been rather cold weather for the last few days. As Christmas draws nearer we are planning our off-duty arrangements. Our last day off we went about 60 miles out of town to a large National Trust forest and reservoir known as the Para Reservoir. This was our first encounter with unsealed roads but Donna managed very well – we only had 20 miles of rough riding! We visited the wildlife sanctuary to say 'Hello!' to some more kangaroos. Saw some baby ones wriggling inside their pouches.

We hardly saw a car or any other people all day. The temperature was in the 90's so we returned to the beach before the sun went down and had a swim. By then we were hungry. Elaine got stuck in a traffic jam the other day in Adelaide. It took her ¾ of an hour to cover four miles. Certainly not too common in Australia. We have a long weekend off next week so we will travel further afield and make our first attempt at sleeping in the car.

Friday 16th December 1966

While I am working Elaine is having a laze in the garden. The weather has been somewhat English and, by all accounts, 20° lower than average for this time of the year. However, it is now in the 70's again. Yesterday was car cleaning day for Elaine as the car was filthy after our weekend in the country and loads of sand was cleared out from the inside, probably piling into her from the beach. It was a great weekend. We went to the York Peninsula, a piece of land that doubles back in the sea almost opposite Adelaide. We went right to the foot, covered about 70 miles of unmade road, not seeing another car all the time. It was a joy to see one when we did! The car put up with the conditions well. We had a picnic supper by a little fishing jetty at a bay called Marion Bay just as the sun was setting across the miles of the bush country and it was flat, very dry and barren. Not really beautiful scenery but interesting to see and full of tremendous unspoilt peace. We moved around the coast to Edithberg, where we slept in a caravan park by the sea. We put the seats of the car down and it made a comfortable bed and we had a good sleep.

The following day we went up the coastal bays, sandy beaches, but they were not very suitable swimming beaches and waters. On our way out we did pass a Cacti Farm so we had a good look. Every kind of Cacti one could imagine and old tree trunks carved into shapes of animals and birds. It was cleverly set out with walls made of old pieces of brick, china and crockery. A plant growing in an old kettle. It was good that we came upon it.

Christmas is getting underway now with decorations going up everywhere. Elaine's ward is decorated as 'Carols', one end of the unit as a Christmas pudding and the other end as a turkey. They had a party on Thursday, given by the bookmakers, who provided beautiful presents. At my Hospital we had a party a week ago. A concert was performed by various different artists. On Thursday we went to a party given by the English girls working at Elaine's Hospital, held at one of physiotherapists' flat – good food, music and entertaining conversation. Last night Elaine went out to tea with a teacher who had arrived from England the same day by air. I had to work. Margaret is holding a party tonight and I shall be joining them. Elaine will pick me up after work at 9.30pm.

Mr Green had a mild stroke this week so it will be good to see him and know how he is getting along. On Sunday we go to 'Carols by Candlelight' which is held in the park by the Torrens River. Elaine's Matron has given her Platform tickets and official car sticker, so we have really gone up in the world! And we should have a good view – it was most kind of her. On Monday we shall both be off again.

Thursday 29th December 1966

Christmas has come and gone so quickly and once again we are about to begin a New Year. Our thoughts have been very much with our homes and families. Between us we have had nearly a hundred cards, so England and our family and friends did not seem so very far away. Well – what about Christmas in Australia? Very strange! I guess it's the weather mainly. There is something about the darker British weather that makes the decorations and festivities seem brighter in contrast. It keeps the family in the home, where they should be, I feel. Our decorations were similar to home but drier and not so much greenery, and much strong sunshine. There is a general exodus to sports and beaches over Christmas but the spirit is there nevertheless – and the turkey and Christmas pudding goes with them. On Christmas Eve Elaine was working late, so I picked her up and we took a brief ride around the town admiring the trees. A local brewery had a good display of illuminations on the back of the river – Santa, reindeers, seven dwarfs, miniature fairground. Quite a crowd watching them too. We then went home and opened our presents which we had saved like good girls. On Christmas Eve the temperature was 108° and the thought of a large Christmas dinner was quite nauseating. However, after opening our presents, we went to Midnight Service and back to bed by 2am. I was up at 5am and to work at 6am, and then Elaine at 7pm – a short night! It was followed with such a beautiful day we didn't mind getting up. Many children were already in swimming using their new rings and floats.

It was grand at work; all the girls were busy getting everything ready. Santa came and gave gifts to all the children and they were so delighted. The dinner was good with all the usual things. We went off to the Greens for the evening and sank with relief into familiar home surroundings. All their relations were there, and after yet another feast, we had a good time singing carols and opening presents from the tree. Tired but happy we then fell into bed.

Next day we had half days, so we took ourselves to the beach where we swam and sunbathed. Then off home to have our own Christmas dinner. We had bought a tiny chicken, very tender, and had a lovely quiet evening by candlelight, eating, listening to records, and generally taking it easy.

The shops and general facilities close down for Public Holidays from Saturday to Thursday so you can imagine the problem of catering. The fridge is a must here. We even have to keep our face cream in it as it melts anywhere else. Nights are spent mostly sleeping on top of the bed instead of in it, but it's only when the humidity is up that we suffer. One thing that made us chuckle was that the postman blows a whistle when he puts mail in your letter box by the gate and it sounds funny going all the way down the street. There are no boys delivering papers. They are rolled up into a roll with an elastic band around them and then they are thrown from a car into the front garden as he drives slowly along the street.

At the moment we have an enemy in the flat – mice! They, or it, chewed up several boxes of matches, so the man next door, Mr Rowe, has set a trap. I am now awaiting the bang, but neither of us will have a look, least of all Elaine, who is there even more than I am. We are going to have a quiet few days off before going on a long weekend trip down to Mount Gambier, about half way to Melbourne. We are going for two and a half days and we have done nearly 3,000 miles in Donna already.

Tuesday 10th January 1967

Elaine has been very busy at work – plenty of car accidents and head injuries over Christmas – but we have been fairly quiet at the Kate Cocks Home and the girls and the children have had a good time.

We went on our long trip weekend going southwards to Murray Bridge, Talum Bend and down the coastal road to Kingston. Here we spent the night in a caravan park. As usual, traffic was light, roads fairly good, and parts of the coast really beautiful. We developed a slack fan belt, which ran our battery down, so we got the other campers to push us. The countryside around here is very flat and not very enlightening. On Friday we reached the little fishing village of Robe. Here we bathed and played tennis – a beautiful sandy beach. We travelled around all the Lakes, through the town of Mount Gambier and spent the night on a caravan site in Port Macdonald. We sleep quite well in the car and use the showers and toilets of the caravan site. We carry plenty of food and clothes and we use an ice cooler for perishable food and drink as temperatures are in the 90's. Travelling so far on dirt roads makes the contents of the boot get completely dust bound. We carry a sack nose bag on

Photo 4 – Robe Sands, South Australia.

the front radiator of the car which cools on route. It looks funny but most people do it! On Saturday we went to Mount Gambier – an old dead volcano. There is a mass of trees and green fertility – such a contrast to the dry barren flatness of the surrounding land. The Lakes lie in the craters, one bright fluorescent turquoise blue, one green, one brown, one dark blue. We climbed up to the peak and had a lovely view all over the area. At this time we noticed the third and fourth gears were slipping a little. We then began our return trip leaving Mount Gambier going northwards to Penola Naracorte. We left the road after about 20 miles to try to find Lake Mundi. Then in the middle of nowhere the gear cable broke. We have got the second gear only so we chugged along very slowly, singing the miles away. Being Saturday the garages were all closed but we managed to get as far as Tarpeena, a little village, and knocked up a mechanic at a break down garage. Saturday was his half day. They had no spare parts, so we were stuck there from 4pm Saturday until 10am Sunday. Certainly a new experience to sleep in a car perched over a pit inside the garage! The bill for overtime charges was tremendous. In fact, he swindled us completely. Nevertheless, he insisted we join him and his family for an evening meal, even though we did not need to, and then he charged us for it!

We did the return trip to Adelaide, 250 miles, with no first and second and reverse gears, just third and fourth. She ran well, praise God. The only tricky part was going up over the Adelaide Hills in a queue of traffic. Elaine suggested I drove and I was having visions of stopping on the hill and remaining there with piles of traffic behind! We did stop off at Naracorte and went round some fascinating caves with stalagmites and stalactites, but actually the Tantanoola Caves near Mount Gambier were our favourite although they were both interesting. If you have a strong imagination you can create almost anything out of the shapes around.

We arrived home at 8pm, very brown and sunburned, satisfied with the trip despite the breakdown. Donna is now in the factory being repaired and we only have to pay half of the bill as she is still under warranty. She used little oil and petrol which was very satisfactory.

Tuesday 19th January 1967

It is a very humid day today - 94°. Elaine has just stewed some plums and apricots. People have been so kind. We have more than we can get through quick enough. On our last days off we spent them quietly at home. We took a picnic to the National Park where we played tennis for a good part of the day on courts surrounded by gum trees with the noisy laughter of the Kookaburra. Tuesday we spent on the beach swimming and playing beach ball. Wednesday evening we managed a quick swim in the sea before dashing off to a Bible Study. The car is now back from hospital. The gears are now fixed but she is still a little difficult to start. All the electrical system has been checked and we have been informed all is well.

Photo 5 – A Kookaburra bird.

We receive gas bills monthly and on average we use one dollar a month which is very good. We have received letters from several couples we met on the way over and they have all had trouble getting settled in their new surroundings and employment. One couple in Tasmania have found it so lonely there they have already moved. The majority of the country towns are very small and remote, and the population limited unless there is industry in the area.

Sunday 29th January 1967

There is quite a wind blowing today, yet it is still warm. We have had some beautiful sunsets recently. We have never seen anything quite like it; we hope the slides will do them justice. Last night we went to the Pictures, second time since arrival and very good films. One was called 'Clarence The Cross-Eyed Lion'. The story is basically about a lion, cross-eyed and so unable to hunt for himself. He was taken into the care of the Animal Doctor, who has many other pets. The animal shots from Africa were very spectacular.
We are off once more to Victor Harbour, a seaside resort about 50 miles south of Adelaide – going on the beach and a good walk around Granite Island which lies off the shores. We are also going to an International Missionary Conference so we shall be sleeping in Donna in the grounds tonight and coming back on Monday. We have been on the beach quite a lot this last week; it is super to be doing so much swimming again.

It was Australia Day on Friday; flags up everywhere. Yet another Public Holiday for the people which means yet another day off work for all.

We do miss the lovely dainty flowers quite a lot – the snowdrops, daffodils, etc. We have plenty of colourful plants, but they are all very bold in shade and size. We are going to a slide show of the Antarctica on Thursday.

Sunday 12th February 1967

It is a beautiful day. There are ants everywhere and in the larder, so Elaine cleaned it out this morning. We keep tinned food in the fridge, in fact, pretty well everything. We went to Morning service then had our lunch of steaks, vegetables and melon. The Conference was marvellous, and we really enjoyed ourselves. There were people of all shapes, colours, types and ages, but the bond between us all was so terrific. We slept in Donna as usual.

A Bishop from Africa and the Archbishop of Sydney, Marcus Loane, took the Bible Study. During the week the weather has become increasingly hotter. Our day off was on Monday and the temperature was 102°! I became very energetic, much to Elaine's dismay, but she came with me around the Zoo. Every time we passed a sprinkler she stood in it clothes and all. We were soon passed caring, and very thirsty, so we went down to Brighton Beach and had a lovely swim in the sea, which was so cool and crystal clear, all blue and calm. What a relief!

On Thursday Elaine went to spend the evening with Audrey Dunn from her Hospital. I have changed my job as the demands upon me at the Kate Cocks Home are rather high. I must say I am very sorry to go and leaving the girls is a real wrench. As my new job is next to the Children's Hospital we will be able to go to work together by car, and also, I shall be in the flat every night instead of living there every other night.

We will be having five days off at the beginning of March and we are going up to Port Lincoln. This is a great fishing and whaling town, situated down a peninsula north of Adelaide. The fish they produce from there seem to be mostly tuna. Donna is going for another service on Monday after doing a good 5,000 miles. Happy Birthday to my sister, Diana, at home in the U.K.

Tuesday 21st February 1967

On reflection it was very hard to leave the girls at the Home, but I was very pleased to deliver Sue's baby before I left. I had a personal chat to all of them and many were upset and deeply challenged personally. I felt I was letting them down, but it is now time to move forward. Sue is coming to stay with us until she gets settled in a job. She wants to do Nursing. Margaret had a Caesarean and a stillbirth, all very unfortunate, but she is taking a job with a family out in the Outback. Adalene has been very challenged by the Lord and has repented of what she has done. Pauline is too enthusiastic about spiritual things so may not last too long, I think, but time will tell. Joanne is quietly searching and I hope to keep in contact with her, that she will come through to know the Lord she needs so much. Elaine seems very depressed and low and I feel concerned whether she is going to contract something.

Sue is now with us and I was overjoyed when she accepted the Lord as her Saviour. It has made quite a change in her and she is so happy. We are going to start a Bible Study in the flat soon so that we can get down to some teaching for those that need it. Sue is now going to work as a Nursing Aid at an Elderly People's Home – I think she will like it.

We are borrowing a fan for the flat from Audrey while she flies to England for a holiday. This will help cool down the place somewhat and lessen the need for so many showers. On our day off we had a lazy morning, then went up the Barossa to Tanunda Seppeltsfield. This is a German part of the State – the towns are spotlessly clean and the people fresh and well groomed. The countryside is cultivated in a European manner with small fenced fields. The slopes are covered with vineyards – wine-making is their industry and livelihood. We went over a Vinery and saw the large vats, distillery, etc. and the huge casks of sherry, port and vinegar. The remainder of the grapes goes to make Cream of Tartar and fertiliser. We had a few samples of wine after our tour and we were given a small bottle to take away, also a pamphlet with all the information. There is definitely a tinge of autumn in the air at night time now.

Friday 3rd March 1967

Elaine and I have just been down to the beach and had some chips! The idea was to have some fresh air and a walk, but the wind seemed to blow right through us. We soon got back into Donna for warmth again. Autumn is in the air at night, but the days still reach the 80's, but comfortably so. We went to the Engel Family Concert last night which we thoroughly enjoyed. An Austrian family of nine, who play several different instruments each. They also did some Tyrolean dancing. Something after the style of the Trapp Family Singers. It made quite a change to hear some good music.

The flat is full of the flowers from the bouquet I was presented with from the girls in the Kate Cocks Home. I treasure it tremendously. Elaine was given twelve huge bunches of grapes; we wish we could send some home, where you never have the chance of so many, so cheaply. Elaine went out with Kathy Godlee, her Surgical Supervisor, the other day, had a picnic dinner and picked some blackberries. It was a lovely day and she got a big billy full! She was afraid of snakes in the long grass but she didn't meet any!

We have had some rain so things are looking a little greener again. We head for Port Lincoln on Wednesday until Sunday, so we hope the weather holds good for us, and the car also – she seems to be running well. The break will do us good; we can do with it at this time.

Sunday 12th March 1967

We have just returned from another 1,000 mile trek. We left
Adelaide on Wednesday afternoon, went north to Port
Broughton and Port Pirie, about 140 miles. We stayed at our
friends, the Lewis's home and had a good night's sleep. They
have such a rambling old place, a farmhouse style, one always
feels very much at home. On Thursday we travelled on to Port
Augusta and then down to Whyalla and Tumbey Bay. Whyalla is
a large industrial area, the fourth largest town in South
Australia. It mainly provides a fishing industry like all the places
around these parts, but here they also have a steel and iron ore
refinery. We ate lunch there on the beach – it was very windy –
and then supper at Tumbey Bay. There is a distinct ruggedness
around these places and a strong smell of the sea and fish. We
arrived in Port Lincoln about 8pm and all the lights were shining
around the bay as we wound our way down the hill towards it.
It is a fair-sized town and a fishing port, after the same idea as
some in Cornwall.
We took a walk down the floodlit jetty and watched the tuna
boats unload. The sky was very clear and the sea very calm –
peace everywhere. There was more activity at night and there
were quite a number of people moving around the streets – a
strange occurrence, as most towns are more like ghost towns
at night. We stayed with Sue's parents for the night which
made an interesting evening. On Friday we continued around
the peninsula – the middle parts are very green and fertile. We

stopped off at Sue's sister's farm and it was lovely to be in the country again. This is a rich wheat farming area. We had lunch at Coffin Bay, a tiny fishing bay with lots of little wooden houses on stilts – all very quaint – and a fine pebbly beach with plenty of our friends, the seagulls.

In season, this is apparently very popular for a holiday, but when we were there it was so lovely and peaceful we could have stayed a few days. In the evening we reached Elliston on the other coast where we saw a lovely sunset and sky. All the roads were dirt tracks, which made it very hard going, and the noise of driving on it is inclined to give you a headache after a while! We ran into a sand well, where the sand is deep, and we did a fair amount of skidding!

We reached Elliston about 10pm, could not find the caravan park, so pulled in by a sand dune just by the sea. Nobody disturbed us and we slept well in spite of it being a hot night. We woke to a bright sunny morning and a view of beautiful surfing waters. After a leisurely breakfast we hit the dirt track northwards once again. At Talia, 40 miles on, we drove off course to see some caves. The rock formations and colours were very interesting. We climbed down a cliff into a type of pit with an open low cave leading to pounding surf. The surrounding land was all sand dunes and flat, dry country. On the way back I drove the car over a boulder and jammed the car. Then as we pulled up the back tyre hissed to a flat state. Although we had seen no one for hours, a young fellow came

Photo 6 – Elaine at the entrance to the cave at Talia.

along and between us we changed the wheel and got the boulder out by jacking the car up on two jacks. We were filthy after our endeavours but continued our trip merrily enough. God is so good in providing all we needed.

Tuesday 14th March 1967

To continue! Then we made for Streaky Bay, but not many miles had passed before we heard an odd noise, but then it went! Then we smelt rubber! We got out to find that the tyre we had changed, which had a new tread, was sizzling in the heat. We drove slowly to Streaky Bay, where as usual on a Saturday afternoon everything was closed. We helped ourselves to the air pumps in one garage putting needed air into the tyre. We then went down onto a shell beach and ate a late lunch. The young fellow who had come to our aid pulled up in his car in search of petrol, so we all picnicked together. About 4pm, the tyre still holding, we set out for Port Pirie about 260 miles away. We did not think much of Streaky Bay by the way; everyone was so disgruntled with life. About fifteen miles out of the town the noise returned and we found the tyre tread had split in half in one spot. We had to drive on it as the spare was still punctured. It was slow progress and we waited for a loud bang as we proceeded along.

Ten miles further on we came to a small village – two houses! A petrol pump stood outside one house so we hopefully stopped. Two young boys came to our aid. The tyre tread had peeled off except for about a foot. So, they mended the puncture and changed the wheels back again. The boys belonged to a family of seven who ran a Post Office, telephone exchange, garage and farm. The parents gave us some coffee and offered us a good wash as we were delightful to behold! They were so interested in us, being Pommies and from the outside world, you would think we had come from the other side of the moon. I guess they do not see many people. They asked us what London looked like, what the latest fashions were. They charged us nothing. Feeling more secure we sped across Highway 1, now a made-up road, arriving in Port Pirie at midnight. We crept into the Lewis's home and fell into bed exhausted but happy, feeling we had conquered the hazards of the Bush. Donna herself ran beautifully. Mr Lewis got us a new tyre on Sunday morning before we returned to Adelaide. I have now started at the Memorial Hospital but I am not as happy as with my girls, but time will tell! It is 89° today and this is supposed to be the autumn!

Saturday 25th March 1967

A happy Easter to you. I hope you have some nice spring flowers to decorate the house. We picked a few Dahlias from the garden, deep pink ones.
We had a wonderful day off on Monday. We went down to Victor Harbour where Kathy Godlee, her mother and sister, had a cottage for the Easter holidays. We took a picnic dinner and

went to a long sandy beach at Goolwa. It was too fresh to swim so we enjoyed cockling, or should I say, learning to do so! Digging your bare toes into the sand, standing in the receding tide, when you feel the cockles you dive your hand in and pull the cockles out. I, of course, had to find a crab, which bit me for my pains. Everyone thought it was very funny! Actually, I bled quite a bit.

We then went across on a little car ferry boat to Hindmarsh Island. On the island we tried our hand at catching Yabbies – these are like large prawns or small crabs. You lay down a net containing a piece of meat, then wait. Patience is a virtue, they say, and we needed it! This was done at the end of the jetty, which is the best place. So, what did we get? One! I suppose it was better than nothing, but good fun, though. I had a couple of days off this week with a mouth full of ulcers and boils. I only needed a bit of sleep and rest, a chance to unwind. Now I am fine again. Hallelujah! Donna now has a slow puncture in her tyre. We are surviving by having it pumped up every two days. We hope to have it mended this week.

Yesterday they had a Good Friday appeal for the Children's Hospital. One of the T.V. channels moved into the Hospital with all their gear, a room with 20 telephones, taking over the third floor. From 7am until midnight they broadcast from the Hospital to raise some money. Some of the children took part and enjoyed the excitement. The Easter Bunny came round and gave out Easter eggs.

We are very quiet with babies coming at a reasonable rate – seem to be having twins – and they are all lovely. I put my foot down about propping bottles on babies in the nursery and insisted it was wrong, but many of the Staff practise this. The Charge Sister was not pleased when I refused to comply. One of the Labour Ward Sisters is from Latvia originally and she has an intense dislike of British people. She practised medicine in her home nation, but here in Australia she is not allowed to. This seems a waste of expertise. I would have thought professionals could be tested to see what they can and cannot do. Later next week we are hoping to go up to the Barossa Valley again, to the Wine Festival and Gala Day.

It is now beginning to get freezing at night and hot water bottles are coming out of hibernation! The cold is not wet like home, but very dry and penetrating and I am very pleased I brought my sheepskin coat – I am going to need it.

Monday 3rd April 1967

We thought autumn had arrived last week, but not on your life. Today has been really hot again and we had three swims and a picnic on the beach. It was great to relax; our days are normally so full. Elaine has just worked a long spell before days off, because of Easter holidays, so she was very tired and spent a quiet day on Friday with a sore throat. We went for a short drive up into the hills and up Mount Lofty to see the so called 'fallen leaves' of autumn, but of course, there are no such things as we understand them. On Saturday Elaine was off duty and is now feeling so much better. In the evening Margaret Green and Elaine made a foursome and went to the Wine Festival and Carnival in the Barossa Valley. I was working, unfortunately, and could not make it this time – it was rather a disappointment. Apparently it was a beautiful evening and it was held in the open air Oval. Quite a colourful sight with German dancers in national costume – the Valley Queen was crowned by the Rhine Wine Queen, flown especially for the occasion from Germany. Elaine and I went to see the film 'Those Magnificent Men In Their Flying Machines'. It had a wonderful cast and we had a good laugh. Elaine, who is not usually amused by comedy films, was very amused by it. It made us rather homesick, especially her, as it was filmed at the White Cliffs of Dover and gave us some aerial views over the Kent countryside on the flight from London to Dover.

Wednesday 12th April 1967

Having just recovered from a sore throat Elaine fell by the wayside with an 'Aussie wog' (Australian bug). I took her home, and she had to take it easy for a couple of days. She even had a temperature. She seems rather low these days. I do trust she is not heading for something worse. We went up to the National Park and picnicked, had a short knock up at tennis and that was about it. She was getting tired quickly.

Anyway Matron is promoting her early, so she is now a fully fledged Sister. So, she is wearing white shoes, stockings, cap and white terylene dresses – it looks very smart. She also received the bill to go with her increased salary, all of 30 dollars' worth (£15).

Had Donna serviced again today and collected her tonight. We got a new tyre to replace the one we lost on our trip to Port Lincoln – safe again!

Elaine is sick and obviously something is wrong. Dougie, a friend from England, came to see her, but it was obviously the wrong time. On Friday we were helping at the Church Fete but, after work, Elaine went home to bed. The leaves are gradually turning brown, but the temperature is in the 80's again – crazy weather. Let's hope we do not get any wogs (bugs).

Tuesday 18th April 1967

Elaine remains unwell and it has transpired she has picked up a virus infection, so she is now in the sick bay of the Children's Hospital. She has Hepatitis, inflammation of the liver. It is comparatively uncommon in England, but much more common here. Perhaps the heat and lack of rain has something to do with it. It makes you feel so rotten, of course, and, as with any inflammation, it is rather painful. She will have to be on bed rest for some time. She is very infectious and so cannot write any letters, so I guess I will do them for her. This means I shall have to have an enormous injection to try and protect me from the same disease. It will be at least two months before she works again.

Wednesday 19th April 1967

Sound advice from Elaine – do not get Infective Hepatitis – it is very sore indeed. Evidently it has been coming on for four weeks, which would account for the depression and tiredness she had been having over that period. Now she is flat in bed in the sick bay of the Hospital looking at Reader's Digest. She has a fan to keep the air cool, lovely red roses on the bed table from Kathy Godlee. Through the crack in the blind the Parkland outside is very green, shining in the hot sun - 86°. The traffic, in fact, any noise, has been bothering her at first but gradually it is getting easier to cope with. She had known blanket baths and bedpans before, so she accepts them readily enough. Great strides today, she was allowed out in the chair, but was glad to return to bed – she is very weak. Everyone seems proud of her deep yellow 'tan', but I think she would prefer to be without it. Fortunately, the nausea and sickness stage has passed and she is starting on the junkets and marmite sandwiches! One of the Nursing Aids comes from Sussex originally and she has promised to buy Elaine some lean ham from Sainsbury. All her colleagues pop in to see her during the day which cheers her up and helps the day along. Another week to go before six weeks convalescence at the flat. It is the slow uphill climb now and she really is so weak. She is more cheery now, but frustrated in wanting to write so many letters, read so many books, but has not got enough 'oomph' as yet. She was able to have her little radio, the only thing which cannot be fumigated from bugs, but what a blessing it has been. Yesterday she listened to a BBC recording from London; Richard Dimbleby taking a tour around Hampton Court.

Saturday 22nd April 1967

Still in Hospital – not so yellow now – her eyes are clearing but she still has a chinsey look about her. She is definitely more cheeky again – able to move and breathe without pain. All pills have gone except night sedation, but not allowed out of bed yet as she is not strong enough. Now Elaine has a round diet of eggs, ham, junket and yoghurt; drinks consisting mostly of pineapple juice, water and Bovril. Fluid charts are now dispensed with. I have just had my injection, all ten mils of it into my bottom and it feels decidedly sore. Elaine had her hair washed. It was practically standing up on its own.
I am jogging along at the Memorial Hospital, but I am not very happy in the job. Too much pettiness and some of the methods are not good. I am afraid propping bottles on babies which I was advised to do I definitely refused to carry out. On the labour wards we never do deliveries and, as there are some Sisters who 'rule the roost' you do not have much look in! We are a mixture of different nationalities, many have been here for some years. Funnily enough I get on better with the German

51

than with many. I must say I miss the girls very much. I have been in to see them, creeping in at night, as I have been refused permission to see them. I suppose it's wrong but I do miss them. Anyway, through the grapevine I hear all the news; some of them have been very ill and I was able to see them in hospital. The others are fine and should be out soon.

Elaine is much better, her liver is not quite its normal size, the jaundice is fading. Plenty of the Staff keep her company but I know how depressed she is at times. I hope to call in at 3pm after work before I return to the flat.

Monday 24th April 1967

It is another crisp clear day – truly autumn. The Park, opposite the Hospitals, looks lovely with its fallen leaves. All the trees in the suburbs are beautiful colours, browns, reds and golds. The peace of Sunday yesterday is now shattered by the bustle of Monday's activities. Elaine is her normal colour again – no aches or pains – eating everything again in small helpings, and Infectious Nursing has now ceased. She watched T.V. for an hour. No walking though, so she was wheeled in the wheel chair which she considered very degrading. She was able to see some of the British news – e.g. the oil disaster down the Cornish coast with all the birds being rescued and washed. It must be a terrible mess and heart-breaking to the local people. Then back to bed and a deep needed sleep. At least she can read now so I have taken in some books and things to occupy her. She keeps up with English 'Woman' and 'Woman's Own'. The question of salary has cropped up and if Elaine gets no 'Worker's Compensation' she will have nothing for two months. We are looking to the Lord in faith and we know He will work it out in the end. Elaine's health is more important than money or savings. The flat is expensive but we have decided to keep it on. It is really home to us and we shall miss it when we have to move on.

Thursday 27th April 1967

Elaine is now up for one and a half hours every day, so yesterday I took her for a ride in the chair to the Park. It was lovely to get her into the sun – one certainly does appreciate the freedom of the outdoors when one is tied down. We got up and down some pretty steep ramps with the chair – it is a good thing I am strong! It was such a joy to take her out and see her so much stronger. I shall try again today before I go on duty lunchtime. We can praise the Lord that Elaine has her Worker's Compensation claim, so we can breathe again regarding the flat. The Doctor, who looks like a dear old Grandpa, had added a postscript in her favour, they really do spoil her. She now has the record player and all the records, so she is playing them all day and sending everyone dotty!
There has been no rain for weeks, so the water hoses are going flat out all day. Looks funny to have water sprinkled on autumn leaves. It was ANZAC Day on Tuesday – similar to our

Remembrance Day – with parades, etc. It was a Public Holiday and so was more like a Sunday. There was a march of the Forces, and the War Veterans with all their medals on their chests, strutting along with backs erect.

Monday 1st May 1967

We had a lovely day yesterday; the temperatures were high and I wheeled Elaine to the Park. The grass was a rich green and the Rose Gardens vivid in colour. We had an hour in the sun which was very nice. The Doctor is very pleased with her and says she has made a rapid and good recovery, considering her severe sickness with extreme jaundice. The liver blood tests were very satisfactory. She is going to watch 'The Seekers' tonight on T.V.

I am doing well at the Memorial Hospital and I have become used to the place. It seems a popular place with the patients. The Matron is very young and charming. I think I have been fortunate to have off-duty, which has enabled me to be with Elaine as much as possible. I think I shall go on night duty soon and apply for permanent nights so that I can be home in the daytime and see to things easier.

Thursday 4th May 1967

Elaine is now allowed up and about so we went for a car ride yesterday to the sea and had a good smell of the ozone down there taking it deep into our lungs. Elaine was glad to get back to bed. The temperature has been in the 80°s again for the last few days. Margaret's brother Philip was late for school today and cycled into a lamp post, so he too is in the Children's Hospital with concussion. Audrey Dunn is taking Elaine for a short drive this afternoon as I am on nights. Elaine is hoping to come home next week. Mr and Mrs Rowe will get her meals for her while I sleep. I can see to breakfast and evening meals.

Wednesday 10th May 1967

Elaine is home again and so pleased to be so. I must say it is great to have her home again after being so long on my own. I had nights off Monday and Tuesday so I slept Monday morning then collected her in the afternoon. The Hospital have offered to have her back if I cannot cope but I am sure we shall be alright. They certainly have been so kind to her and were very sorry to see her leave. It's clinic on Friday for liver function tests. She is steady on her pins now, but two hours up is enough. She has a settee in front of the fire so that she can lie out flat during the day as she wishes and she sleeps from about 10pm until 9am when I arrive home from work. Yesterday we had a drive out into the hills for a couple of hours. The trees are beautiful and the sun makes them shine brightly. Elaine misses driving Donna; she will have to be patient. The lounge gets beautifully warm but there are no plugs in the bedroom so it's warmer in the living room.

Wednesday 17th May 1967

Eight days have now passed and Elaine is much stronger. She now does some odd jobs and we go out for longer runs in the car. She gets deep depressive periods. I only wish I could do more. She is so good and patient. She does sleep much better since being at home in the peace and quiet. We decided to hire a television which is tremendous company for her; we both relax and sit down as we are both terrible at sitting still! With the winter ahead, at least we shall have more rest. Elaine is making me quite envious getting on with her scrapbooks of Australia, and yesterday she drove the car which was great. We went up to the near by Wildlife Sanctuary where we stroked the kangaroos – you could walk among them and I had quite a boxing match with one. There were plenty of koala bears too, mostly snoozing up in the trees. As there were so many children around on school holidays, we gave up any chance of cuddling them. We hope to return later to have another chance. The day before we took a walk along the water's edge. It was a beautiful day and the sea was calm and clear.

Photo 7 – A boxing match with a kangaroo at the Fauna Animal Reserve in South Australia. They are very strong!

Thursday 25th May 1967

Elaine is now back to normal weight and should be back at work within ten days – only mixing with too many people tires her rapidly. Yesterday Elaine, Sue and I went to Morialta Falls where there are waterfalls and a beauty spot four miles out of town. Trees were lovely but only a trickle of water as there had been no rain. As the gum trees lose their bark at this time of year they are shining white. We climbed up the steep cliff a little way but Elaine could not go too far – but the exercise did us all good. Sue and I went on a little further and had a lovely view from higher up. Then we went out for a Chinese meal in town before going home. We saw the Walt Disney film 'Thomasina' by Paul Gallico – his usual excellent form and we did enjoy it. They are going to do a series of old Musical Films this winter so we do hope to see some of them, such as 'Chocolate Soldier' and 'Student Prince'. We spent the morning and dinner with Muriel Leggatt on Tuesday – she was the English State Enrolled Nurse that looked after Elaine in Hospital. I have just had nights off which was great, but, as usual, they are over far too quickly. It is getting very cold, a dry penetrating cold, which is worse than anything we have at home. Even I feel it so that is saying something! Sue is now happily working as a Nursing Aid in an Old People's Home and she really loves it. She is a transformed girl these days and really enjoying her fellowship with the Lord and others. She would like to do her training but I am wondering if she could manage her S.R.N. Or am I being too ambitious?

Elaine has now completed one scrapbook and made a few fancy coat hangers which Sue taught us to do. When I get up at four we shall go for a stroll along the beach.

Sunday 28th May 1967

Elaine has just received her oil painting from England and so she will enjoy doing it as an extra hobby.

Last week South Australia celebrated Guy Fawkes Day. It seems strange it isn't on the 5th November. Of course, there is far less danger of fire at this time of year. With our complaining of the cold we were pleased that they have been the lowest for seventeen years. Trust us to get it! I have Nights off tomorrow, thank goodness, and Tuesday we shall go out into the country. I must say the Hospital is better at night, but I shall not be sorry to leave. Perhaps we may go to the Wildlife Reserve again and cuddle our koala bears. Elaine said a programme on T.V. yesterday showed the birth of a kangaroo. It is an inch long at birth when it crawls out and up into the pouch by instinct. There it remains until it is fully grown.

Sunday 4th June 1967

Elaine is now fit again, depression is going. The temperature went down to 38° the night before last; getting too low for comfort! Elaine cleaned Donna so now she shines bright. Francis Chichester arrived in Australia successfully and there was a big welcome for him. Rule Britannia! With all the unrest in the Middle East we are glad to have come through the Suez when we did spending time in Cairo and Aden.

Just now the shrubs are flowering, the roses blooming and chrysanthemums out. The colour is still in the leaves that are ankle deep in the garden and they blow into the kitchen through the back door.

Monday 12th June 1967

Today is a Public Holiday to celebrate the Queen's birthday – they seem to have more days of this kind than we do. Monday we took a walk in the park and had a go on the paddle boats on the river. We felt quite stiff the following day! Tuesday we drove to Murraybridge and walked down by the Murray River. The trees were magnificent in golds and browns, and we were surprised by so many Willow trees in this dry land. I suppose it would be good to mention the Murray River area is very famous for its fruit farming, a very precious export of South Australia. The fruits are mainly citrus in variety and they are previously treated against fruit fly.

Wednesday we went to friends for a slide evening. Thursday Elaine polished Donna while I slept. Night duty is still about the same, we are not very busy so the nights pass fairly slowly. On Friday Elaine and I, with two other girls, went to see the film

'Fantasia.' Such a delightful film. The music and fantasy were so wonderfully combined.

Saturday Audrey arrived and they went for a walk down the beach. We went to a Doctrine Class yesterday. The sermon was an audio-visual on the disunity of the Middle East and the division of Jerusalem – very interesting!

Saturday 17th June 1967

We saw the first of the musical films 'Maytime' – very old, sad, romantic but utterly charming. We went out to Port Adelaide today and walked around the Docks. Some of the yachts were very colourful and expensive. There were a few English ships in port: two cargo boats from London called 'Alpha' and 'Beta' and a large tanker from Liverpool. Port Adelaide is the really industrial area of the city; factories, power stations and the more slum type of housing conditions.

Yesterday we went down to Cape Jarvis, south of Victor Harbour. We had a snack lunch at Victor Harbour, which was quiet being off season, but there were several honeymoon couples around. We sat in the sun and got quite burned. Going across country on the usual 'B' class dirt roads the car ran well in spite of needing new plugs. We have done 10,000 miles in Donna already, so she has performed very well.

The scenery was green and fertile and there were plenty of hills. We saw plenty of newly born lambs and calves, but it seems the wrong time of the year for the little mites. As we reached the coastal peninsula the land became browner and flatter. All there was at Cape Jarvis was one house, one lighthouse and a fishing jetty with a rocky shore. A pretty deserted spot you might say! On the way back we called at Hindmarsh Waterfall. We did a lot of climbing before we reached the best spot to view the falls. I climbed down some steep ledges and my camera went at one place. I only hope nothing will happen to it! It was good to see some water on the falls – you usually have to use your imagination!

Elaine's blood tests are normal so she should begin work on Monday. She will have a light job for two weeks which will give her a chance to gradually get back to normal ward pace again. They really have been so kind to her.

Thursday 29th June 1967

This week we saw our next musical 'The Chocolate Soldier' which we very much enjoyed. We continue to have bright days, no rain, an extraordinary winter. In the garden we have oranges, mandarins, lemons and bananas growing. It still seems strange to see them growing on trees. On Sunday we have a guest service at the Church. We visited the Greens the other night and had supper with them. Mr Green seems almost his old self after his stroke, though his speech remains slurred somewhat. It is always great to go up and see them and have a break from work and its associations. We have been having a series of Bible Studies at the flat each week going through St

John's Gospel. A few of the girls from the Kate Cocks Home have been coming and its great to have them. Sue is going to do her S.R.N. in Adelaide and I trust she will get on well. Jo has been to a Houseparty Camp from Church and she has become a Christian. She is doing so well. I can really praise God for her progress since leaving the Home. Pauline worries me a little, as to start with she was very keen and seemed to really know which way she was going, but now she is wandering away and being led again into worldly temptations. Margaret has written from her job as Governess and she really is so much happier and really thinking about Spiritual things which we discussed when we were together.

Thursday 6th July 1967

We are sitting by the fire watching the film 'The Desert Rats' and having a lazy evening. As usual I must have something to do so I am busy knitting my sweater. We had a chicken supper which was very enjoyable. I met Elaine from work and we drove out to Adelaide Airport where we watched the planes gleaming in the sun all looking very colourful. Night Duty is getting me down a bit so I am glad to have time off and just relax at home. Elaine is now back on full duties and has been very busy – obviously making up for lost time! The mornings are, at present, dark and very cold. I know Elaine finds it hard. We now have postal codes. Maybe Britain will get them eventually!

Monday 17th July 1967

Bucketing down with rain today. Yesterday we had a dust storm – nothing quite like it really, but it didn't affect us very much. Elaine is busy cooking stuffed heart with stewed vegetables. I must say stews are very good.

We are planning to leave Adelaide in September, heading for Perth in a couple of months. We originally had not anticipated a return to Western Australia, but we hope to see something of the spring which is supposed to be so outstanding over there. We hope to be back in Adelaide for the last week of November and the first week of December before going down to Victoria and Tasmania. This is because Sue and Jo will be confirmed then and we intend to support them in this. Also, they will be baptised having never been done before.

We are on the verge of a postal strike because of wage disputes and because they don't want to work Saturdays and Sundays. Our latest film in the musical field was 'Brigadoon' – a tremendous story and we loved the music though not all of it was familiar.

Sunday 23rd July 1967

On Wednesday we saw 'The Merry Widow', then on to Bible Study. Then on Friday we went to a film evening and a Choir Performance given by Adelaide Bible Institute. We enjoyed it, but the sermon being rather long we got numb sitting down!

Elaine cleaned the flat yesterday while I slept as usual. Then we had the girls round in the evening. We gave them a slide show, had a good old sing song and plenty of eats. Elaine watched the British Open Golf the other day hoping to see Vivien her brother, but no luck this time. The postal strike is now off so at least there will be no delays in the mail. Both Australia and New Zealand do not seem very pleased with Britain considering entry into the Common Market as they will lose 75% of trade. Makes you wonder if there is any contentment and happiness anywhere, doesn't it? We have some more trouble with Donna's plugs – a proper indigestion! But it was soon rectified. We now have a petrol shortage as the petrol tank drivers are on strike and all the city service stations are sold out.

Tuesday 1st August 1967

We have now given in our months' notice as in a month we shall be off to Western Australia to work for two months. We have decided to leave our trip to Tasmania to later on. If we don't leave Adelaide in the spring we shall reach other parts of the country all at the wrong times. For example, the centre in the heat of the summer or Bushland in the rainy season! Elaine seems to be prone to colds at present, but so far I have escaped remarkably well. I am getting tired so I shall be glad of a break. I shall not be sorry to leave the Memorial Hospital now. It is all rather boring really. We are getting quite excited about our 1700 mile trip and we are busy packing all our stuff in boxes.

Sunday 6th August 1967

We went to a Repertory Production of 'The Cross And The Switchblade' at the Arts Theatre last night. It is all about a wonderful working of God among the slums of New York. It was extremely well acted and the theatre was overflowing with all types of people from Beatniks and Rockers to sedate older people.

Today we went to see Barbara, one of 'my girls'. We are so thrilled that she has married the father of her baby Gillian and she has asked me to be her Godmother. It was a responsibility I reluctantly took yet felt it was right, in spite of the vast distance which will divide us on my return to England.

Monday night we have Bible Study. On Wednesday we hope to see our next musical film 'Showboat'. It is a long time since I saw it so it will be good to hear the lovely tunes again.

On Fridays we usually go to Senior Fellowship at Church. It is for the over 21's and we generally have some very good discussions or outings. Well, must get back to work!

Friday 18th August 1967

We have had a very wet day here in Adelaide and the ward maids told me with glee that they are sure a few snowflakes fell. A little did, in fact, settle on Mount Lofty a few days back. Last Friday we went to the Fellowship Dinner and had a beautifully tasty four course meal. 'Showboat' was very good, just as I remembered it. Thursday we had a snack Chinese lunch before Elaine was off to work. Tonight I am taking the Bible Study at Church so I have plenty to occupy my mind. Our packing is still going on and we shall be leaving the bulk of our stuff with the Greens who have very kindly offered to help.

Saturday 26th August 1967

The blossom is coming out on all the trees and we really feel that spring has arrived. There is a lovely almond blossom at the front of our flat. We took a drive around the Adelaide hills and admired the colours. Not so spectacular as the orchards at home, but because everywhere is so dry and barren, it is all rather beautiful. Yesterday the temperatures went up to 73° and the bite has gone out of the air.

Monday evening, we had our last Bible Study and one of Elaine's friends, Lynn Shelton, and a Sister from another Hospital brought along her guitar and we had a good old sing song. On Wednesday we went up to Blackwood for the evening, spent some time with the Greens who are well. The Group from the Blackwood Methodist Church, who have always made us so welcome, asked us to join them for their Bible Study on Wednesday for the last time. We had a wonderful time of fellowship with them and I know we shall miss their hospitality. In fact, when we arrived they had provided a farewell party – such a surprise! Most of them are middle-aged yet we always feel part of their group.

On Thursday evening Mr and Mrs Rowe came in from next door and we showed them some slides of England, which they very much enjoyed. Elaine made a macaroni cheese for the occasion and garnished it with several things. It was much appreciated which pleased her so much. I had the job of making all the cakes and some scotch pancakes which seemed to go down very well also. In the evening we went round to Kathy Godlee's home and saw slides of her tour of New Guinea and all the natives. Elaine and I have restarted our 'keep fit' exercises, with much groaning and a certain amount of stiffness. I must say you do feel much better afterwards, but I wonder how long it will last.

There is a terrible water shortage in many places. At Port Pirie they have been hand feeding the cattle every second day through the winter, so goodness knows what will happen in the summer months. Tasmania are on rationing already, and they fear for their electric supply too.

The brakes seized up on the car yesterday and the only way you can move is to reverse first before proceeding. It can be very embarrassing in traffic, which I found out the other day. When I stopped I had to go back and ask the car behind to move back first. They were mostly, if not all men, and they regarded me rather pityingly, but moved anyway. Elaine got stuck at six sets of traffic lights in a row, so people were not very pleased with her by the time she arrived home. I am off to Melbourne tomorrow to meet Chris Smith off the ship. She is only docking there a few hours on her way to New Zealand. It will be great to see her, even though sleep will be a scarcity to manage it! Well, I had a good time with Chris and Peggy and, of course, we hurriedly caught up on all the latest news. They were very surprised to see me and I was able to join them on the 'Northern Star' for lunch.

Thursday 7th September 1967

It has been such a hectic few days, we hardly know whether we are coming or going. We have just started on our journey and we plan to call upon a friend of Elaine's, Jan Grimm, her husband and family at Clare for lunch today, but we were so weary that she persuaded us to stay the night. They are a lovely family and it was a real pleasure to spend time there. They have three little girls, aged 3 years, 2 years and 1 year old and all very well behaved. They have all inherited the auburn colouring which both John and Jan also have.

We will leave for the Flinders Ranges tomorrow morning. Donna is well loaded but her health condition is excellent, at least to start with anyway. In the boot we have water, food, petrol, a tow rope, shovel and sack. On the back seat two cases, two sleeping bags, four rugs, first aid kit, a lamp, candles, matches, Kleenex tissues and a pile of maps. We must look a comical sight.

We had quite a job getting the flat cleaned and our trunks packed up again. Mr Green took all our luggage to their home to store until our return. Elaine went with him with the station wagon piled full, with the doors having to be left open which was fairly worrying when climbing the steep hills.

We have sent off our Christmas post for England. What a time to have to think of Christmas! I must say I am relieved to have finished night duty for a while and to have left the Memorial Hospital. Elaine was given a lovely send off with a farewell party and they presented her with a big book about Australia and made a special cake for the occasion. She will miss them all I am sure. We went out to evening dinner on Friday night to a lovely middle-aged couple from the Church. The food was delicious; shrimp cocktail, soup, chicken dish, knickerbocker glory and coffee. Thoroughly and wonderfully spoilt! They have a lovely Labrador that looks like Elaine's brother's Kandy.

PERTH

Sunday 17th September 1967

Safe and sound in Perth. We arrived late on Thursday, happy and healthy, tired and filthy! The trip was comparatively uncomplicated. We left Clare on Friday morning and headed northwards for the Flinders Ranges. It was very exciting to be on our way at last. The land got flatter and drier as we drew nearer to Hawker, a fair-sized town, where we managed to get a hot cup of coffee and a cold salad and then we wandered around for some exercise. It was then we came across Geoff's

Headquarters of 'The Overland Tours'. He was the one who used to leave his Landrover in our drive at the flat, a great friend of the Rowe's. He was away.

On leaving Hawker we gradually crept into the hills, mountains and green grass – we nearly go crazy over green grass, it is so rare - and trees. We made our headquarters for the night at Wilpina Pound in the middle of the Ranges. We found a nice spot amongst the trees and made a camp fire. It was a beautiful warm, clear evening and the moon was really bright. There were many other campers and caravanners round about, but not directly on top of us. It was quite a performance getting the car ready for sleeping as we had to move the suitcases from the back seat first. The sleeping bags were really cosy for these fresh spring nights and it meant that we could turn over without losing all the warmth and bedclothes! Getting up the next day we decided to go for a hike. We walked several miles before we started climbing St Mary's Peak, 3,900 feet high. We didn't go right to the top, just to the 'saddle', a flat piece a little way below the summit, and the view was splendid. It took about two hours to climb, but it was well worth it. None of the rivers were flowing or the waterfalls running as the rainfall had been non-existent. About 2pm we moved on and found a spot to camp for a late lunch. It was here we said "Goodbye!" to the handbrake of the car. When we pulled on it, it came away in our hands and a few screws fell out. It proved no problem except that we had to remember not to try and pull it on and to park on a level!

During this meal we realised that summer must be coming as the flies were a real pest. We drove on into Blinman, through pretty country – on a road that was more like a switchback. We went through many floodways, none of them had any water in them, which was probably a good job. There were only a few houses, a shop where we got our thermos flasks filled, and an old hotel. It was formerly an old mining town and the copper mines could still be seen. We took a short drive off the main road where we saw some emus and birds of prey.

The light was failing but we continued through the Gorge to spend the night at the place called Parachilna. This place, on the map was printed in large letters which made it seem bigger and more important. However, we found ourselves on hot, dry, dusty plains again and arrived at the town at 7.30pm. The so-called town consisted of a few houses, a school and a hotel, which was full of men so we decided to push on thinking we would never get a meal there! Just as we turned to go the proprietor came out and said we could park in the back yard to camp for the night. We were given an evening meal with the men and had free use of the bath and toilet. Elaine managed to pull down the shower curtain and we revelled in the bath. We had a hot drink before getting into our bed and had some interesting chats with some of the farmers, long distance drivers, etc. The owner of the hotel was of Scottish origin and he proudly played the bagpipes to us when he learned from where we came. We had to smile because all the pictures on the wall were of water and sea, etc. Perhaps a comfort for them to look at when they have no water at all!

We had breakfast the following morning in the company of a pet kangaroo. Then we headed back to Hawker via a different route with the mountains in the distance en route.

We stopped for morning coffee which we had in a dried-up river bed. Just outside Hawker we came across a notice to some caves. We found them eventually at the top of a hill amongst some rugged red cliffs. In the cave were some Aboriginal paintings and inscriptions which were fascinating. There were two university students there doing research for the museum all the way from Cambridge during their vacation. They were photographing and doing a thesis on them.

After dinner we drove to Port Augusta, passing many ghost towns that were marked on the map but were only ruins, mostly from the old mining days. Just before reaching Port Augusta we made a brief detour to another beauty spot – a green fertile gorge with overhanging rocks, rather tempting with photography.

We reached Port Augusta about 4.30pm and found a caravan park. We dug out some Sunday clothes and made for the showers. There was quite a queue, as a crowd of school teachers had arrived from three days without seeing water, coming down the centre from Alice Springs. Elaine and I decided in the end to share a shower which was much quicker. We then went to Evening Service followed by a good meal at the road house. On Monday morning we got stocked up with food etc. for the next stage of our trip.

It was the first and only overcast day we had, but the roads were bitumen and straight, so travelling was easy enough. We called in to see the farm people who had mended our tyre on a previous trip. They remembered us too!

We arrived at Ceduna that evening, a fishing port and a centre for the 'Flying Doctor' service. We took a walk along the jetty before retiring to bed. We parked in the caravan park – the showers were a bit cold here!

Tuesday we filled up with petrol, water and bread before leaving for our trip across the desert – 300 miles of rough corrugated road to Eucla, just over the border of Western Australia – what an experience! We drove about 100 mile stretches each, and the sun was scorching. The concentration needed in driving made it tiring trying to avoid, at least, a few of the potholes. In spite of the roughness of the road we kept the car going at 40-50 to avoid too much vibration. We stopped at Nullarbor, which was just a ranch station. Here we refuelled and had a picnic lunch, with the flies! We had a game with the beach bat and ball to save us getting too stiff. The afternoon drive was even worse – the road was indescribable, so much red dust making visibility poor at times. Dust coming up through the floor of the car covered everything including us. Elaine's hair was dry and stood on end and my hair changed colour completely. We were filthy and the boot inches deep in dust.

We made quite a few acquaintances en route as you pass the same cars and caravan trailers time and time again. We had camped together at Ceduna and Eucla. On one occasion, when we had run over a boulder, we had got out to look for any damage, four people stopped to offer help! Fortunately, all was well, but when we reached Eucla for the night, there were several cars limping in with broken springs, suspension and exhaust pipes. There was virtually no water at this stop because of the shortage, just a primitive toilet with a sack curtain. We camped here on top of a hill with all our other 'dirty' travelling companions. The hill overlooked a long line of white sand hills. We spring cleaned the car as best we could, and then lit a fire for a hot meal.

The next day we had another 400 miles to go to Norseman, our next stop. Only 112 miles of this was on unmade roads – you can imagine our delight on reaching bitumen again. We felt as if we were floating on air – it was so quiet!

We camped for the night at Norseman where we indulged in long, hot showers, and washed our hair. We felt like new people and all pure again! Norseman was the first civilised and populated place we had come to and was again a mining town. On Thursday morning we left for the 500 mile trek to Perth. The roads were excellent throughout, the day warm and sunny. We did a little sightseeing in Kalgoorlie – the first, and still, gold mining town. We went around the museum and saw all the specimens of the mineral wealth of Australia. We also stopped at Coolgardie to view all the old mining equipment, the pioneer medical wagon, etc. – just like the western films.

The countryside was gradually becoming more colourful with the spring flowers, but we were a little early for the full splendour. Our journey to Perth was from then on straight enough, except for the car becoming very noisy. We had evidently damaged the exhaust pipe at some stage. It is still intact, but will have to be replaced shortly, as we sound more like a fire engine!

I forgot to mention our meeting with Madam Emu and about six little chicks who crossed our path in the bush. We tried to track them down for photos but didn't manage it. All the car doors are jammed with the vibration, and only one door works well. Still for nearly 2000 miles we had no problems and Donna purred perfectly, so we cannot complain.

We arrived very weary at 10pm at Swanbourne where Dougie, Elaine's friend, shares a house with four other Nursing Sisters. We fell into bed ready for a good night's sleep but with the engine ringing in our ears. Friday morning we hosed and scrubbed the car inside and out. In the afternoon we went job hunting – we begin work on Tuesday at a small General Hospital in the southern part of Western Australia, 116 miles south of Perth, at Bunbury. In fact, our address will be c/o Bunbury Regional, Clarke Street, Bunbury, Western Australia. After finding a job and going through all the palaver of registration, we visited my second cousin Paddy, as he is a Master at a public school near Perth. Feeling hungry we had a meal at Perth Airport before returning to the flat. Saturday morning we did all the washing, and then took Dougie up to King's Park for coffee before she went on duty at lunch time. In the afternoon we took a stroll around the university and a short drive to the National Park and Mundaring Weir in the Darling Ranges. In the evening we went to the Pictures and today, being Sunday, we have had a quiet day. We went to Church in the morning; since then, we have been sitting in the garden writing letters. We are off to Bunbury tomorrow and back to work.

September 1967

We left Perth on Monday afternoon after going to the Simca works to collect a new exhaust pipe and silencer, and we are carrying them on the back seat. It is going to be fitted on Tuesday when Donna goes in for a service.
We then called to see Dr and Mrs Dale, who were at Tadworth, Surrey, and they were so pleased to see us. Elaine spent the afternoon searching for Christmas cards and I searched for trousers! Then we left for the pretty coast road drive to Bunbury. The Hospital is fairly large, brand new in every way. There are five floors to the building and it serves all the south-west corner of the state with facilities for operations, both major and minor, children's work, maternity, general medical and surgical cases. The casualty is super in every way, it will be great to work in it. Also, they have a good intensive care unit.

I am starting on Maternity but will be moving around the departments every two days so that I know the layout of the whole hospital. Elaine is busy nursing adults, which she finds very strange being so long with children. We hope to have two days off together soon so we can see the beautiful spring wild flowers, which have a good reputation over here. We have already seen some, which were very delicate and colourful. To see fields and woodland covered with Arum Lilies was something very out of the ordinary.

We went to visit Picton Pioneer Church, which was built in timber about 125 years ago by the first Pastor. There will be celebrations there on Sunday with the Bishop of Perth presiding. He used to be Chaplain at Great Ormond Street Hospital when Elaine was in training there. The weather was very hot when we came, but it is changeable at present. The beach is long and, with beautiful white breakers on the sea, just right for surfing. We hope to start the summer swimming again next month. We will have two days off a week and work either 7am-3.30pm, 2.30pm-11pm or 10am-7pm – at least there are no broken duties.

I just thought I would add some mileage of our trip over here:
Leaving Adelaide – 55931 – round Flinders
Monday – Port Augusta – 56449 – left bitumen
Tuesday – Ceduna – 56761
Wednesday – Eucla – 57092 – reached bitumen road – 57248
Thursday – Norseman – 57551
Arrived Perth – 58090.

Tuesday 3rd October 1967

Elaine is getting accustomed to Adult Nursing again and is finding it all less strenuous than children. Moving about so frequently becomes confusing, but at least it makes one more adaptable. I am, at present, spending two days in theatre, which I am not overjoyed about! My birthday went off very quietly but I enjoyed it. Elaine took me for a meal, we chose our steaks and helped ourselves to all the trimmings. Quite a good place with plenty of atmosphere. We hope to have two days off next week for our long trip, so we have done several small local ones instead. We went to the Shell Museum, which was delightful – it makes one quite enthusiastic over collecting shells. The next day we went along the seashore and found some pretty ones for ourselves. We went to our first 'Drive-In Cinema' in the evening and we saw 'Lilies Of The Field' with Sidney Poitier. You drive in parking in rows facing the enormous screen. The loud speaker is placed inside the car window so that you have the sound satisfactorily.

Donna, the car, was a little sick after her service but we were thankful for the new exhaust as the fumes we were getting on the old one made us sick within five minutes of starting off! Blow me, the next morning she had a flat tyre. They soon rectified that as it was a faulty valve. On trying to start the car we then could not get a whimper from her – so back came the garage men, who proceeded to tow her back to the garage. Apparently a young chap had filled something up with oil that should have been empty. At last she is running well, in fact, so quietly we could hardly believe it.

Elaine did better than me on the income tax rebate forms, but anyway it was a sizeable amount. The forms are huge that you fill in, but they seem more comprehensible than the English ones. We went to the C/E Church on Sunday – in actual fact, it is a Cathedral, something like the monstrosity at Guildford. The service was high church so I do not expect we shall go back. The weather is not quite warm enough for swimming yet we hope it will be soon.

Thursday 12th October 1967

As Suez is now closed we have to rush our Christmas cards through to get them off in plenty of time. We went for a short spell around the coast leaving on Sunday at midday – rather later than planned! We had lovely sunny weather throughout and the countryside is looking so green, very refreshing after the flat dryness of South Australia. There are plenty of forests and tiny caves. In fact, timber is very valuable in these parts and is one of the main exports. There are hundreds of wild flowers of different types and shades. We went on down to Margaret River, where the actual mouth of the river is, where we found beautiful white sands and huge clear greenish-blue surfing waves. There were quite a few skin divers around doing some spear fishing. Then we took the cave coast road which was gravel, but quite passable. We called in at Hamlin Bay, another unspoiled area. We spent the night in Augusta camping ground having taken a scenic drive around the most southerly point of Western Australia, which is a rugged headland covered in creeping red flowers. Leenwin Lighthouse was on the tip and an old water wheel used by the Pioneers. It is at this point that the river with its fresh water meets the oncoming tide of sea water – and this was when I fell into the mud swamp!

Augusta stands at the entrance of the Blackwood River and there is a good panoramic view over the deep blue river to the white foaming sea shores beyond. On Monday we visited some caves called the Augusta Jewel Caves. Beautiful rock formation stalagmites and stalactites and a lake at the bottom, which when lit up with coloured lights displayed some fascinating reflection. We called in at a place called 'Deepdene', which is one of the first pioneering farmsteads set in strange grounds with a huge limestone cliff on one side and the shining white sand dunes and turquoise sea on the other. The fields were full of Arum Lilies. Then we went on to Alexander Bridge, branching off the bitumen highway down the Stuart Highway. This was a real pot-holed road, and you could not avoid them, as there swamps on either side. One car went into one swamp and we tried, with the help of another car, to tow them out. This was the christening of our tow ropes – but it was to no avail – one side of the car was held down by the motion of the water seeping in under the doors.

Donna's footbrakes had decided to seize up on us by this time, so we had to rely on the gears mainly, but the timing seemed wrong too, so that each time we slowed down we stalled. However, we proceeded towards Pemberton, through the valley of giants which is a huge forest of Karri trees, and all the yellow wattle bushes were coming out and the smell was great. Wattle blooms are rather like gorse or mimosa from a distance but are yellow with a red fleck in the petal.

Just near Pemberton there is a huge tree called the 'Gloucester Tree'. With prongs fitted through the tree all the way up 210 feet with a lookout at the top. I managed to climb up alright, but it was a hard pull, and I took some photos from the top over the surrounding countryside. Elaine said she felt safer at the bottom and I think she was right. As you stood in the hut at the top it suddenly swayed and nearly threw me over, and I was hobbling for a day or two as a result of it.

It was half-light in the evening when we took the road to Manjimup, the town known as being the gateway to the tallest hardwood trees in the world. We had two scares when Elaine was driving, when two kangaroos decided to hop across the road right in front of the car and, having no footbrake, it was rather nerve racking. Fortunately, we did not hit either of them. I would not have said much for Donna if we had! Elaine is an excellent driver and I think God was looking after us as well. We spent the night in Manjimup caravan park, and on Tuesday we headed for home through some orchard country. The blossom was all but finished, but we revelled in the green of the hills and rivers with water in – almost like home! We stopped off to see a bird sanctuary at Birdlip and walked among the many peacocks, chickens, budgies, canaries, galahs, parrots, etc. Then at 2.30 it was back to work. The footbrake began to work just as we neared Bunbury, typical! Anyway, Donna went to the garage to be checked and now awaits a new distributor cap from Perth, as ours was evidently cracked. Elaine is enjoying herself in the Children's Ward for two weeks, but the change-overs are frequent. We are going on night duty on 25th October for two weeks – ten days to be exact with four days off. We are going down to Albany for two days on Monday so we hope the wild flowers will last until then.

Saturday 14th October 1967

I have just recovered from another birthday and my Mum sent me flowers Interflora, so many colours – marigolds, anemones, dahlias, poppies, daises and some lovely carnations and sweet peas. The smell was beautiful. It filled our rooms. We managed to get off duty Saturday evening and had a lovely steak. Elaine gave me lots of little things which were so useful, such as talc, soap, powder but her main gift was a lovely book of Australia and the South Sea Islands with plenty of information.
We have met many nice people here at Bunbury, but some of the methods and red tape are really unnecessary. We managed to have two days off together last week and it was great to get away for a change and see some of the sights again. Travelling down the west coast we explored Russeltown, a smallish seaside town, quieter than Bunbury with better sea and

beaches. Then at Margaret River we drove to the mouth of the river where it ran into the sea. Plenty of good spear fishing here, and surfing on the high waves. The countryside around here was covered with lovely wild flowers, every colour you can imagine, growing all down the sides of the roads, in the fields and all over the woods. In some places there were carpets of red flowers and all the gauzy bushes are coming out a lovely yellow. We visited one of the caves near Augusta, where we stayed for the night. A good specimen and well worth viewing. Augusta lies right on the river, but also has the sea with a scenic drive around the headland, where the wild flowers grow in wonderful profusion. We were very fortunate for weather all the time. Donna played up the next day, her footbrake – the garage could find nothing wrong until by chance they saw the brake fluid leaking out – so now it is alright again. We then went out to Pemberton and great forest trees – very tall indeed. Beautiful countryside all around there, and all the way home. Elaine still gets tired occasionally, otherwise we are both well and reasonably happily settled. We do miss our little home in Adelaide and the wonderful fellowship we enjoyed at the Church.

Sunday 22nd October 1967

Elaine has had another week of sick, a flu' injection. She seems to be allergic to the plant life here, as her nose is streaming and her eyes are swollen. The weather is hot now and we are getting rapidly sunburned. We missed our trip to Albany last week as it was too far to go, but we spent one afternoon relaxing on the beach with the delightful name of Peppermint Grove.

Another day I drove Elaine on a scenic drive through the forest plantation to Wellington Weir and dam, and then on to Collie. All the wild flowers were still in bloom, though they are fading fast. Some of the slides we have taken have come out extremely well. We are busy making soft toys for Jan's children at Clare. All our Christmas mail has gone at last – what a job! Today we are off to Perth for a couple of days. We both went to purchase trousers and shorts and feel we shall have a better range for the 'larger bottom people' up there. We now have a new enemy! In South Australia it was flies and ants, but in Western Australia it is the mosquitos. We have nets across our windows, but they still get into our rooms, etc. Elaine had a few bites but nothing to really complain about.

Tuesday 31st October 1967

Elaine had eleven days off sick but is now well and back at the job. We went up to Perth last Sunday and arrived just in time for Evensong at a lovely old Church of England Church, which was a wonderful service and people were very friendly. The churches in Bunbury, and in fact all over the west, are inclined to be high and pretty dead, so it made a welcome change. We found a caravan park and spent the night there. On Monday we spent the morning shopping, then had a snack lunch before driving 30 miles to Yanchep where they have a lovely National Park. On the way we passed a very sick bird – the car behind stopped, found it had broken wings and so took it off with them. We wandered about the Park which had all the facilities for holidays – golf, tennis courts, a swimming pool, boating, a couple of hotels, a zoo, etc. There were caves there to see but we decided not to indulge this time. The koala bears were in large numbers, and so cute, and there were quite a few little babies with their mothers crawling all over their patient parents. Some were asleep with one under each arm, really cuddly bundles. We then went down to the beach which we had to ourselves, had a picnic tea and ran wild on the sand doing our exercises – slimming exercises are easy on the beach as you can anchor your feet in the sand. In the evening we returned to Perth, very wind burnt, and went to a 'Drive-In Cinema', then returned to Bunbury the next day.

Night duty beckons for two weeks, Elaine on the Intensive Care Unit, very busy most of the time, but she enjoys it very much. At least she is left virtually in peace to get on with the work. On day duty there are a fair number of disgruntled Sisters around that can make life rather tiresome.

Friday 10th November 1967

We now have real summer weather here with temperatures up to 87°. We were brave enough to have a swim the other day.

Poor Elaine was so busy on her last night on, in fact, we all were. I was Night Superintendent and we had two boys severely injured in a car crash into Casualty. That kept us running for several hours and the wards had to do without rounds. Then Elaine had to take them into Intensive Care and, because I was so busy, I forgot to send her help until later. We both worked right through and were very tired by the morning, especially her. I felt so sorry I let her down. She had half hourly observations on at least three men all night. In the end next day one boy died from head injuries, one is already unconscious and the other boy will be alright.

We slept late the next day so we left later than intended for Pemberton. We reached the camping ground that night and had another good sleep. We drove Donna up the 'Rainbow Trail' so called because of the variety of flowers. The trail runs amid the forest, beside the river – some rapids and a weir. We had to do a fair bit of scrambling to reach a good vantage point to see them.

Pemberton is a quaint town, all the buildings built of the Karri timber which stretches for miles. We drove all around to see as much as we could before pressing on to Northcliffe. From there we took a track about sixteen miles off course through swampy bush country, low shrubs and poker trees, which are green bushes with a tall poker stick in the middle of a lighter green shade. The road itself was a well-constructed gravel track. At the end was a lighthouse situated on a high limestone cliff. This was known as Windy Point, and it was well named. It didn't take long for us to hop back into the car. The view, however, was worth the goose pimples!

You could see the rough waters of the great Australian Bite, and the coastline along to Albany. Evening was drawing in and the rain was tumbling down – it was in thunderstorms we made our way to Walpole and, on arrival, we could not find any sign of habitation, but eventually we found a café open for a meal and it had a T.V. going, so we watched the play 'The Importance Of Being Earnest'.

After losing the windscreen wiper and, having found it with a torch in the dark, we found the camping site and settled down for the night. Walpole is on the coast but situated in a sheltered inland spot surrounded by unspoilt scrubland and forests. The coastline has miles of pure white sand dunes. The feature of the district was the 'Tingle Tingle Tree' or jarrah timber – this is a type of eucalyptus tree used for building timber – slightly red bark, with enormous trunks in width and height. The inner softer part burns easily if there is a forest fire, but the outer part, being extremely hard, remains intact and very much alive. This means the tree lives on and can still be used. This is their value to prevent forest fire catastrophes and to build safe houses. To give you some idea of the size, we parked Donna inside one of the larger ones.

Then we were off back to Bunbury for a few hours in bed before our last four nights. We finished with two more days off, but decided to remain quiet this time, instead of racing up to Perth to see Dougie as originally planned.

Tuesday we slept in the garden all the morning, cleaned the car, did some washing in the afternoon and had an early night. Wednesday we played tennis all the morning and suffered from stiff arms afterwards! We then went to the beach for a swim – the water was pretty cold at first, but the waves were huge breakers and did not bother to ask us whether we wanted to get wet – they swamped us! In the evening we went to a 'Drive-In' cinema.

Thursday it was back to day duty, where Elaine is doing kid's work, which she likes, and me on Maternity. In the evening we joined two Sisters from Melbourne for a steak meal with some wine at a steak inn.

Letters are mounting as usual, I must get some written. The mosquitoes are being a pest – bed routine is undress, wash, pick up the nearest book and swat any mosquitoes you can see around.

ADELAIDE

Monday 27th November 1967

Safe and sound in Adelaide – all according to schedule. After a busy morning on Saturday we finally packed the car up and left Bunbury about 5pm. We were not sorry to leave really, as we had very little in common with most of the Sisters. They all kept swearing every other word and it sounded so unprofessional – some of the younger Sisters were good fun though. It was a lovely evening and then we had a good run across country to the seaside caravan park of Denmark. We were very ready for bed when we arrived at 10pm, and, apart from having to squat mosquitoes, we soon scrambled into our sleeping bags. Sunday was rather cloudy and inclined to rain. We spent a quieter day roaming around Albany and the surrounding district. A picturesque spot with a fishing and whaling harbour, and many small islands just off the coast, rather like the west coast of Scotland.

Photos were difficult because of the dullness but I did manage a few. We walked to a lookout spot and war memorial overlooking the town. There were hundreds of steps leading to the top with scrub bushes on either side. Plenty of lizards and snakes around too, but they didn't interfere with us. The view was worth it.

In the afternoon we slid down a steep, sandy cliff to find some salmon holes, but although there were some people fishing and many carcasses on the beach we did not see any salmon leaping! Getting back up the cliff was another thing! We crawled up on all fours and got filthy. After tea we changed and went to the Baptist Church for the Evening Service, before settling down for the night.

On Monday we went northwards from Albany up the Chester Pass to the Stirling Ranges – the scenery was so changeable – the high mountains with dark green scrubland, and the flat plains bright yellow with ripening wheat. The day was sunny and very hot and the blue sky just set the picture. We took the car up to a picnic area in the middle of the Ranges, and in shorts, top and sun hat, I decided to go for a walk and a climb. The flies were terrible buzzing around my face as I went. Bluff Knoll was the challenge, 3,700 feet – I only managed 3,000ft but Elaine sensibly decided to do 1500ft. It was so hot and I went so fast that I developed air hunger and so had to rest. Elaine kept in the cool farther below. There were lizards all around me as I climbed, but they were more frightened of me than I was of them. Unbeknown to me I was being cheered on by a Welshman and others down below to reach the top, so they were disappointed I didn't quite make it. Some waited for my return and congratulated me!

We continued our journey to Lake Grace, passing many Salt Lakes, the whiteness of which was fascinating – in the middle of them were skeleton trees growing, that looked like bare twigs sprinkled with artificial Christmas silver sparkle. We then went 50 more miles further north to a place called Hyden Rock – the rock formation we saw was known as 'Wave Rock' because it resembles the shape of a wave just before it breaks. Although it was fairly late in the evening we decided to press onto lessen the mileage the following day. We were travelling on gravel roads and all the way wild rabbits kept running across in front of us – we may have killed one but no more. We stopped at about 10pm at Ravensthorpe. We could not find a park so we pulled off the road by some trees just near the town. In waking up in the morning we found ourselves right in the middle of the local rubbish tip! Delightful!

Photo 8 – Elaine on the 'Wave Rock' at Hyden Rock.

We moved on to Esperance on Tuesday morning and spent three hours lazing on the white sandy beach and had a glorious swim as well. When we went to leave we found the wheels embedded in sand – so we set to and dug them out but used a tow in the end! We moved on to Norseman arriving about 6pm for an early night. We spent a little time on the Copper Mine slag heaps looking for Gem stones, but the flies were so bad they drove us round the bend, so we gave up. About 9am on Wednesday we set off across the plains. It was a hot sunny day and we had to sit on bathing towels because of all the perspiration. We travelled about 300 miles on straight bitumen road, which was very tiring driving, and the scrubland scenery rather monotonous.

We drove a 100 mile stretch each and sang choruses to pass the time. We stopped at Balladonia, a roadside motel, had lager to drink as we were so hot, and this certainly quenched our thirst for a while. The bitumen road had increased by 50 miles in length since our journey across two months ago. The last 80 miles were dreadfully pot-holed and bumpy, we couldn't hear ourselves think!

We were fortunate to reach Eucla as our petrol was getting very low. There was no water available at the petrol station and as the risk of fire was high, we could not make a camp fire as we did coming up.

Thursday we covered 300 miles on gravel roads to Caduna – the loose dust had been cleared so we did not get quite so sandy! It was a cloudy day which was quite a relief, and we had to change our shorts for trousers. Passing through the Lutheran Mission grounds we saw two Aboriginals with their boomerangs. Before entering Caduna we had to pass through a fruit fly inspection and handed over our last five oranges! Caduna marked civilisation to us and the peace of being on made roads! Friday we made our way to Port Pirie after having a minor repair on the petrol pipe of the car. The car ran well throughout, the only loss was a few screws from the window frame. We arrived at the Lewis family very bronze, fit and well, but we very much appreciated sleeping in a real bed.

Saturday we spring cleaned the car before we left Port Pirie because of the water shortage in Adelaide. We stopped at Clare's for tea, and the three girls were thrilled with their knitted animals that we made.

On Sunday we had the baptism of Sue Craige at Holy Trinity Church in Adelaide. It was wonderful to be her sponsors and support her on this great occasion – so Elaine and I have another Godchild. Next Sunday she will be confirmed at St Peter's Cathedral with two of the other girls namely Jo and Ann. Today, Monday, we have been in town shopping and getting our Banks organised – it was so hot and we really felt we were back in the city with a vengeance. We now expect to stay with Mr and Mrs Green until about the 10th December.

Sunday 3rd December 1967

This week has passed so quickly even though there is little to show for our activities. During the early part we had a very hot spell, and it was even too hot to sleep with temperatures in the nineties. The flies and mosquitoes really love this weather and we were quite severely covered with bites. The last few days have been a little better – we play tennis most days and I think, on the whole, our standard is improving. Tuesday we played with the Methodist Guild Club and had a swim in one of the member's pool afterwards. Wednesday we were in the town for most of the day which began about 9.30am. We bought ourselves much needed bathing costumes. We looked everywhere for a roof rack but with no success. However, since then one of our friends from Blackwood Methodist Church came into possession of an old one and has given it to us for one dollar (about 10/-). It will need a few dollars spent on it, but it is a good deal cheaper than a new one costing thirteen dollars, when we only want it for ten months.

On Wednesday evening we were invited to the Methodist Bible Study Christmas Gathering here at Blackwood. We had a very happy evening singing carols, doing Bible quizzes, charades, and eating, of course.

Thursday we pottered around for most of the day and in the evening we went to tea with Audrey Dunn and Kathy Godlee. We had plenty to chat about and we showed some of our slides. Audrey now has a new Hillman Arrow which looks good but seems too big for her needs. We heard yesterday that we have to have a new cylinder for Donna but I guess she has done so well.

Friday we went to a Smorgasbord (buffet type) dinner at the Senior Fellowship of our church at Holy Trinity, followed by a crusade film. Yesterday we touched up the rusty parts on the car – painted the roof rack green and stuck some more pictures in our scrapbooks. We are still not sure where we are going in Victoria – we plan to leave the Greens on Monday 11th December. Confirmation day today and it will be a great joy to be there with Sue and Jo. To see the change in their lives and know they are aiming in the right direction means such a lot to me.

Monday 11th December 1967

I have just been to town for last minute shopping while Elaine had a bath and washed her hair. We have just had three very hot days with temperatures 90-100 night and day. Up until yesterday we had no energy for packing, but today it is raining – what a relief to see it fall and smell the freshness afterwards. We have even had to sleep with the fan going all week.

After having a new valve put in one of Donna's cylinders, she now sounds very sweet. We hope it lasts! We have one new tyre, so we have four good feet for the journey. We have decided to tour part of Victoria and then go to Berni next Monday and see if we can get a job canning fruit for a while.

Berni is actually in South Australia, but only 30 miles from the border of Victoria due east of Adelaide. We shall send some luggage home leaving Adelaide on the 'Ballarat' for London on 22nd December. They allow roughly five to six weeks, so you can watch the newspapers for its arrival in London and is a cash delivery scheme. It will go to Farrows Ltd in London, and all insured with General Accident Insurance for £100-£200 on a policy in my name.

Wednesday 20th December 1967

What a week we have had alternating with joy and laughter, tears and sadness. We have been fit and healthy throughout and have had many wonderful days looking around. After all our goodbyes we left in the end at 6.30pm on Monday evening. We drove south to Tailum Bend in a howling gale and rainstorm – our windscreen wiper fell off three times. We did manage to retrieve it every time and, in the end, we got it fixed securely – so far no more bother!

The wind caused a fair amount of problem to the baggage on the roof; one record player, two suitcases, two boxes and a spare tyre. The tyre became dislodged at one point and dragged the rest with it. At about midnight we stopped at a garage and we noticed we had lost one box – apparently things Elaine had made for me for Christmas which made her very upset. Last time we had checked the roof was 50 miles back, so we made the return drive back at 30mph. With eyes on stalks looking for a box in a polythene bag. At 2am we had to give up and without even removing our jeans, we climbed into our sleeping bags and fell sound asleep. In the morning we covered the same miles back to the garage and enquired whether anything had been handed in. A lorry driver had evidently complained that someone had dropped a 'big rock' in the road. Pricking up our ears we phoned the Police Station en route and, praise God, we found the package intact. Back we went 30 miles to collect it and only one thing was broken!

Tuesday lunchtime we set out once more reaching Narracoorte where three ex-Southmead girls are working (from Bristol). They were pleased to see us and we caught them all by surprise. Joan Holman was just off duty (one of the three who worked with me in England) and we went back to her home for tea and stayed the night there in Lucindale. We had a lovely evening – felt very much at home in the spacious farmhouse. We had strawberries and cream for tea. It was interesting to talk to Joan and hear all her latest exploits in Malaysia. Her parents showed us their photo album, a proud record of how they had worked to build up their prosperous farm. The first pictures show how they begun with pitching a tent on the bush land, how they built their own home, and just last year they could afford the luxury of a T.V. Now with the water shortage he has to buy 1800 dollars' worth of Barley to hand feed all the stock. After our late night the night before, a shower and early bed was welcome. The following morning we were all set to depart when we noticed a huge bulge in one of our new front tyres. We were not very pleased but Mr Holman changed the wheel for us and we then commenced our Wednesday's travels.

We went to Mount Gambier where the same time last year we had enjoyed the Blue Lake. However, this time the lake was not blue, only an inky colour. We picnicked in the old volcanic crater and played a game of bat and ball to keep us from getting car behinds! After lunch we crossed the border into Victoria and headed towards the coast. We reached Port Fairy, a very quaint fishing port, and we were charmed with it straight away. All the fishing vessels were tied up along the jetty of the river inlet that ran parallel to the sea. Houses were built by the waterside with private jetties and yachts. A small island opposite the bay joined the mainland by a wall – we walked around it along the white shell beach. There was a large fish museum in the town where there are all kinds of fish in tanks, even sharks, dolphins, octopi, etc.

We travelled on spending the night in a well-equipped caravan park at Port Campbell. This place marks the beginning of the famous coastline known as 'Ocean Drive Road' – 200 miles of very rocky, rugged, but splendid coastal scenic views.

We were disappointed to find heavy rain falling when we woke up, but after breakfast it began to clear for which we thanked the Lord. The first eighty miles were on winding cliff top roads with limestone formations in various stages of decay with such names as 'London Bridge' which we walked across. It was covered in clay and each step we took we gathered a few more inches of clay on our shoes until our feet were so heavy we could hardly walk! We collapsed laughing so much. We didn't see anyone for many miles. There were about twelve pillars of broken off rock in a row called the Twelve Apostles. We explored gorges and blow holes. The sky was inclined to be cloudy but the sun shone in between, sufficient for some good photos.

The road then headed inland through forest lands and much burned out remains of bush fires. Road works were in progress everywhere and on one corner we had to negotiate about ten miles of mud on a hill – Donna was pretty muddy afterwards! Then thirty miles of hilly winding roads, beautiful trees, ferns – green and as big as some of the trees – and there were many brightly coloured parrots, blues, reds, yellows, greens, etc. Too shady for photos. With so many bends in the road we felt pretty car sick by the end. We soon recovered though and we were back on the coast again.

This time we passed numerous sandy bays, all the creeks we passed were dried up and had peculiar names; 'Sausage Creek', 'Petticoat Creek', 'Lollipop Creek'. We paused for lunch at Lorne, a more residential seaside resort, and watched the surfing enthusiasts. Our next stop was Geelong, Prince Charles' school town, and a large busy one, the next largest to Melbourne. After a Chinese meal, we decided on a 'Drive-In' film which would be the most relaxing evening past time. Friday came and we innocently went to Melbourne for the day. We went first to the Goodyear Tyre Co for advice over our new bulging tyre. We were told that we were sold an 8-year-old tyre as new, which must have perished being in store for so long. The man was most sympathetic as it was irreplaceable, and he gave us a new one for half price. He advised us next time to check the year of manufacture – we shall endeavour not to forget!

A bit fed up we made our way into the city and parked the car as near as possible with all the Christmas shopping rush. Melbourne is just like London – too many people, confusing one-way streets and old buildings. It has a fair amount of culture and atmosphere which Adelaide and Perth lacked. Also, it had a large network of trams. We saw around Captain Cook's Cottage in Fitzroy Gardens which were transported brick by brick from Yorkshire, England!

There were greenhouses full of hydrangeas which were outstanding and we saw around some official buildings including the Cathedral. A lady guide volunteered a great deal of information about the Cathedral and its association with England, such as this came from Canterbury, that pillar from Aberdeen, etc – little realising where we were from. We didn't like to tell her!

On returning to the car we found the back window had been smashed by thieves who had opened the doors and had a good rummage through all our belongings. I lost my handbag and wallet, which only contained one dollar, other contents including a small Bible and my Bush Transistor Radio. Elaine lost her best blue handbag, which contained her car keys, her bank book and our new large car lamp. Worst of all, they took her most treasured possession, her beautiful locket with butterfly wings in it. It was a family heirloom, a bitter blow for her. Although they went right through my suitcase in the car, my jewel case was not found and my writing case which was open with papers everywhere seemed to be intact. We had a hectic hour with the Police, the C.I.D., and cleaning up the car from fragments of glass. The banks were closed but Elaine managed to reach her bank in Melbourne and cancel her pass book. Then we went down to Brighton to visit Ann McRobert and were lucky to find her off duty and at home. Mr McRobert gave us a drink to regain our strength, and we ended up spending Friday night with them. It was good to be in company as it had all been rather depressing.

On Saturday we made for the Grampian Mountains, where we drowned our sorrows. Ballarat is a large town nearby situated on a lake. We had a picnic lunch by the water and fed the cheeky black swans. We went over a little shell house of the Colony days and saw some beautiful mosaic designs made of shells at another private house – it was done to raise money for charity. Travelling through Ararat we went into the centre of the mountains to a place called Hall's Gap. Many falls were marked on the map but few were flowing. We did a couple of walks to vantage view look-outs and had a splendid vision of the miles of brown land surrounding the ranges, broken by a lake here and there.

We slept in a caravan park as normal and awoke to a bright sunny Sunday. We were surrounded by wildlife while we had breakfast. Our first wild koalas were sleeping in the gum trees. Then we drove up a mountain road to a look-out at Mount Difficult, and then took a walk to a point known as 'The Jaws Of Death'. A pleasant walk to two promontories – the jaws suspended over the valley below. We took photos of each other on the edge. Further up we saw a signpost to the Falls, so we thought we would try our luck. There were three lots – at the top 'Broken Falls' which describes them exactly – in the middle 'Pearl Falls' which shine in the sun – then by clambering down very wet steps and getting covered in spray we reached the very large 'McKenzie Falls'.

We were planning to head north for Berri and the fruit canning job after that. We got as far as Horsham, 30 miles away from the mountain, when Elaine glanced again at the Berri pamphlet, we had overlooked the small print "Jobs commence mid-January" – we were unemployed! We decided therefore that it would be stupid to head north to South Australia, so we decided on a hospital job in Victoria. We went to Evensong at Camperdown, a town in the midst of the Plains – we had changed for church in a concrete passage attached to a public convenience! We enjoyed the service, which turned out to be a Carol service and sang heartily.

Photo 9 – Me on the Jaws of Death in the Grampian Mountains.

Photo 10 – The McKenzie Falls in the Grampian Mountains.

Monday was cold and wet. We had no success with jobs on the western side of Victoria, so we made for the eastern side of Melbourne to the Great Dividing Ranges. We are now in the midst of these Ranges at a small District Hospital in Alexandra. Today we have been to Melbourne to sort out Victorian Nursing Regulations, registration, car insurance claim for our broken window, sign various declarations at the bank for a new pass book. Tomorrow we start work.

The news of the Prime Minister Mr Holt's disappearance has been a shock to all here in Australia. Cheviot Beach, where he was swept away, is at the end of St Phillip's Bay, not far from Melbourne. The weather is not very summerlike but we are hoping.

ALEXANDRA

Tuesday 26th December 1967

A Happy New Year to one and all. Elaine and I had a quiet but happy Christmas. We managed to work the same duties so that we could open our presents together and spend the evening together. Christmas Day was really very hot – too warm to even consider sun-bathing. We went to Midnight Communion on Christmas Eve at Eildon, a small town 18 miles away, as that was the only C/E Church having a service at that time. The Vicar rotates his services around the various districts including Alexandra. It was a good service in a little wooden church by the lake – a very pleasant situation indeed. It has been a sad business about Mr Holt's disappearance, but the Memorial Service to him was marvellous, held in Melbourne. The whole affair has certainly given the Christmas Spirit rather a sombre effect. The cultural aspects of life are certainly lacking in Australia.

The Hospital has only 25 beds for various types of patients, geriatrics, children, midwifery, with operations once a week unless we have any emergencies. In fact, a typical Cottage Hospital. For we, who have never done any general work for ten years at least, it is strange to be thrust into all sorts of things again. The Staff consists of five full time Sisters and Matron and four Nursing Aides. A very friendly place, but very quiet after working in larger units. We have both settled down happily and quickly. Being eighty miles from Melbourne, we are close enough to go in if we wish to. Sitting out in the grounds we overlook the town of Alexandria, which has just about one of everything! Surrounding the town are the brown foothills of the Great Dividing Ranges. On our day off this week Matron has invited us to join her at a Convention similar to Keswick. We are contemplating whether to go.

January 1968

The Hospital has been gradually getting busier and from six patients we now have twenty. A few are holiday makers who have picked up some bugs (wogs) while camping, a few elderly

Photo 11 - Staff at Alexandra District Hospital, Victoria, Australia.
Irene Turnbull, Matron, John Macdonald, Surgeon, Norma Price,
Nurse and Raymond Young, Anaesthetist. The doctors were from the
UK.

people admitted for Nursing Care whilst their families take their holidays. On Wednesday we had an Operating List, and Elaine had to assist, which didn't please her very much. Last Sunday Elaine escorted a young fellow by ambulance to Melbourne for emergency chest surgery. The journey was slow because of the windy, bumpy road and the ambulance swung a good deal. One of the married Sisters here trained at Aberdeen with Elaine – what a small world!

We went to the Christian Keswick Convention at Belgrave Heights and met a couple we had known on the 'Fairsky' – in fact, the Chaplain and his wife – and some friends from Adelaide. It was a wonderful atmosphere and we were mightily challenged by the messages from Alan Redpath and George Duncan, whom I knew from England. We stayed in the little chalet homes of the Australian Nurses Christian Movement, tucked away in the hills of the Dandenong Ranges – what a peaceful spot. It could have been in Austria. We met some grand girls, mostly Nursing Sisters from different parts of Australia. The one who shared our chalet was working at the Children's Hospital in Melbourne, so Elaine had quite a bit in common with her. It was Jubilee Day at the Convention and so that's why they had guest speakers from England. The theme was 'Is our submission to God one of partiality or perfection?' I don't think anyone could stay sitting in their seat in comfort. We have just had two days off, had a quiet time on the whole – a few picnics admiring the surrounding countryside. We did go down to the suburbs of Melbourne to see the film of 'The Bible'. We did not get back until 1am so we had a long sleep in.

Saturday 6th January 1968

For Christmas we decorated the sitting room with our crib and the cards we had received. All our presents at the foot of the mantelshelf. We sat quietly and opened them in the evening. Elaine gave me a red velveteen cushion in the shape of Australia with a badge from each state we visited, which I have all stitched on in the appropriate places. I have decided like Elaine to send many of my slides home for Mum to see and, as it were, go through some of our experiences with me. Thinking back, we did have some sad moments on our trip here yet we did see some beautiful scenery – the Coast Road with its unusual rock formation, the beautiful trees and the Grampian Mountains so magnificent and rugged with waterfalls in wonderful splendour – the best we have seen yet. However, when we did at last reach Alexandra, with no success in finding jobs, we camped that night in pouring rain. Before we went to sleep we prayed for guidance and the next day walked into jobs right here. He answered so wonderfully. The Hospital stands high overlooking the town – the peace and quiet are great and the countryside around is very lovely, plenty of hills and little hamlets. We are revelling in the rest and reading plenty. We are hoping to join the Tennis Club, if we feel we are good enough. Everyone is very friendly and we have been enormously busy since Christmas. Both the Doctors here are English and trained at Guy's, one Surgeon and one Physician. Given time they will build up a wonderful practise between them.

We had a picnic the other day beside the lake at Eildon, a beautiful spot. Plenty of lovely black swans swimming around. Elaine seems so much better in health now and it is a joy to see.

Monday 15th January 1968

We have had a postal strike for the past week. The weather has remained hot with temperatures between 90 – 104 degrees. We have been in a melted daze, especially as we have no cooling system in the home. Elaine on nights found it so hot she curled up on the stone floor of the bathroom! The thought of snow just now would be bliss, but I expect in England you have had enough of winter.

We enjoy being on duty just to have a bit of air-conditioning. It's very busy on the wards – two deaths last week and two births, so we feel we are keeping the population steady! One evening, when we were on together, we had two fractured femurs admitted. We came off duty at about midnight. The drought is pretty bad everywhere this year. It has lifted in New South Wales but Victoria plods on. Emergency foodstuffs are being shipped from Western Australia to feed the stock. There is a complete fire ban throughout the area, the hills are mere dust heaps.

We have just had four days off just pottering about. We play tennis when it's cool enough and swim in the pool when hot. We have walked around the district, covering ourselves in fly spray to keep the flies away, not realising we would be invaded by grasshoppers. We spent Saturday evening with a young couple and two children who are from New Zealand visiting her people over here. They are wonderful Christians having met on the Mission Fields of New Guinea and we have some pretty interesting discussions with them – especially as the Churches are pretty dead to say the least. The C/E is rather high and the Congregational is very modernistic. Anyway, Malcolm and Dawn are great and we have seen some slides of his native homeland – she was a Nursing Sister, he a Carpenter.

Wednesday 24th January 1968

At last the postal strike is temporarily settled. Currently the temperature here is 102 degrees, it has been hot and stuffy all the week. It is looking dark outside now and we are getting quite excited at the prospect of rain. We had a day's drive around Eildon Weir and Reservoir and climbed the adjacent mountain road for twenty miles – round and round and round – hairpin bends all the way to Mansfield on the far side of the Ranges. After dinner we took another winding road up to Mount Buller. This was hardly a road and some of the rocks we crossed were more like boulders. Forest land all the way up and some large saw mills. After going for ten miles we came to a village built on Swiss chalet lines, with skiing hotels and chalets and chair lifts – very picturesque. The scene over the hills below was clear and when we saw the road we had come up we felt quite sick! Visiting the Ladies' comfort station, we received a shock – out of the toilet roll came twenty large moths! The drive down was easy and we called in to see Timbertop School situated at the foot of Mount Buller. This was a section of Geelong Grammar School that Prince Charles attended while over here.

Elaine helped me deliver a baby. Just like old times – gave her a thrill. She said she may do the second part midwifery when she returns to England! On Thursday I became ill. Quite a change for Elaine to be running around after me. I had a temperature of 104. The heat outside did not help and they would not admit me to the Hospital where it was cooler as I had a bad attack of Rubella and was considered infectious. Elaine spent frequent intervals tepid sponging me to cool me down. There was no space on my body that did not have a spot – I really looked an awful sight. At last, I am up and pottering about, probably be off another week. The relieving Matron has now left and the permanent one is back – about 35 years and full of life. So work is going very happily.

It's raining, hurrah! A howling gale also. We went outside to cool off and watch the storm come over the hills.

Donna had a service, oil and grease this week and says thanks as she was feeling very dirty. We still haven't got the window fixed. We may go away for the weekend if I am feeling fit enough.

Friday 2nd February 1968

Well, we did take off for the weekend and had a marvellous time. On Friday we went to see Dawn and Malcolm – their third baby will be born soon. Saturday we packed Donna up and went to Bendigo. This was one of the most historical towns we have yet seen. Many old buildings left from the gold mining days – we climbed up an old mining shaft erected as a look-out over the city and had superb views on all sides. The weather was very hot and we attended a special Christian Convention there in the afternoon. We went for a swim before the evening meeting. An elderly couple, Mr and Mrs Wood, insisted on taking us home with them for a night in Castlemaine about 20 miles away from Bendigo. They made us very welcome and we did in fact stay the Sunday night also. We slept better in a bed than in the car! After the Monday morning meeting we headed for Echua. This is a popular holiday town situated on the River Murray and used to be the second largest inland trading and timber port in Australia. A very pleasant place – we watched some junior tennis tournaments and had a swim in the Olympic pool. Many people were swimming in the River Murray but it looked too muddy for us. In the evening we took a paddle steamer down the river – most attractive at sunset. The banks and the trees were brown and dry, but all the gum trees leaning in various directions made pretty shadows on the water. We slept in the car in the caravan park with all the doors open. Tuesday we took our time to get away, even cleaned the car with the hose provided. We crossed the border a short way and put our noses into New South Wales but regretted it when we returned to Victoria and lost all our fruit at the 'Fly and Fruit Barrier'. We followed the river down to Yarra Wonga through orange, lemon and apricot groves and then spent the whole afternoon swimming and lazing under the willow trees by the lake at Yarra Wonga. We left about 6pm for home via Benalla having really enjoyed the trip.

Temperatures over the last few days have been 110 degrees – Elaine now takes salt tablets which really does help her in this enormous heat. I do not seem to need anything even though I actually lose much more fluid than her.

We had an 8 square mile bush fire just a short way out of Alexandra yesterday – we could see the flames on the far hills. We got prepared with hoses but the wind did not blow our way.

Tuesday 13th February 1968

Elaine enjoyed her birthday. She went out water skiing on Saturday with one of the Doctors and his wife at Eildon. She had seven tries but could not stand upright. The level of Eildon Weir is about 50 feet below normal and you can see lots of dead trees poking through the water. We played a game of tennis on Sunday afternoon – I think Elaine was aching a good bit from the water skiing. We went to Church in the evening and round to supper with Dawn and Malcolm. We went to tea with Elaine McNichol, one of the Scottish Sisters, on Friday evening – Elaine had a wonderful discussion with her about old times. She and her husband are managing a large grazing farm and would not think of returning to Scotland again – they are so happy. This weekend we are going to Mount Buffalo and the snowy mountains – also to a Rodeo.

Thursday 22nd February 1968

We are still sweltering in the century temperatures and feel like a melted piece of dripping. We have had dust storms and gales which have caused bush fires and disaster everywhere owing to the drought. Thinking of cold and snowdrops at home sounds positively blissful – perhaps a little of both might be the ideal. We have been very busy and the baby business is booming. Our friends Dawn and Malcolm Blackie have just had a little girl to add to the two little boys they already have. She is in hospital here, so it is good to look after her.

We had a lovely time our last four days off. On Friday we played tennis with Malcolm and then joined two other girls for an evening swim in the pool. Saturday we packed the car up and went off to Benalla to the Rodeo. A very hot day and we got burned being out in the sun all day. It was exciting to watch all the Rodeo Riders trying their skill at riding bucking bronks and bulls. They fall pretty heavily at times yet always seem to be alright. Some were real Cowboy types with fancy leather saddles with 'Australian All-Round Cowboy for 1966-1967' written on them. Another item was roping the calves – very skilled piece of work indeed. We got through many drinks that day, 15 altogether! We left Benalla at 4pm and drove on to Wangaratta. Here we scouted around to see which Church we could attend on the Sunday. Then we headed for the banks of the River Ovens and had a refreshing swim, followed by supper. We then considered going to a 'Drive-In' but we were too weary, so we just lazed on our rugs under the stars and talked until bedtime.

On Sunday we attended 11am service at the Baptist Church after an early morning swim. We were a little hesitant to swim in the river, not being used to it and not knowing what our feet were going to step on next! However, it was too hot to be choosy! After Church we drove to Lake Hume near Albury on the N.S.W. border, but only one end of the lake had any water in it. We drove to Tallangatta and had a picnic lunch on the banks of the so-called lake. Young chaps in old cars were charging over the floor of the lake which was all dry with cattle grazing on part of it. Then on southwards to Omeo. The heat was terrific. Elaine had her head out of the window to catch any breeze as I drove along. We stopped at Mitta Mitta where we bought a bottle of lager and that did at least quench our thirst for a while. We had a lovely swim in a really deep river, had supper and felt generally refreshed. On the road we passed flocks of sheep being herded along the roadside, so eating up the grass along the edges as there is no food for them in the fields – real roving shepherds with them in old Bush wagons and horses, boiling their billy cans as they pause for shade under the trees. They have to move six miles per day by law – but they proved a real typical Aussie sight.

Saturday 24th February 1968

Still too hot, and by all accounts we have another two months of it. After Mitta Mitta we decided to head for Omeo 80 miles south along very winding hilly roads. It was getting dark, but with a breeze it was just right for travelling. Somewhere, miles from anywhere, Donna just faded out. We had no torch to examine the trouble as ours had been stolen. However, we pushed her off the road and decided to walk a short way for help. We changed into trousers from shorts and made tracks up the road. We knew the last house back was 5 miles, so, after hearing a dog bark, we went forward feeling like Babes in the Wood. Walking about a mile we came to a farmhouse where there was a young couple who came to our rescue. We then found out that their house was the last one for 50 miles! They gave us coffee and brought a torch to look at Donna. Her fuel pipe had become dislodged and got a split in it. We mended it with insulating tape and then all was well. We decided to stay put and camp near the river for the night. In the morning the flies nearly drove us mad, so we were forced to move before breakfast and came across a couple of Melbourne businessmen who were on a fishing camping weekend. They were very interesting to talk to so we didn't get going until quite late. The country around was involved with timber and the logging industry and as we drove along there would be notices to 'Dug Outs' meaning saw mill settlements. Omeo was a dreary place, so we didn't stop, but passed straight through on the Alpine road to Hotham Heights. This was a rough mountainous track, very winding, a bit nerve racking with precipitous slopes. We passed through such places as 'Whisky Flat' with mountains called 'Little Baldy' and 'Big Baldy' which we had a chuckle over. We reached 6,000 feet above sea level and had splendid views of the mountains all around. We were disappointed that it was not photographic weather. The long 20 mile descent was a bit sickly with all the bends, but it brought us safely to a resort town called Bright where we spent Monday night.

We had a lovely swim in the Ovens River at Bright and found the whole town very attractive – nestling in the hills, not unlike Ballater. One of the tourist attractions are the trees – many are English – Poplar, Oak and Willows mainly, quite a change from all the Gum trees. On Tuesday we drove up to Mount Beauty through a private road owned by the Electricity Company as there is a large lake and dam half way up the mountain at a place called Bobong. We drove way up to Falls Creek, a skiing resort on the mountain top and came across yet another lake said to be the highest one in Australia called Rocky Gully, which describes its setting exactly. The weather was becoming

overcast and visibility was not too good so we went back to
Bright for dinner and then drove up Mount Buffalo, but we
could see nothing from the top of the peak – only the chalets
and well organised skiing slopes. We passed a lyre bird on the
way. By this time our ears were ringing with the constant bends
and hills, so we decided to make tracks for home. As we
reached Benalla we got into a nasty dust storm blown down
from the north. It surrounds you like a blanket. We were filthy
from the dust and Donna was just the same. We arrived at
Alexandra about 9pm for a good scrub and clean up.

Sunday 3rd March 1968

Elaine has half an hour to spare before the next Sister takes
over for the afternoon shift. I am sitting beside her doing a
crossword. Donna has just spent a week in hospital, we missed
her very much. She went to have a new brake cable fitted and
the radiator cleaned. We had to have a new core put in the
radiator and we had to await the spare part from Melbourne. It
was good exercise for us, however, to do more walking. We had
two days off and so were a little lost and stuck without a car.
On Wednesday we attended Ash Wednesday Communion
followed by the beginning of the Lenten discussion 'Is the
Church doing its best?' A very orthodox Anglican congregation
but most of the comments were very stimulating. Thursday we
slept in late and strolled down to the shops and on to the pool
for a swim. With all the children back at school we had the

place to ourselves and we had a good long swim. Afterwards
we played a game of tennis – we seem to be getting back into
better form again with all the practice – then on to tea with the
Blackie's where we enjoyed their own delicious 'Corn on the
Cob' grown in their garden. The temperatures seem a little
cooler, now 80-90 degrees, and certainly more comfortable.
This gives us more energy to do things.

We have decided to remain here in Alexandra until the end of
June thus completing six months. We like it at this Hospital and
we will have earned our bonus. After the disappointment over
jobs we do not feel like uprooting again. However, we have two
weeks holiday from 20th April. During this time, we are going to
tour New South Wales, stay with Ruth near Sydney in the Blue
Mountains and attend the Billy Graham Crusade. On leaving
Victoria we shall head straight for Queensland.

We have had plenty of work to do, a busy spell indeed. We had
a severe accident case admitted last Sunday evening, young
lads driving to Melbourne. The driver died after we had done
everything we could at 7am in the morning, but the passenger,
who was asleep in the back, just received lacerations – such is
life. We were talking to one of our patients who works on a
sheep farm. She was saying the usual price of sheep when sold
was fifteen dollars or £7 10/- each, but because of the drought
and lack of food etc., they were being sold for 10 cents or one
dollar or else given away – a terrible loss indeed. Tomorrow we
are going to see the film 'To Sir With Love' with Sidney Poitier.

The weather at home must be getting brighter now – spring must be truly on the way.

Tuesday 12th March 1968

The weather here is muggy, but not too hot just now, which is wonderful. We need the rain so badly – it is desperate – most of the rivers and dams are down to their last few week's supply. I think bath restrictions will be next. We spent the day on Friday at Eileen McNichol's farm and they have been carrying water by the bucket since Christmas! It makes us appreciate the everyday facilities. We had a good day there. We helped to do a little painting of the outside of their house thoroughly enjoying ourselves. Sunday after Church we were invited back to one of the women's flat for coffee afterwards. Our circle of friends seems to be growing, although at the end of next week Dawn and Malcolm are going back to New Zealand – we shall miss them very much.
We spring cleaned Donna last week, inside and out, but almost straight afterwards we found ourselves on a dirt road overlooking the weir. Hence there is dust all over the inside again. Every time you sit down you get covered and the clouds nearly choke you. The view was tremendous so it was well worth it. Work has been very quiet – only seven patients – makes the days seem a little tedious when there's little to do.

Friday 22nd March 1968

Saturday we got up at 5am and travelled to Melbourne, parked the car in a public car park within the city and were ready to shop by 9am. We bought a few odd things, trailed the Travel Agencies for literature on ships to New Zealand and the U.S.A. But most of all Elaine bought her new camera which she was so thrilled about. At lunch time we flopped exhausted into a restaurant – south sea atmosphere – candlelit, dark and peaceful. In the afternoon we wandered around the Botanical gardens which have suffered from the drought badly. We then drove southwards down the Mornington peninsula to the tip at Portsea. Some of the beaches are fine for surfing, whilst others were quiet swimming bays. The farther we got away from the town the less people there were, but in some places with temperatures in the 90's the beaches looked as packed as Bournemouth!

We found a Bay of Sorrento which we had to ourselves. We had a lovely swim and supper on the beach. It was great to see the sea. In the evening we went to a 'Drive-In' and saw a film of Aboriginal customs, which was interesting – did not see the second film as we mostly fell asleep. We camped on the foreshore that night and got up refreshed the next day. Had a swim before breakfast, then went to the local C/E Church for Matins, a very informal service. The Vicar stopped the service half way through to spray all the pews which were full of ants.

Afterwards we noticed that we had a bulge in the front tyre so we put the spare one on. It was a stifling humid heat so it was with much speed we drove to our next spot through San Remo across the old Bailey bridge to Phillip Island. We found a pleasant resort at Cowes where we had a late picnic lunch, swam and spent the afternoon digesting all the travel literature. About 6pm we drove in the dusk across the other side of the island to where all the penguins parade each night. This was fascinating. The sands and the sea are floodlit each night and at the same time each evening the penguins return from their fishing at sea. They eat enough for the babies and are so fat that they cannot even waddle up the sand. We saw about 30 come in to their nests.

We spent the night in the woods of a koala reserve. It was still very hot so neither of us slept too well, but we did see a few little bears. On Monday morning we finished exploring the island, a few strange rock formations called the Pyramid and the Nobbies. A nearby island is called French Island and on it a town called Tankerton, so Elaine was thrilled, just like home. The island is used as a prison so did not think we would call! On Monday afternoon we made our way southward again towards Wilson's promontory. We found ourselves on the usual unmade roads so Donna got filthy, but in passing we found a sweet little bay called Walkerville. We had the place to ourselves, so after eating we spent the whole afternoon in and out of the water. That evening we made for Yanicke where we had been invited to stay with a Mr and Mrs Weeks from the

Photo 12 – The Fairy Penguins landing at dusk on Phillip Island, Victoria.

Church at Alexandra. They were having a holiday there in the boathouse. We had a delicious fresh whiting fish for supper which had been caught that day. On Tuesday Mrs Weeks drove us down to Wilson's Promontory to have a look around. It belongs to the National Trust and is a Game Reserve except for a very organised large camping site at Tidal River. After the comparative flatness of the land it was good to see some mountains and this promontory was full of them. We went to Squeaky Bay, thinking it was a funny name, but the sand is almost pure white and when you walk on it, it really squeaks! The next bay was called Whiskey Bay and we wondered what we would find there but did not investigate. After dinner we went out in their motor boat for a couple of hours crossing to a little island where there were hundreds of Mutton Birds. I do not know much about them other than after hatching out in their nests of mud holes we could see grey fluffy bottoms sticking out. The nests were so close together in the adjoining soil was thin mud and we kept falling through losing our thongs in the holes.

We returned to Alexandra that night feeling thoroughly fit and intoxicated by the sea air and happy days off. Last night we made the great effort and attended a Country Women's Association meeting to which we had been invited. We had a pleasant evening, met lots of people, ate too much and had to judge the novelty hat competition.

Tonight we are at home quiet, but tomorrow and Sunday we shall be out to tea. Elaine has a sudden urge to sew so she is very busy tonight while I am working. Matron is off sick with a bad back so the atmosphere is less tense. She seems very nice, only 30 years old, but talks non-stop about herself and has a different complaint each time – a rather spoilt only child.

It rained yesterday – headline news!

Saturday 30th March 1968

Yesterday evening history was made. We were forced to light a fire in the sitting room and we felt quite excited about it. It was a cold night and it was lovely to snuggle down under the weight of blankets and sleep, instead of in the nude fighting mosquitoes. There was even a frost on the ground this morning. I think we can bid farewell to the century temperatures until we go to Queensland in July.

On Thursday we went out to Norma Miller's farm and spent the afternoon in the shearing shed watching the shearers at work. It was fascinating to watch the skilful way they handled the sheep, the way the fleece came off in one piece, and is then graded according to the wool's fineness of texture, not the thickness of the coat. It was, however, a hot humid day and Elaine picked up a sore throat and felt rather groggy, so we did not stay out too long.

On Friday we went to Swanpool about forty miles away to spend the day with Margaret Daws, one of our colleagues, yet another day spent on a farm, but certainly an interesting day. Part of their land has been used for damning water so in front of their house is a huge lake of water. The water level is pretty low through the period of drought. They must find it strange to see sheds and fences re-appearing as the water level drops. We were taken for a bush drive into the Blue Hills nearby and saw a few blue and scarlet Parrot Birds and some Wallabies. Unfortunately, there was a mist and visibility from the top was too poor for photography. We have had a few bouts of rain and if you look closely the hills do have a slight tinge of green. Elaine has now recovered from her sore throat and is fighting fit again. The bedrooms here are minute and we have so far been fortunate in having a spare room for all our camping and travelling junk. Unfortunately, the room is now needed for a new Trainee Nursing Aide so we have cleared our things out. Elaine has been going mad sewing up bags and covers so that the picnic things don't travel loose in the car boot and get filthy with the dust. Next job is to make seat covers with large pockets on the back of the front seats of the car.

Tuesday 9th April 1968

We have just had four days off and thoroughly enjoyed them. I took Helen back to Melbourne today while Elaine had a rest in preparation for work tomorrow. She had stayed with us here at the home in Alexandra for the weekend. Makes us feel quite old 'Aussies' showing new 'Pommies' around.

Tuesday 16th April 1968

We set off on holiday on Friday and we are really looking
forward to it. We hope to make Canberra by the weekend,
south of New South Wales during the week then to Sydney to
stay with Ruth and June. We hope to attend the Billy Graham
Crusade there and sing in the choir. The weather is still fairly
good, a little variable and the nights will be rather cold for
sleeping, so back to winter nighties again.
On our last weekend we went to Melbourne on the Saturday
with Dot Phillips from Alexandra and we had a lovely day. After
picking up Helen we went to the open day of a handicapped
Children's Home. It was a really homely atmosphere and Elaine
especially felt enormously at home. There were eight children
there of varying ages and types. They had a modern building
with no regular income, but completely run by faith in God's
provision.
On Sunday we showed Helen around our beautiful countryside
and she quite understood why we were so taken with the
place. Monday we climbed up Mount Cathedral, 2100 feet,
which is a few miles away. Tuesday I took Helen back to
Melbourne while Elaine remained behind rather bunged up
with a cold. The hospital has been really quiet over Easter, in
fact, desperately boring. Our main nursing problem patient
died and we were left with a mere handful of patients. We had
a peaceful Easter. We were going to a Convention on the

Sunday evening but I was so tired I had a sleep before we went to Church locally instead and it was a great service.

Wednesday 24th April 1968

Today is the first warm day comfortable enough to sit out at a picnic table beside the river near Shell Harbour N.S.W. To begin at the beginning – we were very slack on duty so we were let off about 1.30pm. After a few last-minute packings and a good bath we began our journey. Our aim – to reach the N.S.W. border by the Snowy Mountains. We drove hard for 200 miles pausing only for tea at Wangaratta, then arrived just over the bridge of the River Murray which marks the boundary at Corryong at 9pm, where we settled for the night.
On Saturday morning we began our tour around the Snowy Mountains. It was a chilly day, but plenty of blue skies with scudding clouds. The Mountains were beautiful and their slopes very green after the lack of grass in Victoria. We followed the never-ending winding roads, only pausing at the various look-out positions. We passed a few dams and followed large water pipes, all part of the vast electricity and power water scheme in the Snowy Mountains. At a place called Gechi we came to a stop. The bridge was under repair and the makeshift one across the river had subsided. We watched them shovelling in rocks for a while, then took ourselves off for a walk, collected a lot of wood which we tied onto the roof rack, and we picked a huge bucketful of mushrooms. There were hundreds of them and

our mouths watered. After waiting two hours a kind of bridge was completed and we ploughed through the water to the other side.

We were on the Mountain Alpine Way, about 5,000 feet above sea level, and it got colder and colder. Some of the Passes were not unlike Glencoe in Scotland. About lunch time we arrived at Thredbo, a skiing resort with typical chalets and chair lifts. We found a spot for dinner but the wind was freezing and it was a case of rushing to the boot and jumping back in the car. We heard later that they had their first fall of snow that night. It would have been spectacular to see it.

We were now skirting the slopes of Koscuisko, 7,000 feet high and the highest mountain in the area. Visibility for the peak was poor so we did not bother to drive up to the top. At Jindabyne we took a photo of a large dam just opened and then we went to Cooma to inspect the Pioneer Pilot Memorial. Along the Snowy Mountain Highway we sped toward Kiandra. We found by the wayside a hut called Sawyer's Hut. It was very windy and cold – in the days of carriages, if the horses couldn't make the Snowy Pass, the passengers used to stay in the hut. Now it is used as a skier's rest. It has a huge fireplace with a pile of logs. We carry candles so we lit them to save the battery of our torch and made a huge fire. It was very welcome and warm. Just as we were going to cook our mushrooms and sausages, a young man came to the door, he had run out of petrol. Elaine drove him five miles to the nearest ski village, whilst his wife kept me company. On their return we all enjoyed a huge supper. After they had gone we heated some water and had a strip wash in front of the fire. We parked Donna next to the wall for shelter and snuggled into our sleeping bags.

After cooking breakfast in the hut, on Sunday morning we began another day trip. The countryside was pretty bleak and barren and, as we descended into the valley, it was sad to see all the farmhouses vacated – fertile farmlands about to be flooded into another huge lake. The wages of progress and the desperate need in this country for water. We paused a while at a very Englishy place called Tumut. All the trees were changing colours, autumn shades. We got quite excited about seeing Poplars, Beech and Oak trees.

At Tumut we took a Forestry Commission road clearly indicating Canberra. We started off on bitumen, then went to gravel roads with a fairly good surface and after forty miles got to a single track with pot holes. After a while the petrol gauge showed empty and we met up with a car going in the opposite direction. Their description indicated worse to come but only thirty miles to go, so we decided to plod on. The hairpin bends and rocks have to be seen to be believed, but the views were magnificent. One could almost say we followed the electricity cables over the Ranges. After ascending a rugged pathway at the Peak, we then gradually descended onto a wider road. In the far distance we could see Canberra. We pulled off the road and had lunch, getting changed from jeans into Sunday clothes at the same time. Before entering Canberra, we paused to see the great Cotter Dam nearby.

Canberra is a splendid capital city, all very modern and beautifully designed. We had a job finding a Church for evening service but ended up in a Baptist one in the suburbs. After the Service some people invited us to use their garden to park our car so we had the use of a bathroom, etc., and somewhere warm to sit for the evening as by now it was raining.

Monday dawned windy and cold but we began to tour around the city, saw the Civic Centre, the shopping area, went over the War Memorial which was excellent, also St John's C/E Church of pioneer days, the U.S.A. War Memorial, a round tour of Parliament House and then a drive around the various Embassy Buildings and Universities. The colours of autumn were lovely, the buildings were ultra-modern and some were exceedingly ugly. However, the spaciousness between buildings did not give you the impression of a busy city, but a peaceful residential area. We cooked dinner up on Black Mountain where there were plenty of look-out picnic spots supplied with gas stoves, etc. We were very impressed with how organised it all was. By the end of the day we were pretty weary so we went back to our acquaintances, Mr and Mrs Brook, for the evening and night.

On Tuesday morning we took ourselves out to the Royal Australian Mint and went around the works, had a quick look at Government House and, after cooking dinner on the Black Mountain again, we bade farewell to Canberra.

Since then we leisurely drove into New South Wales and up the coast to Wollongong. Today we are having a quiet morning washing smalls, writing letters, before taking a deep breath and pushing on into Sydney itself. We hope to meet Ruth this afternoon and go to the Billy Graham Crusade this evening with her. The car is running well and we are both enjoying the trip – coffee time!

Thursday 2nd May 1968

From Wollongong we made our way across the Bulli Pass with its splendid view all down the coast of N.S.W. and then we gradually drew nearer to Sydney itself. We never reached the city in Donna as in the suburbs we were involved in a car accident. It was not our fault at all and fortunately we were only shaken. We were pulling away from some traffic lights at 10mph when a vehicle swung across our path coming from the opposite direction. The result – one completely smashed nearside wing. I was fine, Elaine had just a small cut on her knee and a hard hit on the middle finger of her left hand. The offender was drunk, unregistered and uninsured, and was taken away by the Police who were so interested in convicting him that they were no help to us at all. We had to trust the tow truck men who were extremely kind. Donna was towed away to their garage and we followed to sort out our things. The garage men were wonderful, helped us with insurance claim forms, allowed us to ring Ruth at the Children's Hospital, and then drove us with all our things down there to meet her. The Matron took pity on us and gave us rooms for the night. Thursday was a public holiday for Anzac Day and Elaine and I took a bus into town to see the Military Parade, a morning spectacle – they take it all very seriously. Afterwards we walked miles around the city, through Hyde Park, the Botanical Gardens, all very green along the water's edge, by the new Opera House, still only half completed and up to the great Harbour Bridge. Then in the evening we went with Ruth to the Billy Graham Crusade, as we did each evening until the final meeting on Sunday. What a tremendous Spiritual uplift it was. We were members of the 2,000 Choir and to be part of the singing from the heart was a wonderful experience, so beautiful it moved you to tears. We used to have Choir practices half an hour before each meeting – wish you could have been there. The Showground was packed each night with thousands of people. About 4,000 went forward to enquire about commitment to Christ as Saviour and Lord, 90% were under 25 years. Whether it was in the heat of the moment or not, many people realise their need of Christ, someone more than themselves. We met many people and enjoyed the fellowship with other Christians.

On Thursday night we slept at Deaconess House, the Anglican Ladies College who kindly opened their doors to us for a night. On Friday we did a little more sightseeing in the city. We saw many soldiers just back home from Vietnam. We went to the top of a huge building up 48 floors and had a panoramic view of Sydney.

After the meeting Ruth drove us out to Lawson, her home, about 60 miles from Sydney in the Blue Mountains and here we will stay until Donna is repaired. As the man was uninsured we have to cover all the expense and, when assessed, the repair came to 400 dollars – more than the value of the car. They were going to tow her away and dump her, but the garage man pleaded her cause and they have consented to pay. We are more than thankful as we would have really been in the soup! The Rev and Mrs Smith have been so very kind and have offered to have us stay and use their house as home for the next ten days. With a bit of luck we should be back in Alexandra in time to start work on the day arranged. God is so good and has looked after us.

Saturday and Sunday we attended the Crusade meetings but returned each night to Lawson. Monday was rather overcast but Ruth took us to the Blue Mountain beauty spots and we went down in the scenic railway which goes down at a perpendicular drop. The colours of the autumn leaves are breath taking, especially the red maple leaf. Tuesday we spent inspecting the Jenolan Caves with all their rock formation, stalagmites and stalactites. Yesterday Ruth was due back at work so we went into Sydney with her. We took the boat ferry across the Harbour to Manly on the far side where there are beautiful surfing beaches. It was a hot, sunny day. We ate a picnic lunch on the sand and wished our bathing costumes

Photo 13 – Sydney Harbour with the Bridge and Opera House.

Photo 14 – The Billy Graham Crusade in Sydney where Elaine and I sang in the Crusade Choir.

were not still in the car. We went back to Sydney in the new fast 'Hydrofoil' which was great fun. We would have liked another go! We then called at the P&O hire office and made provisional reservations for a ship to America. We have a cabin for the ship 'Arcadia' May 1969 but we are on a waiting list with a good chance for February. The voyage goes via Singapore, Hong Kong, Japan, etc. They only do about three a year – that is why we had to book so early. We then saw a film before catching a train to Lawson.

Monday 13th May 1968

Well, here we are back in Alexandra. The car was just ready in time and we had a swift but safe journey home. We have received our Passports early. They must trust that we will not leave the country before the two years are up. The winter weather is really here with thick frosts and fogs and large wood fires. With descriptions of spring in full swing in Britain, we cannot but comment on how beautiful the hills look, so green they look artificial. We walk on grass as if it is something precious and strange. The land is softer to the eyes.
Now to recap on the end of our holiday in more detail; they were so kind to us at Lawson, we really felt at home. Saturday we took a train into town, a long slow trip stopping at every station en route. June met us at Sydney in her Mini and off we went for the day on a conducted tour of all the famous surfing beaches. We crossed the Harbour Bridge, about eight lanes of

traffic controlled at a toll bridge. We drove around Manly, Mosman and up to Palm Beach where all the 'classy' people have their homes. They certainly are gorgeous with a beautiful view of the sea. We had a picnic lunch, pottered around all the other little boating inlets. In the evening we treated Ruth and June to a dinner out. It was about 1.30am when we travelled back to Lawson. Sunday we spent quietly again, attending Morning Service and had an early night. Monday we went into Sydney, did a little shopping and wandered around the famous King's Cross area, very similar to Chelsea, a place full of atmosphere and very bohemian. Then we called at the garage to get the car. They had done a good job, it appeared, she ran well, only the bonnet catch was loose. We drove through Sydney and picked up the camping gear in Ruth's room at the Hospital and then back to Lawson for the night. Tuesday we had a long 500 mile trip back to Alexandra to make it in time for work.

We left Lawson about 8.30am and made fairly slow headway across the Blue Mountains because of the winding roads and the constant stream of lorries. We stopped at Bathurst, a picturesque old gold-mining town where we saw some beautiful Botanical Gardens. Soon after leaving we noticed that Donna's bonnet was loose and in danger of flying up. We tied it down with a piece of tow rope. We picnicked at lunch time in a glade of Poplar trees with changing autumnal leaves. As dusk came we unfortunately ran over a kitten, a horrible experience. A lady crossed the road right in front of us and quite out of the blue the kitten jumped from the bushes to follow her. We crossed from N.S.W into Victoria at Albury where the car was searched for any fruit – the Victorian fruit fly restrictions. Their search was in vain, as we had none, being wise to the loss of one picnic lunch on one occasion!

We had a hundred miles to go with 400 now behind us. After an evening meal at Wangaratta we drove out of the city but soon found we had a Police car on our tail. With blue lights flashing they hooted us down. We could not think what the matter was as we were doing about the right speed, etc. the Policeman came up looking all official, attempted to book us with one headlight only going, but found both were on. Since the crash one had been slow to come on, but a bump in the road usually fixes that! Poor man felt a little silly. We also found a piece of wire entangled in the back wheel and had to jack the car up to free it. In all, it was an eventful journey. We arrived at about 10pm, started work at lunch time the following day and have been kept busy ever since. We were glad to get back to familiar surroundings again and start work.

Tuesday 21ˢᵗ May 1968

We have had plenty of rain over the past week and hail too. Snow fell a few miles away. Elaine's room had no wall fire and she froze! She managed to get an old Nursery radiator which she leaves on low so her room is now cosy all the time. The Officer Cadet School have been on exercises in the mountains and we had loads of them here at the Hospital coming in by ambulance for treatment of various strains. Several were admitted with exposure having spent six days and nights in the rain and snow in the same clothes. We have two days off now and went to Melbourne yesterday via the Dandenong Ranges. The trees were so lovely, a joy to see. We got a puncture in the middle of the main highway but it was changed in ten minutes and not one driver or pedestrian offered to help us.

Friday 31st May 1968

Today is the last official day of Autumn and June 1st begins Winter, although the weather has been cold enough for that already. It is milder today. The leaves are falling fast and Eildon Weir is filling quickly. We have been very slack at the Hospital with too many staff – I think it must be the penalty we pay for being used to rush in the wards at home. On Saturday evening we went out to dinner with a farmer and his wife, a good feed of stew and dumplings. We were interested to see some of their slides of Alexandra snow covered, also of the Hospital before and after it was burned in 1958. These people have a dairy farm, so we ploughed our way through mud to watch the mechanical milking set-up.

Sunday was Church Unity Day and all the various denominations came to the C/E for Evensong. It was good to see the Church so full. Tonight there is a combined service at the Roman Catholic Church, so we are going out of interest. It actually was good and we enjoyed the evening of fellowship with the people there.

We now have four days off and are thinking of going to Mount Buller to see the snow and skiing. We will have to see how far Donna will get up the hill without wheel chains.

Saturday 15th June 1968

When people get to know that you are leaving there seems to be a large rush of invitations! We went to Mount Buller and the Alpine Village during our days off. We borrowed gum boots and put on all the thick clothing we could find. It was a pretty wet day down here in the valley but as we climbed the Mountain it changed to snow. Donna got within four miles from the top and then wouldn't grip the snow-covered roads at a steep gradient. We turned her around and parked her, taking the four-wheeled drive Land Rover service to the top, an expensive business – one dollar each for four miles.

At the top the village was black against the snow being in the middle of a blizzard. Visibility was nil and only a few brave people were skiing. We saw plenty of snow and decided to go into the warm Chalet Hotel where we enjoyed soup and rolls before walking back to the car. The trees were beautiful, heavily-laden with snow. Donna was now almost completely covered. It was lovely to see snow again and we felt very young and childish again!

That was Tuesday. Then on Wednesday we went to dinner with

Photo 15 – Elaine with Donna in the snow on Mount Buller.

a friend and then to Bible Study at lunch time before going to work in the afternoon. Thursday we attended a talk on European immigrants, that is Greeks and Italians, which was most enlightening. They have so many different customs and tend to live together in order to maintain them. In numbers they acquire strength and communities grow, which tend to become outcast to the Australian people. The Australians maintain they have no racial problems but this is not true in practise. They are not conscious of the problem, any more than we are in England. They still exist unfortunately.

We were both on duty during the weekend and had a 28-week baby born weighing 1¾lb only. It lived for about two days and was so perfect in every detail. Then we had a sick old man admitted whom Elaine escorted by ambulance to Melbourne for special treatment with lung collapse.

Thursday and Friday we were off duty and we went to Melbourne. We nearly lost part of the engine – the automatic choke from the engine but fortunately it got lodged on the way down. This was soon screwed back into place. We called in to see Ann McRobert first and had coffee with her. We then went into town shopping. In the evening we had a Chinese meal and then we went to see 'Camelot' which we very much enjoyed. A mixture of history, drama, romance, farce, all beautifully photographed. We stayed the night with Pat Pither who used to be our Matron in Alexandra. In the foyer of the cinema we met a Sister we had worked with in Western Australia – what a small world!

Saturday 15th June 1968

To continue – we left Pat Pither after 'brunch' and continued shopping. It sounds as if we are rolling in money, but we are not! Elaine bought herself a pair of trousers, took her alarm clock for repair and did quite a bit of Christmas shopping. We have to get everything off early this year as we are travelling into 'the back of beyond'. We then made our way back to Alexandra.

Thursday 20th June 1968

We went to supper last evening with two other English Sisters working nearby. We had a slide evening and exchanged experiences and adventures – one of them comes from Woking. I bought a little camping stove the other day so we can cook our meals as we travel around this vast continent. Donna's feet are all well shod again and we have booked the car in for a complete overhaul next week. We cannot take too many chances when she has done 75,000 miles on the clock!

Tuesday 2nd July 1968

We got Donna back on Friday evening and bravely paid the bill! It is a terribly wet day today and very cold and the fire is very welcoming. The Home is like an ice box as the plumbers have been in all day making a mess re-plumbing the entire building.

They collected sacks full of Sparrows' nests from the roof. It will be so quiet without them. I forgot to say that the car needed an overhaul, one blown gasket, clutch and starting system – 115 dollars' worth! We have considered selling her but public transport and hotels would be far too expensive in comparison. We would like to see the rest of Australia, so Donna is spending a little time resting – we have become very attached to her. We are having smallpox re-vaccinations tomorrow for our International Travelling Certificates – they have to be done every two years. We have been quite busy at the Hospital overflowing with ladies and only two men. We had a skiing accident in yesterday which made headline news for our little Hospital on the T.V. and newspapers. We only have three more days to go here and it seems strange to be going in some ways. We have no job booked in Queensland, just taking each day as it comes. We shall be meeting friends from here in Queensland where they are on holiday.

Last Wednesday at the Bible Study and Prayer Meeting we were very overwhelmed as they had prepared a tea party for us and presented us with tea spoons and key rings to take with us. I believe there is a small article about us in the Paper – we shall have to see what they have said when it is published on Thursday. We look to the Lord for safe travelling.

QUEENSLAND

Friday 12th July 1968

We spent Saturday and Sunday packing and visiting a few
people. Sunday afternoon Norma Price took us around the Golf
Course and we played nine holes. We really enjoyed it too, in
spite of the mud and the many misses! In the evening we went
out to dinner with one of the Sisters, which was fattening but
very satisfying. We finally left at 11am on Monday, called in at
the farm at Benalla where Margaret Dawe, another Sister, was
spending her days off. We had lunch with her and all the family.
The car ran well and has done so far, even though she is very
laden inside, in the boot and on the roof. We went to Albury
and over the border into New South Wales, north to Wagga
Wagga and then on to Gundagai where we bedded down for
the night by the river.
Tuesday we went to see the marble model of a French
Cathedral made by a craftsman in his spare time over the last
28 years. We drove northwards to Grenfell, Forbes and Dubbo,
the scenery getting gradually browner and drier as we went.
The days were bright but fresh and we have had no rain.
Tuesday night we camped at a place 50 miles from a place
called Walgett, right out in the wilds near an opal mining
district called Lightening Ridge. With the cold nights we were
glad we had the stove to cook hot food and drinks.

On Wednesday morning we went down an Opal Mine and it was fascinating to find out where they came from. In this area the Opals are found in 'nobbles' or 'clusters' whereas they normally run in seams. We examined all the different kinds and then went and hunted for some ourselves among the numerous heaps. Everywhere you look there are white clay piles as if a lot of moles had been burrowing! We looked around and found a few chippings, which we have kept in a bottle. The rough shacks that the people live in have to be seen to be believed and some of the Aboriginals in their tents are a truly typical 'outback sight'.

We bumped into civilisation again for 50 miles. What a joy to be on 'proper' roads again. We spent the night at Tamworth, then on Thursday we went to see the Apsley Falls near Walcha, a truly lovely drop of water. Then on to Armidale, a big town full of churches, schools and colleges. Then up to Glen Innis which has a rock formation similar to that of Stonehenge, though not nearly so fine. Also called in and examined the Sapphire Mines but decided not to stop and try our luck. That evening the moon was full and bright, so we cooked a huge barbecue supper on an open wood fire – delicious! We treated ourselves to a Caravan Park that night at Tenterfield with the luxury of showers and hair washing.

We visited Ghost Gully – a dry river bed with tremendous erosion of the soil forming funny shapes and effects. We climbed to the top of Bald Rock, 4,196 feet above sea level, the second largest single rock in the world. Then we drove over the border into Queensland where the sun was bright and warm. We came across many banana plantations, followed by pineapples – so we ate plenty and they were delicious. We are now at Coolangatta, the first seaside resort of the famous Gold Coast. We met our friends from Alexandra who have a caravan site on the sea shore, so after travelling 1600 miles in five days we shall stay here for a few days rest. We shall soon be swimming again; the sea looks very inviting.

Saturday 20th July 1968

On Saturday we went to see the performing seals and dolphins. We fed the dolphins with fish and had our photos taken in the act. A skin diver showed us his skill at feeding a man-eating shark. Afterwards we lazed in the sun on the beach. Later we went further up the coast to the Parakeet Feeding Gardens. It was a wonderful sight to see thousands of green, red, orange and blue plumed Parakeets flocking down over you when the food appears. The noise of their twittering is tremendous and they wait impatiently on every twig and tree available. The food consists of honey and bread placed on plates which you hold. We were covered with coloured birds as they descended with a great rush on our plates. This procedure occurs every morning and evening.

On Sunday afternoon Eddy and Millie Weeks, our friends with whom we have been staying, took us for a drive through the banana plantations and down to the Natural Arch, which is a

Photo 16 – Feeding the dolphins.

Photo 17 – Feeding the birds at the Bird Sanctuary on the Gold Coast.

bridge formed by rock formation set in a deep ravine.

On Monday we left Coolangatta after a visit to the Car Museum up the coast. 'Genevieve' the vintage car from the film of the same name was there in place of honour. We saw many other models and had some rides in them which was great fun but rather bumpy. We drove through the Gold Coast resorts – reminded me of Blackpool, very commercialised, filled with neon lights, fish and chips and candy floss. Admittedly the ninety miles of golden sands and surfing seas are beautiful.

We arrived in Brisbane on Monday evening, took ourselves to a 'Drive-In' Cinema before bedding down for the night. Brisbane is the capital of Queensland, is situated on many hills and is a typical busy centre with trams running down the road intersection where no one knows who is going to move first!

We attempted to get employment but nothing doing. They would not register Elaine until they had a board meeting in the month because of her Children's Training with her General training being slightly different to theirs. It was all completely stupid and unreasonable but perhaps it was for the best.

We were rather worried as this penalised our chances of work greatly and we really needed the employment very much. We hoped and prayed we would be able to get other types of work but this proved to be a complete fallacy. Tuesday evening we drove to Caloundra where we caught up with Eddy and Millie again. This proved to be the beginning of heavy rains. In fact, we had five days of solid rain together – it poured in sheets – come to sunny Queensland!

Wednesday we headed northward again and came into Sugar Cane country. The little Cane Trains running in and out of the fields taking the cane into the factory. We went into the Ginger Factory, one of the greatest in the world. It was most interesting and we were able to get many samples afterwards. Then we continued our drive up to Maryborough and Bundaberg, then to Gladstone until we arrived at Rockhampton on Friday morning. By this time we had clocked 2,500 miles in the last ten days. Just before we reached Bundaberg we heard a loud bang and found that one of the new tyres had lost a section. We managed to acquire an exchange new one, thank goodness.

Rockhampton is one of the nicest towns we have seen yet, fairly large but classy with lovely houses all beautifully laid out. All the houses here are built on stilts, off the ground to allow air to circulate as a cooling system. Sometimes it is covered in as garages with lattice work. Near the town is Mount Morgan, a very large Copper and Gold mine. We went on a two hour tour of the factory which was most interesting. We seemed to have walked miles but it made a nice change to driving. Meanwhile Donna was having an oil change.

Friday evening we travelled 180 miles up the coast to Mackay. A very wet road with one lane in the middle. The verges are soft but when a car comes the other way you have to veer off the road and pray that no stones or grit will smash the windscreen. We passed an overturned oil truck in flames. It must have skidded and sunk badly on the soft verges. By this time it was 8pm and the glow of the flames showed up for miles.

Today we have spent touring Mackay and we have booked a caravan park for two nights. We have been rather depressed with the continual wet weather – living in the car can get rather uncomfortable, you seem to eat, sleep and dream water. The weather did improve with the new week – praise God! We went to Church on Sunday and then we drove up to Hillsborough with its untouched beach. We got a puncture of course!

Sunday 28th July 1968

On Monday we spent the morning going round a Sugar Cane Farm. We were shown the various stages of growth and implements used. The Cane grows to about 10 feet high and has an arrow shaped grassy head. One machine cuts off the heads, the tops, cuts the cane, chops it up into pieces and drops it into the wire baskets on wheels. We chewed a piece of raw cane, but it was rather sickly. They showed us how the men used to chop it by hand before the machines took over. This has cut down employment considerably in these parts, even for the locals. There certainly was no chance of us getting work. We managed to get our puncture mended and in doing so the mechanic broke off a wheel bolt, so we had to wait for that to be done. We gave Donna a good shampoo as she was mud all over and packed up to leave Mackay.

On Tuesday we took a boat trip from Shute Harbour to the islands of the Whitsunday Passage near to the Barrier Reef. We had a wonderful day and a welcome change from driving. We left at 9am and called at South Molle Island, a peaceful unspoiled tropical island with coconut palms and little chalets looking out over the beach. There were brightly coloured shrubs everywhere, sandy beach and lovely walks over the hills behind. The only main building was a hotel which contained everything you needed, plus a beautiful swimming pool outside.

Then we went on the Hayman Island which has the reputation of being a rich man's paradise. A little train took us from the quay to the hotel, all gaily printed. There we enjoyed a magnificent barbecue lunch all prepared. We were very piggish and took full advantage of it all. We could sit under palm trees or on soft green lawns.

Saturday 3rd August 1968

We have spent a lovely restful week here in the North. We have had time to receive our post from Adelaide. On Monday Donna had a grease and front wheel alignment – the latter the result of our Sydney accident. We took a mountain train ride seventeen miles north of Cairns to a picturesque railway station at Kuranda all covered in ferns. The scenery on the way up was splendid with the overhanging tropical foliage, water cascades, etc. Tuesday we did a round trip of the Atherton Tablelands,

Photo 18 – Butterfly Fish on the Great Barrier Reef, Green Island, Queensland.

again a mountainous district with panoramic views over the sugar cane, dairy farming and tobacco district. We visited a few lakesides and an old crater which was far too dark to photograph. Also found a huge over-hanging fig curtain tree in the middle of the forest. The ferns grew out of the tree trunks in all kinds of directions but mostly high up where it is difficult to examine closely. We called at Herberton and Atherton Townships and passed an orange grove on the way back. A garage mechanic offered to repair the noisy exhaust for us in the evening – a chap we met at Church. We always have exhaust problems!

On Wednesday we leisurely took ourselves northwards and stopped at Port Douglas, about forty miles north of Cairns along the Cook Highway. The drive took us right up the coast adjacent to the sea. We made a big camp fire, cooked supper on the beach. When we collected the wood we met so many Toads – they were everywhere, even when we went to the toilet they were on the doorstep, so we preferred the woodlands. Which reminds me, we could write a book on toilets, but I will not waste space here!

Thursday morning we wandered along the sandy seashore and collected some beautiful shells. The beach was deserted and looked lovely. About midday we went thirty miles on to the farthest point of Australia with bitumen roads to Daintree and Mossman. The flora of this district is by far the most outstanding in Queensland that we have seen. Mossman is a sugar milling centre and has a small hospital built in Spanish style. Close by we saw an Aboriginal Mission Settlement. It consisted of a cluster of prefabricated houses in a palm glade. It seems impossible to improve their lot as they have little idea how to live in them. The little children have such lovely faces in spite of their runny noses. We camped again at Port Douglas and cooked chops over the fire.

On Friday morning we drove the car over four miles of sand then found a good spot and stopped. We had our first swim of the year. Then in the afternoon we drove back southwards to Ellis Island Beach, about fifteen miles north of Cairns, then we camped for the night. We took ourselves to a Café to have a coffee before retiring which we greatly enjoyed as there was a negro pianist playing Calypso music, which was rather appropriate to the setting of coconut palms and a moonlit beach.

Saturday we came back to Cairns where we once again had a wash day, that is clothes, hairs and Donna! In the evening we went to a 'Drive-In' Cinema and saw 'The Blue Max'. Today is Sunday and we shall be off to Church shortly. It is a lovely day and we are sitting in the sun, having got quite brown over the past few days. Plus 50 gnat bites, which are not particularly welcome! Tomorrow we are going to begin our trek of 2,000 miles to Darwin. We are getting rather tired of travelling so we do trust we shall find a job soon. We are so short of money now, we are dipping into our savings, but we have seen and done so much – we are so thankful.

Thursday 8th August 1968

We are still nomads on safari, but we have got well adjusted to our living conditions. Monday we left Cairns and commenced our long trip – we are about half way at Mount Isa, a large industrial mining town in the midst of dry scrubland. We started off across the Atherton Tablelands in wet weather which caused our windscreen to leak again, but as soon as we left the Mountains we found the sun again. We drove about 250 miles on good bitumen roads, then we pulled off into the scrub just outside Georgetown, where we made a large camp fire and cooked supper. The next day we drove from Georgetown to Karumba via Normantown, another 300 miles or so. The roads were rather rough, consisting of sandy unmade roads and we got covered in red dust as usual. The countryside was pretty monotonous, mainly flat with a few creek beds that were dry. Normantown is a typically cowboy town, very hot, very dry and dusty with the majority of the townsfolk 'living at the hotel' or loitering about. The men actually dress like cowboys with jeans and Stetsons. We can appreciate why they love their beer as it is the only really good thirst quencher. The Aboriginals now have free licensing but cannot hold the liquor and are always in trouble with controls – it's sad to see it. The white man has taken so much from him and given so little in exchange which is helpful to them.
We drove to Karumba, a prawn fishing resort on the Gulf of Carpentaria, an awful road of bumps and sand drifts but we

managed to manoeuvre Donna through without getting stuck. When we arrived we discovered a support missing from the exhaust pipe, but we managed to tie it up until we reached a garage. The sea breeze was so welcome in the heat and there was a magnificent sunset over the sea with all the fishing vessels in port. We camped there for the night, rather rough, we felt grubbier all the time! On Wednesday we tried to get a job at the prawn factory but, as the season finishes in a couple of weeks, we had no luck. We did, however, buy a pound of fresh King Prawns, the biggest we had ever seen and ate them with relish for lunch. We then bumped our way back to Normantown where we persuaded someone to put a support on the exhaust pipe.

About lunch time we started south for Cloncurry. The first 120 miles was on good bitumen road, then we hit the gravel again. We passed over many grids which divide up the herds of cattle and on one occasion we met a gate instead. Elaine tried to get out to open it but found herself locked in. The door had stuck with the vibrations and mine had done the same. We just sat and laughed imagining ourselves clambering into the back to get out. Eventually we managed to unstick Elaine's and on we went. We camped just outside Clonclurry that night. On Thursday the car had to go into the garage again to have the exhaust put right. Then on down to Mount Isa where we found it was a Rodeo Week – the biggest in Australia – so we decided to remain there for the weekend and watch some of the main events. We were looking in a really good Christian bookshop when we met a lovely Christian fellow. He opened his home to us and we were able to have a bath, use the washing machine and have a meal with his wife and family. So that night we 'sparkled again' and smelled a little sweeter by the end. We felt pounds lighter and almost civilised again. Sunday we shall make our way to Darwin, another 1,000 miles and probably reach there by Wednesday. Well made roads all the way, thank goodness. We are tanned and well, the temperature is now 98°.

Friday 16th August 1968

We are both well, still brown and covered in mosquito bites. At Mount Isa we had an interesting time. We watched the Mardi Gras parade, similar to our carnivals but without the more polished entries. Some floats were humorous though. The streets were full of people and, with the side shows and the background of an illuminated mining industry, it was a colourful spectacle. On Saturday we went to the Rodeo for the day and really enjoyed watching the buck riders, bull riders, etc., a real cowboy day. Unfortunately, it was spoiled by many drunks who had been steadily drinking all day. Aboriginals and Whites were alike in this and brawls were not infrequent towards the evening. A man was knocked out cold at our feet when we were buying a coffee. The litter on the ground was ankle deep! Many of the kids were collecting up all the empty beer cans. They get paid so much for certain numbers. Things were quieter in the evening when we watched the Pony events and wood-cutting championships and then heard Slim Dusty singing Western songs. We met a couple of German chaps with whom we spent the evening and we found them very interesting company.

Sunday after lunch we began our journey to Darwin. We camped by the roadside 80 miles south of Tremena and the second night we camped in a huge sand pit near Harrimah. On both days we drove on good roads but, when meeting other traffic, you have to swerve off in order to avoid broken windscreens. The numerous road haulers have about four trailers for carrying cattle and they kick up a great deal of dust. The road was pretty straight and flat and the scenery much the same – dry scrubland and quite a number of dead cows along the way with the good old vultures flying overhead waiting for the pickings. Lots of burst tyres and hundreds of tin barrels could be seen by the road, presumably used for petrol and tar when the road was made. We acquired a puncture at Elliot and we were not very impressed when the garage watched us take the tyre off and charged two dollars for repairing it. What made it worse was we had to have it repaired again the following day as a piece of nail was left in. The drive on Tuesday was more interesting, undulating with more trees and rocks. We visited an unspoiled resort at Mataranka where there is an old Homestead. In the tropical grounds they have a thermal pool which maintains itself at 84° all the year round. The minerals are very concentrated in the water which are supposed to be beneficial to health. However, if you remain in too long it makes you rather weak. We had a beautiful swim and picnicked in the woods. There was practically nobody around. Some of the rock formations were unique – one, in fact, was called 'Churchill's Head' and there did seem to be a likeness. Tuesday night we camped at Pine Creek outside the garage. The countryside has a plague of rats and much of the woodland was being burned out in order to exterminate them. As evening drew on we passed huge bush fires – controlled we supposed, although we saw nobody. On Wednesday we arrived in Darwin.

ALICE SPRINGS

Wednesday 28th August 1968

Darwin is the only place in Australia with any evidence of war damage. There are still a few bombed houses, the remains of aircraft hangers and numerous hidden airstrips in the bushland. The actual city is growing in the usual modern fashion with some lovely buildings being erected. The bungalow type houses were again built on stilts for the heat to allow circulation. There was an area of poverty in the housing estates of corrugated iron shacks. The city caravan parks were crammed full of families who use them as permanent homes. The prices of homes are so high in cost for many of the people. In fact, the cost of living was terribly high due to all the freight charges to bring foodstuffs, etc., so far north. We attempted to get employment of any kind but after three days of trying we could find nothing. We had Donna serviced, purchased a new tyre for the one we had ruined on the way up. We explored the sights of Darwin. The Cathedral was Roman Catholic, large, majestic and modern. The C/E Church was an old pioneer Church, similar to our parish churches. We attended the United Church on Sunday, a combination of the Methodist, Presbyterian and Congregational, again a very ultra-modern building, the A plan style. The place is very cosmopolitan with mixed cultures, religions and nationalities. A Chinese Temple was one of the formations with all the little idols and images. The Chinese are descended from the Gold Rush days and they are taking no more immigrants. We liked the Harbour, well-sheltered by the Peninsula, quite a busy trading port and exporting Uranium. On Saturday we took a day trip across the other side of the Peninsula to a place called Mandorah – about an hour's boat trip away. Rather a disappointing place with only one café, shop and a hotel. We had a lovely swim in the sea and collected more shells and we are getting very burned on the shoulders again. After lunch we watched an Aboriginal Corroboree. The Natives were all in their paint and they danced for us. A 'Happy Dance' first to get them in the mood, then dances to illustrate the way they hunt crabs and kill bullocks. We enjoyed it very much and I was able to take some photos. It was good to see the didgeridoo in use. They had funny names such as 'The Prince of Wales' who was, incidentally, the champion dancer in the Northern Territory. On the ship back we met a man who told us that four English Nursing Sisters were on the cargo ship going round Australia and it was in dock at Darwin. They turned out to be Kay, Liz and Lyn, with whom I worked at Southmead Hospital in England. We went on board their ship and had a good chat; it was good to see some familiar faces. Afterwards we treated ourselves to a huge Chinese meal and felt thoroughly full.

We camped each night at a place called Howard Springs, about sixteen miles out of Darwin. A beauty spot with a natural spring for swimming and after the day's temperature of 90°-100° a cool swim was wonderful. We also visited an animal zoo where I held around my neck an 11 foot Python, an experience indeed! The baby Emus were lovely. We left Darwin on Sunday and drove out to a place called Humpty Doo where there are rice fields. We drove around the farms and saw the rice in various stages of growth – what a bright green the shoots are. Nearby, as part of the irrigation, was Fog Dam. We drove across the middle and there were thousands of birds – Ducks, Herons, Storks, Cranes, etc., a wonderful selection. The noise was deafening at times, Peter Scott would be in his element here. After lunch we drove to another beauty spot called Berry Springs, where we enjoyed another swim in natural reserve surroundings. I must say I was very glad to get away from the Darwin heat as I had been eaten badly by the large mosquitos there. Sunday night we camped at Pine Creek outside a garage as we did previously. Monday we went to Katherine and took a little flat-bottomed boat ride through some magnificent gorges. There are about fifteen discovered so far but we only touched two of them. We took the boat so far then climbed over rocks the rest of the way about 800 yards. Then into another boat to go round the second gorge. The people in the boat were very chatty, one man particularly had travelled all around the world and was very enlightening about some of his observations on 'pubs'. Another two boys were travelling by jeep and had crossed over the desert from Western Australia, had a great journey and had taken some good photos of the sunrise across the desert. The sides of the second gorge were sheer, 1,000 feet up and 1,000 feet down under the water, red rugged rocks which shone vividly in the sun. The water was cool, clear, deep and reflected everything like a mirror. We saw some fresh water Crocodiles, about 3-10 feet long, but they were very shy and kept darting away when we got too near them. Underneath the overhanging rocks you could see the swallow nests built in the exact shape of a bottle – these birds are known as the Bottle Swallows. It was a lovely two hour trip but we couldn't resist a quick swim before we continued our journey.

We camped Monday night in a palm grove on the property of A. Gunn, who wrote the book 'We of the Never Never'. The actual homestead, known as 'The Elsey ', was supposed to be 40 miles inland but we could not find it in spite of searching pretty hard.

Tuesday night we camped at Renner Springs Hotel garage. Wednesday we drove back to the crossroads where we had turned northwards for Darwin but this time we were southward bound. We went through Tennant Creek, a mining township past an area known as the 'Devil's Marbles' which are clusters of huge boulders piled on top of each other over acres of ground. We camped about 20 miles north of Alice Springs on Wednesday night, thus arriving in that famous town on Thursday. We have now passed the central spot of Australia where there is a monument to Stuart, the man responsible for the road – the Stuart Highway. The weather has been awful and it rained for about five days making all the roads to the various beauty spots impassable. So all the tourists are having to wait around until the buses and Land Rovers can get through. We were told there were no jobs at the Hospital here when we enquired at Darwin. We learned later there were plenty of vacancies and we were not very pleased! We acquired a job for one month at a motel starting on Friday with food and accommodation provided. This will enable us to see something of this interesting area. We have met two other Nursing Sisters who are touring like us and also are stuck waiting for the roads to clear. We now have all got jobs. We have made a four and make huge camp fires at night and cooked together. This is in a Caravan Park nearby. We attended Church, the Memorial Church of the Rev Flynn who started the Flying Doctor Service and who should we meet there but some friends from Blackwood. The couple, in fact, who gave us a roof rack. It was wonderful to see them and we were able to catch up on all the news. They are camping in another caravan park waiting for the roads to clear to continue their trek to Adelaide, a thousand miles away, all dirt roads.

Tuesday 3rd September 1968

One thing is for sure, after two months of camping and really roughing it, we were very thankful to find some form of civilisation. It was lovely to get our bags unpacked and give everything an airing. It is rather nice being a working girl again, though the type of work is an experience in itself. We are now Housemaids in a Motel which possesses 50 bedrooms, all twin or three bed and there is usually about four of us to do them out each day working from 8am to 4.30pm. Most people only call for one night. The first few days we were pretty tired as the divans are low – I feel as if I am bending double. We have to change all the beds, dust, brush and mop each room and then clean all the toilets, showers, basins, etc. However, it is good fun for a short while and we meet many interesting travellers in the course of the day. There is a swimming pool here and we are allowed to use it after work. Sometimes it is wonderful to fall in when you ache all over.

Today the rain is heavy again and all the trips to the beauty spots are off. Of course, there has been a drought for eight years but, now that we are here, it has broken. Our accommodation is nothing wonderful, single rooms, known as tin shacks, but clean with the usual bed and furniture. My door doesn't close, so apart from being able to gaze out at the stars, it is a luxury after the car. We have the same meals as the guests, which consists of four meals, so I suppose the weight will appear again! We hope to counteract the food with work. By working at this motel we get free tours around the area as this is the aircraft and pioneer centre. We are hoping to take a trip on Thursday through some gorges. We see quite a bit of our two friends. They are fine Christian girls; it is a joy to share fellowship with them. They have remained in the caravan park, with their beautiful dog Zara, a cross between a Golden Labrador and Alsatian. One of the girls is a kitchen maid, the other a waitress. Tonight we are going to the film festival to see some of the award winning films. Really well done, a bit of culture very hard to find in this country. They seem to have more here than most other places.

Saturday 14th September 1968

We have been very busy with our scrapbooks, catching up with our travels through Queensland and the Northern Territory. Last Thursday we had our tour of the gorges which was really great. Quite free – it costs 14 dollars usually. We left at 6am in a little bus which held 27 passengers. All the buses have names – ours was called 'Lavapinta' which means 'Flowing Water', an Aboriginal name. We drove firstly to Ellery Creek, which was very pretty. There was plenty of water in the gorge and we had some vivid reflections of the red rock faces and the trees. We built a camp fire and boiled a big billycan of tea to have with our packed salad lunch. Then we went on to Serpentine Gorge which appears as its name describes. We climbed up a high cliff and took some good photos looking down the narrow winding gorge. Next stop was Ormiston Gorge which was perhaps the most magnificent because of the great height of the mountains on either side. We caught the sun on it as it went down. We enjoyed a steak barbecue supper at Glen Helen Gorge. I climbed up over the gorge, almost sheer, and met a fellow on the way up. He was on a camping safari and we could see the tents clearly from where we were. The sun was setting on the red rock and it was a lovely sight. We arrived back about 9.30pm. Friday and Saturday we were back at work, although on Saturday we got off early to attend the Henley-on-Todd Festival. During the rainy season, which is very rare, the River Todd runs through Alice Springs. Most of the time, as now, it is just a river of sand. Each year they have boat race entries as with the Henley-on-Thames Regatta at home. As it is on sand they have bottomless sailing boats. The crews hold bars attached to the boat and they run along the sand with the sails flowing in the breeze. A team entered from our Motel called 'The Mount Gillon Babes'. They managed to come second. It was very hilarious.

Sunday and Monday we worked. Tuesday we had a day off, decided to clean out our rooms, scrubbed our suitcases which have a well-travelled look! In the afternoon we drove to the Old Telegraph Station which was the original site of Alice Springs. They are now renovating the old buildings and making a

Museum to keep a little of the history. The memory mostly concerns the Pioneers who built the telegraph wires from Darwin to Alice Springs and south. There was apparently great loss of life and great hardships at the time – probably at the beginning of the century.

On Wednesday Elaine was able to go on a bus tour to a Lutheran Mission to Aboriginal People at Hermansburg on the Finke River. It was founded about ninety years ago and is very well established. I was able to go the following week and we all enjoyed it very much. They were very proud of the Church that the Aboriginals themselves had built. They also showed us their artistic works which were on show. There was, of course, the Christian influence which was not as alive as I would have liked but it was at least part of their lives. They were fairly strictly controlled as regards leaving the Mission, but very generously and comfortably kept on the whole. Other than the Mission, the Aboriginals have been housed in Government settlements and also their own free areas to which very little control is given. As a result they appear rather wild and slummy to our eyes. The Government settlements, however, have lovely schools to teach the children, homes for the families, jobs for the men. They also have facilities for cooking and washing and ironing, etc. We did visit one of these and we were shown around by one of the natives. The children were so delightful with their runny noses. They pick up our bugs so easily and they seem to stay. There were plenty of dogs around, apparently the more they own from a native point of view, the better family

Photo 19 – Me with some Aborigine children at the Lutheran Mission.

you are supposed to be. Afterwards we drove twelve miles to Palm Valley across rocks and sandy creeks, very rough indeed. We were thrown all over the bus, the last two miles took half an hour to negotiate. It was well worth it, however, as these particular Palm trees, which are the only ones of their kind in the world, grow very wild. It was intensely hot in the valley and really very interesting. We went for plenty of walks and I took plenty of pictures.

On the way back we passed some fascinating rock formations, one in the shape of a Cathedral, one in the shape of a Battleship. I got rather sun-burned on the shoulders! Tonight we are going to a Barbecue party to celebrate the departure of several of the girls here. After the heavy rains we have had the countryside, normally very dry, has become a garden. The wild flowers spring up, almost overnight, a pretty sight everywhere we go.

Saturday 21st September 1968

There has been some delay with the post as the 'Ghan', the train from Adelaide only comes twice a week. We are Housemaids for one more week only as we leave on the 30th September. We are hoping to go to Ayers Rock with Jan and Penny, our nursing friends, plus their dog Zara. With two cars going if one gets stuck the other will have to pull them out. We are making sure we have the car checked and that we are stocked with plenty of food, petrol, water, tow-ropes, etc. We hope to drive on south after the Rock over very rough country to Adelaide, about 1,000 miles.

I have been very busy working in the Motel by day and three evenings a week at a Milk Bar in town. I wasn't back from Palm Valley until late and Elaine filled in for me. She was exhausted but she really enjoyed it. I must say it has been very hard work but I have done many things I have never done before. Selling confectionary, milk shakes, making sandwiches and serving hot meals, washing up, cleaning tables and making expresso chocolate and coffees. Variety is certainly the spice of life!

On Thursday the Girls treated us to dinner out and the local drama production to celebrate the anniversary of leaving England. It was a lovely evening. On Friday Jan and Elaine went to the Cattle Sales which were very interesting to see with the great cattle owners in town wearing Stetsons, the lot. I was able to sneak down for a short while. The weather is getting hotter now as the summer is getting nearer. We both have plenty of swims in the pool but with the heat come more flies and they drive you mad! The nights are cold so it's easy to sleep. In fact, Jan and Penny sleeping in sleeping bags on the ground woke up one morning to find themselves covered in frost. Elaine and I decided to buy an Opal for each other. I had been meaning to buy a stone to replace her stolen pendant and this seemed a good opportunity. Elaine chose a 'tear drop' shape and I had an oval shape. Mine was for a ring and hers, of course, for a pendant. We shall have them set when we get back to England.

Sunday 29th September 1968

Donna the car is now ready for the off and we are loaded up all ready to go. Yesterday the ignition fell apart. The Coach Mechanics mended it for us. Tomorrow we are off to Ayers Rock about 300 miles and we hope to stay at The Lodge, an annex to this Motel – we should have free accommodation for working here. Jan and Penny will be with us.
The weather continues very hot and we have lived in the swimming pool to cool off. It has been hectic the last week as it is the end of the season and all the staff have gone mad. Everyone throwing everyone else into the pool. One of the Mechanics, an Austrian by birth, threw our Head Receptionist, a Canadian, in. She took it all very well and was fully prepared. We made sure we didn't get caught! Well, we are now off to Church, the Flynn Memorial as usual.

AYERS ROCK

Tuesday 8th October 1968

Here begins another great adventure on leaving Alice Springs. Both Elaine and I are blooming in health and are very tanned. We left on Monday after packing the last things into the car. We drove about 80 miles south to our place of rendezvous with Jan and Penny. They were two hours late as they had had to get the car re-registered which they thought would be straight forward. However, having had N.S.W. licences previously, they had to go through a driving test and car fitness before acquiring licences in the Northern Territory. Elaine and I were sitting on the side of the road having lunch, saying we would give them five more minutes and along they came. We hadn't driven far when we heard a rattle in our engine. On examination we found that the bracket holding the battery in place had broken. We managed to secure the battery with rope but it quickly worked loose so every few miles we had to check it.

On the way we looked around for the Henbury Craters which were made by meteorites but we were unsuccessful. Then we turned down a deeply sandy track with sand high on each side. It drove into the undercarriage of the car throwing up a lot of dust. In order to get over quite steep rises in the road we had to go full speed in order to get over the top. It made a change to driving on corrugations. About 40 miles along the track we paused to put some fuel in the tank but when we wanted to start the engine, Donna was as dead as a doornail! The generator light would not even register. After a while we had practically given up, when everyone was praying frantically for a miracle to happen, she suddenly decided to go, praise to God indeed!

About 3pm we came to Wallara Ranch which is a small Motel/Garage/Homestead run by an English couple. The man tied our battery on more securely for us and we filled up with petrol before continuing. The track was just wide enough to get one car through and was like a switchback. The wild flowers were very spectacular, all colours and varieties. One particular yellow flower carpeted the shrubs like buttercups and another one which they called a 'Poached Egg' flower resembling our daisy. Jan and Penny managed to drive in this thick sand very well considering they had only been driving for ten months. They used to keep about half a mile behind us out of our dust. On one occasion they seemed to be a long time catching up, so we turned and went back. We found them bogged in a mound of sand having swerved off the track. In order to get the shovel and sack out of our boot we emptied it completely. It took about an hour of perseverance and perspiration to get it dug out and onto the road again.

Then on to Angus Downs where we had hoped to get the bracket mended but the Aboriginal mechanic had gone 'Walk About'. The actual station consisted of a few shacks and a field full of camels. Shortly after leaving here we joined up with the main road leading to Ayers Rock. This proved to be no better, a wide gravel sand track and very bumpy. We drove both cars as far as Curtain Springs Homestead and then we left Donna to have the bracket mended. We took our sleeping things and left everything else in the car. We drove the last 50 miles to Ayers Rock in 'Victoria', Jan and Penny's grey Holden van plus Zara the dog, of course. It was quite a tight squeeze with three of us in the front and the fourth plus luggage, food and the dog sat in the back. We arrived at Ayers Rock at 10pm so we could only see the enormous size by silhouette in the dark. On arrival at the Motel where Elaine and I were supposed to be staying we found the Manager who was most put out as he had not been told we were coming. They had not sent out coke to heat the water for the guests' showers, etc. and there was barely enough food for guests and certainly not enough to feed us. That just about finished our day! We decided we would just retire to bed and worry about everything else in the morning. Elaine and I slept in beds and Jan and Penny on their li-los in our room. On Tuesday it was Penny's birthday. We got up at 5am to watch the sunrise. It was magnificent and our first real view of the Rock. It goes a bright orange at sunrise and there is colour in the midday heat and deep orange to dark silhouette in the evening. After breakfast we started to explore. The problem of food was solved as Jan and Penny shared their food with us so we managed very well. It is rather difficult to describe the Rock. It is made of reddish rock which looks like sandstone at first glance but is definitely not. It lies in the flattest desert we have ever seen. It is about five miles around the bottom and 2,000 feet above sea level. It was the centre of Aboriginal culture and so much of their myths and legends are portrayed on the walls of the caves in paintings and diagrams. The names of the caves were 'Maternity Cave', 'Fertility Cave', 'Initiation Cave' which describes the different uses of each one. In fact, their primitive way of life was quite civilised in some respects. There are marks to be seen on the Rock. One is in the shape of a brain or human skull. Another piece tagged on the side is called the 'Kangaroo Tail'.

One of the greatest challenges is to climb the Rock and there is

Photo 20 – Ayers Rock in the Northern Territory.

an organised route with chains erected at the steep parts to haul yourself up with and a white line to guide you up and across the top to the centre. You would get hopelessly lost if you didn't have it to guide you. Whew! What a climb! It was pretty well perpendicular for the first half of the distance and on reaching the top you find you have to walk a few miles across undulations in the Rock to reach the centre. There is a pile of stones in the centre with a book perched on the top. Of course, we filled in our names and some of the remarks in it were a scream, such as 'Where is the helicopter to take us down?', 'Wouldn't do it again', 'What about an ice cream or a drink?' I must say we would not choose to go up again and coming down is not my favourite part as it is very sheer in places and we landed up with blisters on our toes. It was worthwhile though. We had a lovely view of the Olgas, the only other rock formations in the area and they were thirty miles away.

In the evening we watched the sun go down on the Rock, then had a meal and fell exhausted into bed. The next day, Wednesday, was my birthday and we spent it touring the Olgas. We joined one of the Pioneer tours. The Olgas are made up of large rock formations of the same substance as Ayers Rock. Against the horizon they looked very impressive, Mount Olga is equally as high as Ayers Rock itself. We explored some of the gorges and walked up to view the Valley of Winds. Very impressive with the solid walls of red rock on each side. While waiting again for the sunset a mini bus came along and the driver let us climb on the roof so that we could have a better view. We also met some of our acquaintances from Alexandra so we were able to catch up on all the news in Victoria. When we arrived back at the Rock we built a huge camp fire and had a wonderful meal to celebrate three of our birthdays, mine on that day, Jan's the day before and Penny's on the 10th October. Elaine had made me a lovely cake and had sneaked it into the car without me seeing. It had remained remarkably whole after our very bumpy ride from Alice Springs. With some bottles of Cider it finished it all off very well. On Thursday we were up early after our lovely and precious evening of fellowship and treated ourselves to a flight over the Rock in a small four seater plane. We went up at 7.30am and the early morning sun made the Rock shine. We then piled into the car and made our way out of the National Park and back to Curtain Springs where Donna was all fixed and waiting for us.

We had a picnic lunch at Angus Downs in the scorching sun and then onto Wallara Road. Just before we reached the place, about two miles out, we got bogged in a sand creek. While two of us dug the wheels free, the others prepared to attach the tow rope. The task was quickly done except that I had attached the rope to the steering control bar and our wheels therefore were pulled out of alignment. We drove a very crooked path to the Ranch where we again left Donna and all piled into Victoria once again. Then off we went towards the great King's Canyon. Previously we had been told that only four wheeled drive vehicles could go, but we have since discovered that ordinary vehicles could get through. The actual canyon was sixty eight miles away along thick sandy tracks. About twenty miles out from the Ranch we hit a pothole which punctured the back tyre and dented the rim. Out we all got once more to change the wheel only to find their jack would not lift the car off the ground high enough. We ended up digging a hole underneath. By this time evening was drawing in and darkness descending but we managed to get the tyre changed before pushing on in the dark. This entailed ploughing through many creek beds but the Holden Van did a grand job being higher off the ground and having a more powerful engine. We were more than a little relieved to leave Donna at home. About 9pm we got bogged in a creek bed. It was a scream to see us scrabbling away underneath the car trying to dig out the wheels with our hands by torchlight. Of course, our shovel was in Donna! We managed it in the end. Reaching King's Canyon we found a young couple was there and they had built a camp fire. We were able to join them and cooked on their fire. Before long we realised we knew the girl. She had worked at Bunbury Hospital W.A. with us. While Jan and Penny slept outside, Elaine and I curled up in our sleeping bags inside the van. We washed in a rock pool in the morning and did not realise until afterwards that the place was known for its deadly snakes. We did see one with his head buried in the sand and we were glad he decided to remain that way.

We began our climb of the Canyon about 9am as it gets too hot to do anything by midday. From the bottom the view shows an ordinary gorge with nothing out of the ordinary. We were beginning to wonder why we had come through so much for nothing when we reached the top and realised how fascinating the rock formation is. Along the top you could see hundreds of cone-shaped towers which looked something like Chinese temples. This was all natural rock but one wonders how they ever reached such shapes. We came to many deep crevices in the rock and a deep valley with water and palms in the bottom. The sides of the gorge were made up of strata of different coloured rocks which made it all rather colourful. By lunchtime we were exhausted and, after an afternoon siesta and watching all the wild budgerigars mate and build their nests in the trees, we drove back to the Ranch, this time with no mishaps. The man had managed to straighten out our steering bars and refused to take anything for it. We camped the night outside their Ranch enjoying the luxury of a shower and clothes washing session. We had a game of Scrabble and then slept like babies we were so tired.

Saturday we drove back to the main road, had some lunch together and a time of fellowship before Jan and Penny went back to Alice Springs and we began our southward drive once more. It was sad to see them go. We had been through so much together and had really had a great time. We said farewell with a laugh. We all looked like lost orphans – Penny with split jeans, Jan had odd sandal thongs, one red and one blue. My sunglasses were cracked and looked odd, Elaine had one green thong and one blue thong and her sunglasses were taped in the middle as someone had sat on them. We did, however, possess clean respectable clothes and a pair of new thongs each but everything gets ruined in the bush so we did not worry until we reached more civilisation.

Saturday was a hot and humid day and so it was not surprising that Sunday brought torrential rain. We drove on some very stony roads and pulled in at Welbourn Hill Homestead for petrol. Soon after leaving the Homestead Elaine smelled petrol and on investigation we found we had punctured the petrol tank with a heavy stone. Unfortunately it had knocked it on the drainage nut and there was very little we could do. I tried to gum it up with chewing gum but no good. In pouring rain we grabbed everything that could hold petrol as our tank was leaking rapidly. We managed to save about five gallons out of the eight. There we were surrounded with saucepans, water carriers and buckets, all full of petrol. A couple of cars drew up to help, they also tried to seal up the hole but had no success. In the end they cut a piece out of Elaine's leather belt and used it as a washer around the screw. Still it persisted, but we reckoned with care we could drive the 150 miles to the next garage at Cooper Pedy. The men were wonderful and drove behind us all the way in case we had any difficulties.

However, the rain had done its damage and the road ahead of us had become very badly flooded. Large trucks and long trailers with their huge wheels were badly bogged down and having much difficulty getting through. The roadway was actually blocked with water and if you came off the road you usually sank in the bog. On the worst patches Elaine walked ahead testing the ground all the way on the hardest spots. In one spot she fell almost knee deep so we were thankful it wasn't the car. By going off the road we had to cross dykes as well which was rather hazardous for Donna. In order to get through and over these obstacles we had to maintain a good speed. The bumps were bad and as we jumped a dyke the roof rack leaped out of its sockets onto the car nearly throwing all our luggage into the water and, of course, denting the roof as well. Draining the very last drops of petrol, as we had fed it in little bits every few miles, we arrived safely at Cooper Pedy. Very few people apparently got through, but without our faith and trust in God and our prayers for His continual care, we would never have made it. We arrived on Sunday evening very tired but praising our wonderful Lord.

Cooper Pedy is an Opal mining town and lives in a world of its own. As the heat is so intense most of the people live in underground dug out houses which are fascinating to see inside. The population is about 2,000 of very mixed types and nationalities. The main visible buildings are shops and garages and a motel. We parked behind a garage and slept in the car as usual. We met an English mechanic who had only been over here 8 weeks and in exchange for our company and meals he mended our petrol tank for a smaller fee than normal. The average normal rate per hour for a mechanic in Cooper Pedy is £4.10. In fact, the cost of everything is out of this world, mostly because of the isolation and distance from civilisation. The town consists of Greeks, Italians, Canadians, all out to acquire as much money as possible. The atmosphere is rather like a rat race and the town is known as the 'town of sin'. One Greek boy stopped to talk with us and he drove us all around the mine shafts and we were able to collect plenty of Opal chips. His friend offered Elaine an Opal for 20 dollars (£10) and she thought there was a catch in it and I feel may have lost a bargain. About six different men asked us out to different places but we ended up joining a few for a barbecue supper. It was rather difficult to shake them off so we locked ourselves in our car for the night.

Tuesday morning we were all set to go but no generator light and a flat battery. After a morning of getting nowhere we were given a tow start and by lunchtime we were away once more. We had only gone 80 miles when the car stopped dead. As we prayed a jeep came round the corner with two men inside, so they towed us to their Homestead Sheep Station about four miles in the bush. They found the problem at once and what had caused the battery to get low. The cog in the centre of the distributor had cracked right across. So here we are on a real Australian outback station stuck for two or three days while the spare part is flown all the way from Adelaide by the AA. It is flown to Woomera from Adelaide and from there by private airline to this station twenty miles away. The dear man here is going to fetch it from the airfield and, as our AA subscription has expired, he used his to fly it all the way from Adelaide. We just trust it is the right size when it reaches us. They are very kind to us here and it's great fun to live with them for a few days. We had an evening meal from them with the family but otherwise we just had enough food in our boot to last for other meals. We slept in the car as usual. We even had a Church service with the C/E Minister who only gets round infrequently as he has to cover such wide distances. He was a true Christian and we enjoyed lovely fellowship all day Sunday. The Lord knew we were coming and provided every detail. We learned a lot about the Aboriginals which was very useful. They know and love them very much in the bush.

Sunday 13th October 1968

The distributor cog arrived, was the correct size and Mr Stephenson, the Boss here, put it in for us. We were safely on our way by 2pm. About twenty miles down the road we met our English Mechanic from Cooper Pedy. He had two burst tyres while going to a semi-trailer whose steering had broken. We stopped to ask if we could help and Donna decided she wouldn't start again. The Mechanic thought it was the timing device and after altering it he found it was air in the petrol filter pipe. It was soon fixed and we moved on our way but after only ten miles she began to smell and wouldn't pull properly. After investigation we found that the Mechanic had made the timing devise too fast which had boiled the radiator dry, overheated the engine and blown two head gaskets. We could have wept. We were reasonably close to the Mount Eba Homestead so we drove in sounding like a tractor. Finding the Mechanic he made a list of all the things he would have to get up from Adelaide and as it was a long weekend to celebrate Labour Day, we would be stuck until next Tuesday. Apart from that we had insufficient food and money with us. A young chap working on the Station came to our aid and said he had a tin of Chem-i-weld which you can pour into the radiator and seal all the leaks temporarily. Anything was worth a try, so we did, and in twenty minutes Donna was running quietly again and there was no leaking through. The chap said that if we got into any further difficulties along the road his brother worked at the next Homestead. It was here the timing was reset accurately and all was well. We checked the water every ten miles and as we were using a great deal we called on the brother at the next station called Bon Bon Homestead. We drove until midnight on the Friday and then pulled off the road and slept like logs. We were in desert scrubland but we found enough wood to make a fire for a cooked breakfast, our last camp fire in the bush. Saturday and civilisation here we come! We drove fairly slowly so as not to do too much damage to the engine. It was quite interesting as our road took us round the edge of the top secret Woomera Rocket range. We could see some of the Rocket Towers on the skyline but we could not get very near. Evidently Britain is withdrawing shortly from there. We arrived at Port Augusta about 1pm and I don't think we could believe it either! After a cup of coffee and a snack we drove on down to Port Pirie. It was wonderful to be driving on bitumen again, though

Donna was beginning to sound like a tractor again. We arrived at Mr and Mrs Lewis' home and spent the evening showing slides and also seeing some of Ruth's slides of New Guinea. They were very impressive, it made us wish we could go there. Sunday we went to the Congregational Church with Mr Lewis and then out to their farm for a barbecue dinner. Afterwards we left for Adelaide arriving just in time for Evensong at Holy Trinity. It was great to see all our friends again. We went up to Mr and Mrs Green to see if it was alright to stay with them as they had previously sent us a note to say that due to ill health Mr Green had had to retire and that their house was up for sale. However, we found them still at Blackwood, so here we have been ever since.

On Monday we took all day to clean the red mud off the car, cleaning the engine and inside also. It was a day with temperatures in the 80's and by 6pm we had had it. However, Donna looked great for all our efforts. On Tuesday we went to town to collect our post and do some shopping.

Wednesday the car was made in good running order by our reliable garage in order to sell her and we spent the day unpacking and packing. In the evening we had a good wash up of clothes.

On Thursday we went to town for another wooden crate for my luggage and in the evening we went to say goodbye to Mr Rowe, the owner of our previous flat. As our flat was vacant, we would have loved to have settled in once again. Today, Friday, I went to town to buy a new suitcase as mine had been ruined by the rain when travelling. Elaine had to throw out the large revelation zip bag as the zip had rotted and there was a hole in the bottom. It was quite unmendable. In between all these things we have written and posted off all our Christmas cards and our hands are dropping off! We are planning to go to Tasmania next week sometime and maybe work until Christmas, depending on how employment is over there. This is our last visit to Adelaide, so we have many people to say goodbye to. We have certainly had a grand two year circuit round Australia. We are hoping to sell Donna. Well, we shall miss her very much.

TASMANIA

Monday 28th October 1968

At N.E.S.M. Hospital, Scottsdale, Tasmania 7254.

The last two weeks have been very hectic travelling around. Saturday we went to our last 'Drive-In' Cinema in Donna and it was kind of sad. Sunday we went to the Methodist Church in Blackwood in the morning with the Greens. In the afternoon we looked up Muriel Leggat and family and they came with us to the guest service at Holy Trinity Church in the evening. It was for the last time and we shall miss such an active Church full of young people. A well-balanced combination of C/E and Evangelical. Monday we went out to supper with the Senior

Fellowship Group. Tuesday evening we went to dinner with Audrey Dunn and she also held a small reunion of Sisters from the Children's Hospital to bid Elaine au-revoir.

Wednesday was a messy sort of day but in the evening we joined our friends in Blackwood for their Bible study evening. Thursday all our last minute arrangements were done regarding the car and bank, etc. Donna has not yet been sold so we have left her in the hands of our garage owner, an English couple, and very reliable. He was in Customs work in London and had been a River Pilot in the Police Force. We had to get our travelling luggage at the required weight of 44lbs for air travel, so we sent small parcels home by post to cut down the weight. We left Adelaide for the last time by express overnight coach to Melbourne. Audrey Dunn and the Greens saw us off, goodbyes are never easy. We left at 7.30pm and arrived in Melbourne at 7am. It was a good trip, we managed to sleep on and off, although there was not very much space to stretch your legs. The seats reclined and were very comfortable. After breakfast we flew to Tasmania by plane. We had a good flight over the Tasman Sea and arrived at Hobart, the capital, about lunchtime. We went to the 'Tourist Nursing Service' for employment and we were fortunate to acquire positions immediately. After all the red tape was over we looked in at the Nurses Club for the night. Then tea, a bath and bed for 12 hours – absolute bliss!

Saturday we had a brief look around Hobart. All the streets were deserted as the shops were shut, so we had plenty of space to tour the sights. We saw around St David's Cathedral, only to find relics of most of our main cathedrals in England. We climbed up the tower and enjoyed a splendid view of the city, the bridge, the estuary and docks with the mountains all around, Mount Wellington being the highest. We wandered through the parks to Battery Point. It was similar to England, narrow winding streets and the typical little cottages. One of the differences was that many of them had tin roofs rather than tiles. The gardens were full of flowers and very colourful. We met one of the Pioneer coach drivers we had known in Alice Springs. Then, after lunch, we caught the Express Coach to Launceston on the other side of the island. We were about four hours travelling and we passed through green and mountainous countryside. The weather was inclined to be 'rain with sunny periods' – very home from home!

While we were pondering over a map in Launceston a young man came up to offer us a Bible tract. He noticed we were wearing Scripture Union badges and welcomed us very warmly. He was attending the Missionary Training College in Launceston run by the Worldwide Evangelisation Crusade (W.E.C.). He asked us to go and stay at the College, so when we arrived there we did just that. We spent all of Sunday with them sharing in college life and discipline, meeting many people, learning much of the work expected of them. They all shone with the presence of Jesus in their lives and we felt we belonged to this wonderful family of God.

On Monday morning two Sisters from the Hospital where we were going came to pick us up. I found, to my surprise, that one of them trained with me in Bristol Royal Infirmary. It was a forty minute drive to the Hospital through really beautiful countryside and winding mountain roads. The name of the Hospital is the North East Soldiers' Memorial Hospital, Scottsdale, N.E.S.M. for short. The population of Scottsdale is about 3,000 people and the hospital is about the same size as the one in Alexandra. The garden is full of Rhododendron bushes in bud. They should show a splendid display later on. The Sisters' quarters are modern with all conveniences possible. We commence work tomorrow morning and hope it won't take too long to settle into a new routine.

Wednesday 30th October 1968

We have commenced work. We have to wear veils instead of caps here and they are very cumbersome. They seem so large. We all take turns on nights and I have offered to do permanent nights to save Elaine and the others as they find it so much harder to sleep than I do. The mountains are all around us as we lie in our rooms. They must look very impressive in the winter with the snow. Just now the Spring is in the air and the birds are singing merrily. We changed the clocks at the weekend for daylight saving. Tasmania is the only state which carries out this alteration but at least it makes the evening lighter.

Photo 21 - Nursing in North East Soldiers' Memorial Hospital, Scottsdale, Tasmania. Back Row Left to Right: Myself, Carol Jay, Jean Borman, Joan Chugs, Elaine, Ann Chibbett. Front Row Left to Right: Liz Pullin, Matron Smith, Ann Winter.

Thursday 7th November 1968

A fortnight has gone by and we have settled down extremely well. We work the same shift system here: 7am-4pm, 2-10.30pm, 10pm-7am on night shift with two days off a week. On Tuesday the Children's Welfare Sister, who holds baby Clinics in various parts of the district on different days, took Elaine and I down to Bridport for the day while she did her work. Unfortunately the day was rather overcast so we didn't see the seaside town at its best but we enjoyed it very much. Bridport lies on the coast, fifteen miles from Scottsdale, and our nearest seaside resort. It has a sheltered inner harbour which is ideal for fishing vessels to anchor. They have a Trout Farm there which is providing a decent supply of trout and it also handles a lot of research into the life of this fish. They keep the ponds filled with half fresh and half sea water. The local inhabitants of Bridport are few but during the summer Christmas holidays the caravans pour in and they have approximately a 7,000 population. The Sister took us for a drive around some of the holiday homes and they are rather lavish! In the evening we came back to dinner with her.

Yesterday the Chairman of the Board, Bert Farquhar, took Elaine and Ann, the other English Sister, out to his property which covers thousands of acres for cattle grazing. He owns the majority of the Tomahawk Bay region of the north east corner of the Tasman coast. On arrival at the property they left the comfort of the car and travelled for the rest of the day sitting on bales of hay in the Landrover. The ride was very bumpy through fields, bogs, creeks, etc. an exhausting ride. While Bert inspected all his cattle, they helped to light fires to burn off the bush and grass which if left can be a danger with fire. This enables the grass to produce completely new growth which is green and therefore not so likely to burn in the hot season. They found a few wild orchids as they went through the bush. I was quite envious of their sunburned, healthy appearances on their return while I had been slogging it out at work! Elaine has had a medical but she is A1 again, praise God. We have a few cases of Hepatitis in the Hospital at present and all of us who have not had the disease have to be inoculated against it, including me. It was a whoppa!

Monday 18th November 1968

We are enjoying a fairly lazy time here after the rushing around and much travelling. Actually having time to do some reading and watch T.V. Elaine has made some slippers which are light to carry. I must make some dresses as I have very few for the summer months just starting. At the moment we have been having rather wintry weather, gales and plenty of rain. Everywhere looks greener than ever but the wind played havoc with the Rhododendron bushes. There is talk at the moment of there being another postal strike over Christmas which will mean chaos once again. We have finished all our Australian Christmas cards so they are all ready to go.

We attended the Scottsdale Annual Show last evening and it was well represented. There were the usual side shows and fun fairs, pavilions for agricultural machinery, household furniture, plenty of crafts on show, entries to the cake competition, floral decorations, preserves, art, etc. all of which was a high standard. We enjoyed the woollen fashion show best, some beautiful dresses. One particularly very nice one in buttercup yellow with black accessories. We are planning our next days off in Launceston in order to visit Jack and Elsa Riley who shared our table when we first travelled over. They are now happily settled in the area near to their only son and family. I am busy on nights but all is going quite well so far. I am afraid I have just had a cold, not very usual for me.

Saturday 30th November 1968

I can hardly believe it is now the last day of November, how time flies. Elaine had a turn with flu this time and was quite poorly with a temperature of 100+. She has been well stacked up with dispirin and fresh orange juice and was much better within two days. Just a sore throat and earache now. We are still having plenty of rain, just like England. We are contemplating remaining here longer than two months now as we have settled in so well. Last weekend one of the Sisters lent us her car for a couple of days. We left Scottsdale at 8.30am, drove down the eastern coastal road. The roads were very narrow and winding so we took a long time to cover a few miles. We detoured slightly off route to view some magnificent waterfalls called St Columba. After so much rain the cascade was terrific. We walked along the path overhung with trees with large ferns growing each side and reached the foot of the falls where we were sprayed with water. After about another 50 miles there was a marked change in the countryside. It was brown and dry having suffered very severe drought for several weeks. The sheep were very thin and bony and vegetation was very sparse. Many of the sheep were sold for a pittance, otherwise they would have died. The east coast is the fishing side of the island and all the harbours are naturally sheltered from the high seas by peninsulas of land. St Helen's was the most attractive of these little townships. We stopped and had some coffee in an old hotel which had a large log fire blazing. We were fortunate as the sun was shining even through the wind and cold. About 4pm we arrived at the pretty little church at Buckland. This is noted as one of the oldest churches and was built by a clergyman from Sussex and is very much patterned on the English style. The windows were delightful. We arrived at Port Arthur at the bottom right corner south of Hobart. This is where all the convicts came from England and elsewhere. It was a beautiful spot but one in which it would have been difficult for anyone to get away as it was joined to the mainland by a narrow piece of land known as Eaglehawk Neck. It was just wide enough for a road. Port Arthur reminded us of an old English estate. All the buildings surround a large green and they were actually playing cricket when we arrived.

The actual Penitentiary is in ruins, also the church and hospital, but many of the other buildings still stood. I think, perhaps, this was the first historical place we had visited since arrival in Australia. The atmosphere made us rather conscious of dear old England.

In the evening light we explored the Eaglehawk Neck area, a very rugged rocky coastline full of caves, blow holes and the famous Tasman Archway with the sea pounding underneath. There was a tessellated pavement which was rather unusual. The sea has smoothed out the rocks making them flat into a pavement of square rock slabs. We slept in the car that night and we managed to sleep well, someone had lent us sleeping bags so we were not cold.

Sunday was a real April showers day, one minute pouring rain and the next bright sunshine, so we tuned our photography accordingly! We had a look around Richmond, especially at the old bridge built by the Convicts. We noticed that many of the houses were Georgian and Elizabethan style.

We then drove up Mount Rumney and enjoyed a good view of Hobart and the estuary. We had our morning coffee in the Botanical Gardens at Hobart. The flowers were very variable, very English-looking and we could have remained ages enjoying such plants as ferns, lilies, roses, pansies, etc. The Government House at the back of the Gardens is built like a Scottish castle. Then we went to the other side of Hobart to a model Tudor Village which was thrilling. A family who had emigrated out from Romney Marsh had a son crippled by polio and he had built the whole village himself. It included many copies of Chilham village and its church, also Cranbrook Windmill, all out of Kent. We then drove up Mount Wellington, the highest mountain overlooking Hobart. Half way up the clouds were very black and the snow came suddenly down. We sat and ate our lunch whilst it blew over and the view cleared. We then drove down to Huonville and the Huonville Valley, a very pretty ride, mountains all snow capped and underneath miles and miles of apple orchards. It must have been a picture in the Spring with all the blossoms out. We managed to do a few miles up the Derwent Valley which is the valley for hops but everything was too wet so we didn't see many in evidence. Then we proceeded up the centre of Tasmania in time for evensong at Launceston church before returning to Scottsdale at 10.30pm. A very full two days, we covered about 500 miles but had seen very much and enjoyed it all. We did pass through a village or town called 'Doo us' and all the houses were named as follows: 'Doo Write', 'Af 2 Doo', 'Didgeri Doo', 'Thistle Me Doo', 'Doo Rest', 'Doo I' – all rather quaint. Now we must get back to work.

Tuesday 10th December 1968

It is a lovely day here, quite a change from the average rainfall. Everyone keeps saying that Summer is coming but we still are pretty cold at night. Each weekend they have a Staff Hospital Request on the local radio station. We listen to our name and choice of record played for us, rather like Family Favourites. We had a bit of excitement here the other day – a man of forty had fallen off the ladder and fractured his base of skull. He joined us in the hospital for about four days and he appeared to be improving when he suddenly collapsed. Everything we could do was done but in the end they decided to send him to Launceston as an emergency. Elaine had the job of escorting with drips, oxygen, suction and breathing machines. They only just managed to squeeze everything into the very small ambulance. The chances of getting him there alive were very slim and he decided to die before departure.

We have finalised our plans about our return trip home. We have decided to leave Australia on 1st May flying to Hong Kong and Thailand, then picking up a Penn Overland Coach in Calcutta, India, then travelling by road to London. We will pass through countries such as India, Pakistan, Afghanistan, Iran, Turkey, Greece, Yugoslavia, Italy, Austria, Germany, Belgium, then across to Dover. We expect to arrive on July 11th 1969.

We attended the Worldwide Evangelisation Crusade Bible College in Launceston to join the students on their open graduation day. We had plenty of fun, fellowship and spiritual refreshment. The personal testimonies of the students were lovely and heart-warming. Len Moules, British Director of W.E.C. came to present the Diplomas, it was great to meet him again. We shared one of the College flatlets and it was very encouraging to see how close he lived to the Lord. Before he took up missionary work in Tibet he had been involved in an

Everest Expedition so he had plenty of tales to tell, plus the twenty years he spent in Tibet. He showed us slides of the new W.E.C. Headquarters at Gerrard's Cross, the old Earl of Somerset's mansion and grounds just off the Oxford Road.

Wednesday 18th December 1968

We are expecting a call from Matron to decorate the Home. Elaine went into Launceston to shop the other day, catching the bus there and back. Others who went carried most everything back with them – milk, post, cases and even T.V. sets which had been in town for repair.

On Sunday we had quite an eventful day. Our little district with the help of the Rotary Club have started a Home Nursing Service. This has made history being the first one in Tasmania. We had T.V. cameras and the Ministry of Health department present to officially hand over the keys to the little mini-van to be used by the Sister chosen for the task. Her duties will mainly be home care of the older people thus relieving hospital beds. We spent most of Saturday preparing chairs, tables and arranging flowers for the party afterwards.

We have now heard that Donna, our car, has been sold to a Vicar at Blackwood. It seemed to be a good price considering how much wear we had given it. Most people wanted it on hire purchase but Elaine, of course, needed a cash settlement before we leave.

Monday 30th December 1968

Well, Christmas is now over for another year. Elaine did some nights but slept pretty well with all the chaos. On the Friday before Christmas we prepared for the party to which all the Hospital Board and Staff were invited. We worked very hard preparing food under the supervision of the Matron who was not a little hypertensive and confused driving us all a little silly. By the evening we had had enough and locked ourselves in our rooms.

Elaine and I then went to the Carols by Candlelight Service which we enjoyed but it was rather poorly supported. It made us feel much like Christmas. We then joined the others at the party which went very well. There was an outside buffet meal under the lights of lanterns, a few games and some folk singing by Jo, the Path. Technician, who plays the guitar. Everyone mixed well and seemed to enjoy themselves. When everyone had gone we all had to set to and do the washing up! Quite a mountain to do.

On Christmas Eve we were asked round to have a drink with Doctor North and his family. They are a wonderful family and made us very welcome.

Elaine was then on nights and apparently had a dreadful night. Plenty of patients, a Midwifery case, the milk fridge burst and blew frosted gas everywhere. At 6.15am one patient died and at 8am another patient died. She was very glad to finish and we went to Holy Communion at 8.30am as it was the only one of the day. When we arrived back we had to entertain the Board to morning coffee followed by Father Christmas giving out presents to the Staff and all the children. We really felt there was too much interest in the Staff and the patients seemed to be in the background. We are used to it being the other way round.

When we had a few moments of peace Elaine and I withdrew and opened our own presents. We both felt a little homesick but felt thoroughly spoiled by all we had received. Sister Chugg collected us both to share in a homely Christmas dinner with her family. We really enjoyed the peace and relaxation away from the Hospital for a while. Then it was bed for Elaine.

Tuesday 31st December 1968

On Christmas Day Ann, one of our Sisters, was rushed to Launceston with an Ovarian Cyst. She was operated on Boxing Day and is now progressing well. In the evening we finally got Matron off for a three week holiday in Alice Springs. Now we have more free time to ourselves and it is a welcome rest, even putting in some early nights. Having felt rather cheated of some of Christmas we all cooked a special dinner in the Home, all the mad English Sisters together. We all ate it by candle light and the menu was sherry with cheese and biscuits and olives, mushroom soup, stuffed turkey, new potatoes, cauliflower, peas, sausages, Christmas pudding with brandy sauce, coffee with cheese. We had it all with white wine and felt at least six pounds heavier when we finished. To celebrate the New Year we are going to a beach barbecue at Bridport. We hoped to have a swim but the day is overcast so I am not sure if we shall be brave enough.

Thursday 2nd January 1969

The barbecue was great, the weather kept fine. We ate plenty of sausages, steak and chops, then went for a long walk down the beach in the moonlight. We got back to camp in time to bring the New Year in remembering you all at Home. The children went in for a swim but we decided it was too cold for the older ones like us! The Hospital is very quiet, the lull before the storm I expect. We have days off together and we hope to spend them in Launceston. We are both well and saving like mad for our journey home.

Sunday 12th January 1969

We have a run of accident cases in the Hospital this last week. Everyone had to get up at 1am for the seven victims of a car smash. Elaine escorted three of the worst seriously injured to Launceston by ambulance. Not a very good journey, one died, one went delirious and the other had to be constantly reminded to breathe, all seventeen in age. I was out of uniform so I went into the Nursery in my nightie and fed some of the babies.

It has been very much warmer and we have managed to have some time in the sun. We are still making dresses for the tour home. We will be flying to Calcutta via Hong Kong and Thailand in order to reach there for the bus and we shall be leaving on May 1st.

On our days off we had a car lent to us again and we went along the coast via Bridport and Georgetown, all dirt tracks, and then across the new Batman Suspension Bridge. We explored the Tamar River Valley with all the apple orchards and a little harbour full of yachts. We stayed with Jack and Eva Riley in Launceston and then took a drive up a mountain road to Ben Lomond and Ben Nevis, all very peaceful, the birds singing, the wild flowers in bloom.

Monday 27th January 1969

The first of the English Sisters leaves for Sydney at the end of the week so it seems as if the happy party will soon be breaking up. Ann goes off to Perth two weeks later. She hopes to return home at Christmas. Elaine is doing some more night duty next week which she is not overwhelmed about! She has booked her starting date in England as July 27th. We have been on another four days off and have now toured most of Tasmania. It was very wet on Sunday so instead of touring we decided to have a nice restful day. We left 5am Monday morning, drove to Launceston, down to Cresey, then across the central part of Tasmania by the great lake. The road was winding and hilly and the scenery was like dry scanty scrubland. We had dinner by the Lake of St Claire in the Cradle Mount National Park. While we were eating a tame Wallaby came and ate out of Elaine's hand. Along the precipitous unmade road we drove up and down and round and round until we arrived at Queenstown, the largest town on the west coast of Tasmania. We have never seen anything like it, it is very difficult to describe in words, but it did have a majesty, an attraction, but rather ghostly. It is a mining town and the mining is for sulphur and iron ore. When sulphur fumes have been evacuated into the air long enough all vegetation in the whole area around was completely destroyed. There was not even a weed growing. It looks like mounds of slag heaps where houses are built around. In the sunlight the various colours of the deposits shine beautifully. Normally it rains for 75% of the year and I can imagine how depressing it must be. It is almost as if one had landed on Mars!

After having some coffee we drove the 26 miles to Strahan on the coast by the sea. About ten miles out of Queenstown vegetation and scrub appeared as normal. It was a sweet little town, a sleepy fishing port with sandy beaches. It used to be an important busy port for the livelihood of the mining town but since roads were built it had been almost forgotten. We were feeling rather weary after all our driving so we camped for the night on the sandy beach. One of the Sisters had lent us a lean-to tent which we fixed to the side of the car and two mattresses. Matron had lent us her primus stove, so we had everything we needed. We were sleeping peacefully when I awoke and felt something moving around my neck. First of all I thought it was Elaine as she is so restless but when I realised it wasn't I let out such a yell. We put on the torch and, of course, whatever had been there had dashed off in fright. We slept peacefully then until 9am on Tuesday morning and, after breakfast, we began driving northwards through scenery not unlike the Canadian Rockies with forests and deep river gorges. We passed through Rosebery, another mining town, and on to Waratah. Built on the side of a deep valley, Waratah was a large derelict wooden mine which looked as if the wind would blow it over. However, on passing the place we heard signs of life so knew it was working. On enquiry at the garage we were told that it was no longer functional but a few lads did a bit of mining for iron ore as a private enterprise.

We drove inland forty miles to Savage River again across winding tracks. On arrival we found a very nice modern community with some very nice shops, etc. It seemed out of place with the local situation and rugged terrain. It was a prosperous mining organisation which pipes the iron ore 60 miles across newly pioneered land to Port Latta for export. The temperature was 80-90 degrees so we made for the coast, then, as we drew near to Wynyard, the country changed to gentler slopes and rich dairy farms. A welcome softness to the eyes and mind after all the rough mining districts. We drove up Table Cape and had a magnificent view along the northern coast of Tasmania. In the cool of the evening we drove along the coast and camped by the sea at a place called Somerset.

There was a gale force wind and we had a job to secure the tent, quite a change from the heat of the day.

Wednesday we drove further along the coast to Cooee-Burnie, rather industrial with saw mills and paper mills, then to Wivenhoe, Penguin, Ulverstone and Leith, all typical seaside places, mostly unspoiled with sand and rocky beaches. We had a look around Devonport which is where the ships dock from the mainland of Australia. In the afternoon we drove to the top end of the Cradle Mountain which describes itself. The mountain is 5,069 feet high with snow along the top. We had a walk and then drove back to Launceston via Deloraine. We arrived there at 8pm in order that I could take Elaine out for a birthday meal. However, there were only two places where you could get a full dinner with wine, etc and they served from 6-8pm only. I was very disappointed but we did find a nice café, bought a bottle of wine from the shop and had Tasmanian Trout to eat. It was very tasty and we enjoyed it. Then we drove back to Scottsdale feeling rather tired, very red from the sun, but happy. We had covered about 600 miles. The flies were now becoming very clinging and are a nuisance in the heat, so I think I must make for the fly spray!

Wednesday 5th February 1969

We attended another beach barbecue on Saturday. It was a lovely day and we all had a swim. We had not been in the sea for some months. We cooked chops and steak over the fire and then played beach ball to work off the excess food eaten by us all. Joan and Colin Chugg are very kind to arrange these barbecues for us as she knows we enjoy their informality. Sunday bought a change in the weather and Monday we had a thunder storm all night and day. The rain was so hard and fast, it seemed like a monsoon. I have just got to have my ten days owing from night duty and I must say I feel very tired and am glad of a rest. I decided to spend a few days at the W.E.C College and it was a refreshing time spiritually and a good rest physically and mentally. I met Helen who was in Tasmania for a month. She had come over mostly on holiday with her parents. Helen may work here for a short while before returning to Melbourne. Elaine goes on nights tomorrow for five nights and it will probably be the last time which pleases her very much. Our little band of English Sisters here is soon breaking up, the second one leaves at the end of the week. The place is beginning to feel very empty.

Saturday 15th February 1969

Elaine had a lovely birthday. She had worked all night and then received a lovely bouquet of flowers in the morning. She slept in the morning. I woke her up at lunch time when she had her lovely flowers, gladioli, dahlias, carnations, etc. They were beautifully arranged in a fan shape and were very fresh. I gave her an Opal which I had bought her earlier in Alice Springs in the shape of a tear drop. She knew about that, so I gave her a little native vase and two Christian paperbacks. I had managed successfully to prepare a birthday tea for her and the kitchen staff had iced a cake for me. On Wednesday six of us went into Launceston for the evening. Elaine and I went to the Crusade Bible Class and the others went to see the film 'Star' – the life story of Gertrude Lawrence. We would have loved to see it too but perhaps another time.

Saturday 22nd February 1969

Elaine began to get a sore throat during the afternoon and after the bus journey to Scottsdale felt full of flu. On the Tuesday she got a stiff neck and spent the day in bed. Doctor North came in to say hello to her in the evening and told her to stay in bed. She had blood tests done and it seems as if she had caught Glandular Fever. The unfortunate part is that the liver appears to be affected and so is enlarged again. No jaundice but some nausea. After five days on glucose fluids she gradually began to get back to normal and eating again. Every gland in the body seems to ache and she seems poorly again for a little while. I have five nights off and it is good to have time to care for her. We came down to the beach shack yesterday where I hoped she would have some good sea air but it has rained so far. One of the Sisters lent us a car so we can move more easily. It has been nice to be away from the Hospital especially as this weekend they are laying the foundation stone for the new Hospital by the Minister of Health and pandemonium reigns everywhere. Here all we have is a beautiful view over the bay at Bridport and all is very peaceful

Saturday 1st March 1969

We have had a severe frost during the night but the day has turned out clear, crisp and warm. Elaine has been sitting in the garden watching all the small planes spraying the valley fields. The garden is full of dahlias which are so colourful. Elaine has seen the doctor and her liver is now back to normal, her spleen a little enlarged, but she is very fit again, praise God, and can be up all day without tiredness. She will return to work on Monday which she is very pleased about as she gets rather bored with nothing much to do. We only have five more working weeks to go before we leave the country. I have been very busy driving into Launceston for evening Counselling Classes to counsel during the Lane Adams Crusade quite soon now. Elaine has had to miss some because of illness but will be singing in the Choir as she did with me in Sydney.

We are now starting our injections again for Cholera, Typhoid and Smallpox. As Monday is 'Labour Day' everything comes to a standstill until Tuesday. Elaine has made two dresses and is going to make two more. Someone only said the other day "Faith is not only what we get out of quiet times and Church but that God loves us and desires to have fellowship with us." We should enjoy being with Him too, not just to get blessing for ourselves.

Monday 10th March 1969

Elaine is staying with Eva and Jack Riley in Launceston while we attend the Lane Adams Crusade. I have nights off and went down on Thursday while Elaine joined the Salvation Army Car Convoy down on Friday evening after work. So far the meetings have been well attended and very encouraging. Last night was Youth Night and it was packed to the roof. The last afternoon is being held today in York Park. It is a beautifully hot sunny day so we are hoping for a superb attendance. We shall probably both sing in the choir today. I have been counselling and had a difficult time with the Seventh Day Adventists. We have met many of our friends from the W.E.C Missionary College and made many new acquaintances. We shall return to Scottsdale tomorrow evening by bus. Jack and Eva have lent us their car since we have been here so we have not had to wait for public transport which has been wonderful.

The towns are going through some changes. The latest is that the shops only work five days a week but remain open until 6pm at night. They have been contemplating erecting another casino in Launceston but there has been great opposition from many people.

We have now applied for our tickets Launceston to Melbourne on April 9th, Melbourne to New Zealand on April 14th, New Zealand to Sydney April 29th. April 30th will be the last day for collecting post until we have postal addresses for the Tour.

Saturday 15th March 1969

We are now in the middle of all our injections, Cholera, Typhoid and Hong Kong Flu – the joys of travelling! We have been very slack in the Hospital so we have been able to take it easy. Jean Boorman, one of the other Sisters, is also off sick and very poorly. She may be moved into the Hospital with suspected Rheumatic Fever. I am better than the others, I just have two sore arms so turning in bed becomes rather hard. We have now sent in our resignations so we feel we are coming to the end and our departure is near.

Last week on Tuesday we went to Joan Chugg's home and had a wonderful buffet dinner party. Chicken and salad followed by pavlova and strawberries with cream. Last night Dr North collected us and we had a very enjoyable slide evening on New Zealand. A little preview of what we hope to see ourselves. We have planned to spend one week in the South Island and one week in the North Island where we have friends both sides.

Saturday 22nd March 1969

It is bright and sunny again, warm enough to sit outside. During the week the Kraft Factory have been processing onions and, as the smell has been rather overpowering, we have not been able to sit outside. It has been so strong at times the patients' eyes have been running. Apart from that it has been cold and we have needed extra blankets and hot water bottles at night. I am now back on days and I am beginning to feel civilised again. We went down to Bridport yesterday and had a walk along the sand. There was not a person in sight. The sea was choppy and a deep green colour. In the evening we had a game of tennis. Jean is still in Hospital with a confirmed diagnosis of Rheumatic Arthritis, her joints are really swollen, not a pleasant thing to have at 25 years. Elaine and I hired a T.V. for her which helps to pass the time.

Our Tour home has limited luggage to one suitcase only of the required weight and size, so we are very busy sending off full boxes through the post to relieve ourselves of most of our luggage. It seems never ending.

Monday 31st March 1969

On Wednesday April 9th we shall be flying to Melbourne from Launceston. We are staying at Alexandra from the 10th-14th April. On Monday April 14th we shall be flying from Melbourne to Christchurch, New Zealand, spending the first week in the South Island followed by one week in the North Island. On 29th April we shall be flying to Sydney from Auckland. We hope to spend the 29th and 30th in Sydney. On 1st May we fly to Hong Kong, then onwards toward home.

On Thursday Elaine and I went to do last minute shopping in Launceston. Joan Chugg lent us a car, which was wonderful. We did shopping in the morning, then had some passport photos done which as usual are not very inspiring. We treated ourselves to a lovely smorgasbord lunch in a hotel. You can have as much as you can eat which usually means you eat too much. We went to the W.E.C. College for tea and to say goodbye to all our friends there. We then had our final Cholera and Typhoid injections and we took it easy on Friday!

Monday 7th April 1969

We have just completed our last day's work in the Hospital after a chaotic weekend of Easter road accidents. We have just done a whole heap of washing which we hope will dry before the rain comes but the sky is looking rather black over the mountains. We are going out to dinner even though Elaine has just recovered from a cold during the last week. Saturday evening Matron gave us a party inviting many of the people we have been acquainted with here. It was very enjoyable although I think we would have been glad of an early night. Last evening we were invited out to a meal with the Chairman of the Board, Mr Bert Farquhar and his wife. They have a beautiful home and after a lovely evening we reached home by 9pm which was just right. Tonight we are going to Joan Chugg's for dinner – it's all go these days! Tomorrow, Tuesday, we have left for ourselves, to pack and generally get organised. Elaine received a good stack of income tax rebate, 120 dollars. Mine was a little less, I think. Knowing me, it will not go very far.

Friday 11th April 1969

After a last minute rush of goodbyes at Scottsdale we eventually left on the 9.30am bus to Launceston. Matron made us buttonholes of roses, Mrs North came to wave us off with the Chuggs and Polly. Bert Farquhar collected us from the Hospital so we felt we had had a tremendous send-off; it was very sad to leave them all. In Launceston we fetched our air tickets and traveller's cheques and then spent the afternoon with Jack and Eva Riley. She was thrilled to see us, yet a little sad to think we were on our way home and she was not. At 3.30pm we caught the bus to the Airport and had a comfortable flight across the Tasman Sea to Melbourne. It was really much hotter there and, as we were wearing suits, we felt overdressed to say the least. We had a meal out and then went and enjoyed the film 'In the Shoes of the Fisherman'. An excellent portrayal of the influence and power, both spiritually and politically, of the Pope in Rome. We slept the night in the People's Palace which was the Salvation Army Home. This is not just a place for down and outs and drunks but an official Bed and Breakfast place for travellers and many people use it. It is all very reasonable and, of course, they can use the money for their work. We found it rather hot at night so found ourselves sleeping with only a sheet when we had five blankets in Tasmania. Tuesday we caught the bus at 3pm out to Alexandra. Eddie Weeks met us with the car. It was lovely to see him and Millie again and we caught up on all the news. In the evening we went to the Church Hall and saw a film on the modern interpretation of the Gospel. This morning we have had a lazy time talking and enjoying the peace of farm life. We shall be doing a bit of visiting in the town this afternoon. There have been quite a few changes around the place, by all accounts, since we left.

SOUTH ISLAND, NEW ZEALAND

Sunday 20th April 1969

On Monday morning we left Alexandra in mist and coldness but as we drove through the countryside the sun poked its face through and it turned out to be a beautiful day. Driving with Eddie and Millie we were interested to see the farm damage around Alexandra. Apparently the fire had encircled the town, the people gathered in the middle and they were all saved. It must have been a terrifying experience, a miracle indeed. There were signs of burned down fences, farmsteads, charred tree trunks and places where the fire had singed all the trees around the house yet the house was intact. The once blackened little hills are now sprouting with bright fresh grass and the farmers are making a gallant effort to start again. If their homes were gone with stock intact they were alright but if their livelihood was taken away they were left with nothing. The fires reached Alexandra in the evening which was a blessing as the dampness had set in by then and this must have saved them to a large extent. Flames completely surrounded the town and the outlying houses were lost. Eileen McNichol, our Scottish friend, her husband and child lay under wet blankets. The roof went from their home but, thank God, they were alright. It was an experience we were thankful to have missed, yet it was a part of Australia we needed to know and appreciate.

We arrived at Melbourne Airport by 11am to be told that our 12.30pm flight had been postponed to 3pm due to mechanical failure. We checked our luggage through, 14kg overweight which cost us an extra seventeen dollars. Hence we shall be sending another parcel to England I expect! We left the Airport and went into the city with Eddie and Millie. After an Australian snack lunch of pies and coffee we said goodbye to the dear couple who had well and truly adopted us as their daughters. We were quite glad the plane had been delayed because it gave us a chance to visit our ex-Matron Pat Pither who was in Hospital after having an eye operation after a road accident. The impact of the crash sent a piece of glass into her better eye causing damage and loss of sight, she already had bad vision in the other eye. She was very pleased to see us and she has booked a trip to England soon and will probably arrive there about the same time as we do.

We then returned to the Airport and awaited departure. If we had left a half hour later we would have met Mrs North flying over from Launceston, Tasmania, and if we had gone a day later we would have met Audrey Dunn on her way to Japan. We travelled by Air New Zealand, a white and turquoise

218

aircraft, Electra model. We left about 4pm eventually. We were waited on by three male stewards and one stewardess smartly dressed in turquoise uniforms. Before take-off we were given fresh orange juice to drink and then a 'quickie' to wipe hands and face. The flight took four hours in all and we had a delicious meal while on board. Too much really when we were not having much exercise. The menu was salad and eggs stuffed with shell fish, steak with mushrooms, beans, carrots and potatoes, roll and butter, a sweet, biscuits and cheese followed by two cups of coffee and cream.

We enjoyed a clear view of Melbourne and the Victorian coastline. We flew very near to the coast of Tasmania and had a lovely view of Flinders Island just off the coast of north east Tasmania. We had to put our watches on two hours which upset us a little as we had hoped to fly over the southern snow-clad Alps of New Zealand in daylight but we were not destined to see that this time.

We arrived at Christchurch Airport at 10pm and were met by Joan Cuttriss with whom we were staying. We got through international formalities quickly which included long explanations about the fact that, although we had been staying on a farm in Victoria, we had thoroughly cleaned our shoes and ourselves also. The Agricultural Officers were satisfied so we were allowed through. First through, but our cases were unloaded last! They had large baggage carriers so you did not have to carry cases at all. About 10.45pm we found a taxi, drove into Christchurch, where Joan and Henry have their home with their three year old son Trevor. We met the couple in Tasmania while they were students in the W.E.C. Missionary Training College. We nearly died when a small meal was served because we were full to capacity but we managed a little. Our beds were all warmed and after a bath, we slept soundly until we awoke for breakfast at 8.30am, now Tuesday.

In the morning we went by bus into Christchurch centre. Immediate impressions, old cars on the road out of the ark almost and long forgotten at home. The houses have two storeys like English ones, the trees like ours with all the trees changing colour as autumn sets in. The poplars, in particular, are a golden glow. We made our travel arrangements for a fortnight's time and then bought some hot soup to have with our sandwiches for lunch. Although the day was bright and sunny there was a bitter wind. We went into Christchurch Cathedral and climbed up the bell tower for a good view of the city. The wooden step ladder was rickety and steep, to say the least, but it was worth the effort. Surrounding Christchurch are the Cashmere Hills which are dry and brown from the summer drought. Running through the centre of the city is the River Avon which is picturesque with little bridges and overhanging willows. We took an afternoon tour of the city and surrounding countryside which was most interesting. The port for the South Island and Christchurch is Littleton about seven miles from the city. It is a naturally shaped harbour but after a launch trip round it we learned of many disadvantages. Being a flat shaped sea bed instead of a normal V with silted shelves, all the ocean

Photo 22 – Christchurch, South Island, New Zealand.

currents come in relentlessly. So the harbour needs breakwaters, but anything permanent is hard to erect as the sea bed is soft mud and everything sinks. There were boats of all kinds in the Docks, yachts, cargo boats and also the 'Maori', the one and only passenger ship that ferries between the North and South Islands. It was at present lying idle as the Deck Crew were on strike. The other ship was wrecked in the hurricane last year and that was called the 'Wahinne'. The crossing from North to South by this route takes all day. There were other ships out of use too, especially those run on coal, now out of date. Surrounding the harbour were high hills which made it difficult to reach the inland. There is a pathway leading over the top, very steep, known as the Bridal Path where the earliest settlers carted all their belongings. There is a roadway now and a tunnel to facilitate communications. We had afternoon tea at an old grey Mansion House 'The Sign of the Takahe'. It was very beautiful inside with wall murals of English history.

Wednesday we caught the bus to the railway station at 8am. It was crowded with school children as well as others and we noticed how polite they were on public transport standing sedately to allow other passengers the seats. We caught the train which is divided into four classes: 1st, 2nd, smokers and non-smokers. When you purchase a ticket, you sit on an allocated seat and above it is a ticket indicating your destination. We arrived at Ashburton at 10am and were met by Dawn and Malcolm and their three children. It was a joyful reunion and Roseanne had grown so much from a new baby with long black hair to a lively toddler of one year with fair hair. We clambered into the huge black car, about 1940 vintage, and you feel as if you were travelling in a Black Maria. They took us for a ride around the township which was a typical country town. Large sprawling layout, plenty of trees and lovely residential homes with well-kept gardens. Dawn and Malcolm have to be admired for their courage. Originally they had a wooden house which they have now demolished and they are in the process of building their own brick house of their own design. No interior decorating has yet been done but the bedrooms, bathroom and kitchen are sound structurally. The lounge and dining room have yet to exist. Quite a tough time for them with three children, 4, 3 and 1 year old and all into everything.

After dinner, Malcolm's father came and took us out for a drive, about 110 miles in all. We went over the famous Canterbury Plains which were flat and like a patchwork quilt, though very dry because of the drought. We drove up through Methuen to Mount Hut, Windwhistle and Lake Coleridge. The autumn colours were breath-taking, the photos were enhanced by Pampas Grass (known as flax) and of sweet Briar Bushes (Redberry Bush) and the Tussock Grass which grows in clumps as is described. We had afternoon tea by the river and gorge which was wide to allow for spring flooding following the melting snows. We passed the evening chatting to Dawn cosily by the fire.

Thursday we said 'Au Revoir' to our Christian friends who had been so kind and packed us up a packed lunch to save expense on our travels. We caught the 9.30am coach, Mount Cook Service, from Ashburton to Queenstown arriving at 6pm. It was a long hot day travelling but worthwhile for the views. We quickly left the plains behind and got into rolling hills and undulating country. The autumn tints were still our highlights as we have not seen English trees to that extent since leaving home.

Our route took us to Geraldine and we had morning tea at Fairlie before crossing Burkes Pass to Lake Tekapo. Just before reaching the lake we crossed some rough barren land which was quite unexpectantly full of bulldozers, etc. This evidently is the first stage of building a new hydro-electric village which they are going to call 'Twizzle'. This is a gigantic project when they will be damming the rivers with five dams. Lake Tekapo appeared a vivid blue and most attractive and overlooking it is an old church called 'The Church of the Good Shepherd'. The coach did not stop so we could not go inside. However, we did stop at Lake Pukaki where we ate our sandwiches overlooking the still waters.

As the afternoon progressed the mountains came nearer and we were soon climbing up the Lindis pass to a height of 3,300 feet. Then began the gradual descent to Tarrio for afternoon tea and then across to Lake Wanaka where we were allowed to get out and stretch our legs and take some photographs. Behind this attractive township and lake there were snow-

Photo 23 - Lake Pukaki & Mount Cook, South Island, New Zealand.

capped mountains and all along the road we kept passing fast flowing rivers and suspension bridges. From Wanaka we drove via Cromwell to Queenstown. We drove down the Kawaura Gorge which in earlier days had been a wealth of gold. This was the reason for the original settlement of the area. Evidence of the gold mining towns and shacks can be seen along the gorge. One famous area was at Shotover River where some people still have gold claims and hoses spray continually the rock and soil faces and this runs down through sieves which separate the gold from the debris. I don't know how prosperous these gold mines are these days. Just before our arrival in Queenstown we passed Lake Hayes, the most photographed lake in New Zealand. The reflections in the nearby still water are also identical. The bus went by too fast to take a picture for which I was very sorry. The reflection was so perfect that it would have been one of the best. Our approach to Lake Wokatipu, Maori for 'Breathing Water', as the level is supposed to go up and down like respirations and Queenstown was absolutely awe-inspiring. Elaine and I thought it was the most beautiful place we had visited since our whole journey began 2½ years ago. Any description in word would be inadequate. We found a restaurant and had some tea, then climbed the hill to our Guest House where we had booked Bed and Breakfast for two nights. We met two young girls, one from Canada and one from Australia. It was interesting conversing with them and hearing about their travelling experiences. We also met a Swiss couple and we had a lively discussion on wages, income tax and the cost of living in England, Europe, Australia and New Zealand. The Guest House was the cheapest rate available at $3 and 25 cents, yet it was excellent, modern, comfortable, clean, electric blankets on the bed, T.V., etc. We were most impressed. Friday morning we were called at 6.30am for an early breakfast, 7.30am we began an all-day coach tour to Milford Sound and return covering 400 miles. A long day but well worth the effort. There were only four passengers for the day. Elaine and I, Gail, a Canadian girl, and a middle aged lady from Wellington called Mrs Gwynfer Rousella, a highly entertaining lady, very well educated and having travelled around the world absorbing all she had seen. She loved England, especially Canterbury Cathedral. In fact, she had enjoyed all the cultural and historical aspects. So we set out on our long trip. Driving down the side of Lake Wakatipu beneath the foothills of 'The Remarkables', a mountain range, we drove to Kingston, Five Rivers, Mossburn to Te Anan. The journey was comparatively uneventful as there was a low lying mist and fog and other than the fact that now and again we saw a glimpse of snow-packed mountains, all we could see were grazing fields packed to capacity with millions of sheep. We have never seen so many thousands all in one place. They had all been mustered from the hills for shearing. Wool is the mainstay of these farms and sometimes they are able to shear them twice a year.

At Te Anan on the Lake Te Anan this is the gateway to the great Fiordland and National Parkland of the south west corner. The road was gravelled but well graded. The scenery was mainly beech forests, pine trees and lakes backed by rugged hills and snow-peaked mountains. The weather remained overcast and disappointing.

At Cascade Creek we stopped at 11.30am for late morning tea and lunch and we felt somewhat bottom sore from four hours solid sitting. We felt much better with food in our stomachs. We were very fortunate as over the last 26 miles into the Fiord the cloud lifted and, although it was not sunny, it was absolutely clear. The road became steeper, rougher and more winding, the views were majestic. There was more snow, steep cliff faces, hundreds of waterfalls, small and large lakes, deep gorges, avalanched snow, deep blue glaciers, overhanging valleys. The forests became more dense and, because of the permanent moisture blowing through the valley, there is moss hanging from all the trees like cobwebs. We came to the Homer Tunnel, a wonderful piece of construction by pick axe and shovel three quarters of a mile through the mountainside. When we came out the other side there was a slow eleven mile descent to the Fiord and on arrival the reflection was perfect. A peak called 'Mitre', due to the shape, reflected exactly in the water and we took several photographs. We then had an hour's cruise on the Fiord. It was freezing cold but we stayed up on deck in order to get the best view. We cruised within two miles of the entrance of Milford Sound and the Tasman Sea. This area was first pioneered by a man called Sutherland and his wife who died 1919 and 1924, their tombstone can be seen. The Fiords were then taken over by the NZ tourist board for promotion. We passed under two waterfalls, the Bowen Falls and the Stirling Falls, both huge cascades. At one stage we were directly underneath 2,000 feet of sheer precipitous rock face and it was a strange feeling to know there was another 1,800 feet below the water. Other mountains had strange rock formations like a lion and an elephant's face.

After the cruise we had a very welcome hot drink in the Hotel before boarding the bus once again. We stopped at the far end of the Homer Tunnel as there were some tame birds. A similar size to a Hawk with a mottled brown and green plumage but when they opened their wings it was a bright orange wing span. They were called Kea birds and we fed them with chocolate by hand and they ate it delicately but greedily. We then returned to Queenstown arriving about 9pm.

Saturday dawned a bright clear sunny day and we had ideal conditions in which to rapidly explore Queenstown. Such a pretty lakeside township with masses of autumn leaves surrounded by mountains. We took a chair lift up one mountain to a restaurant overlooking the town and had a breath-taking view of the lake. We could have stayed up there all day. We visited a quaint C/E Church Hall decorated out for Harvest Thanksgiving and we had a lovely chat with the Vicar, a man from Coventry called Rev. Glover. He explained that the church had been built in the 1930's during the depression years when labour was inexpensive and was paid for by a legacy. It looked much older.

At midday we caught the bus out to the airport where we boarded a Mount Cook Airline plane for a flight back to Christchurch via the Southern Alps. Again we were fortunate for the weather, although there was a fair amount of low cloud but that did not prevent us having a splendid view of the Alps. We took some lovely photos of the snow-capped mountains, glaciers and especially a close up of Mount Cook, the highest mountain in New Zealand, 12,349 feet. The flight took 2½ hours and when we arrived back at Christchurch we found cold wet wintry weather and we thanked the Lord for enabling us to have three such wonderful days. We had to take a taxi from the airport to Joan's home as there was no public transport. Sunday we had a quiet day, going for a short journey in the car in the afternoon and then church again tonight. Tomorrow we leave for our journey to the North Island.

NORTH ISLAND, NEW ZEALAND

Tuesday 29th April 1969

Monday morning 7am we left by taxi for the Coach terminal and our journey northwards began. The countryside was variable, undulating and open. Elaine slept most of the way as she was very tired after all our dashing around. I sat quiet and dreamed the time away. We had much to think about and so much to remember and thank God for His wonderful love and protection with us every step of the way. We looked forward now to the next phase, meeting new people and always experiencing new things. We changed coaches at Blenheim for the last twenty miles to Picton which is a smallish township situated in the crest of the hills and spreading down to the water's edge. Again we found ourselves in Fiordland and after boarding the Ferry Boat, it was a pleasant hour's cruise in still waters before we reached the open sea. We watched the baggage and cars being loaded onto the ship for some time. Baggage was placed on trucks and driven straight on board so that it need not be handled. When you disembark your luggage is driven off with you so that there is no delay at all. Once out in the open sea we had a brief glimpse of the North Island coastline in the distance but it was too cold to stay on deck. We had a hot cup of soup and then retired to the Observation Lounge where Elaine returned to another two hours sleep while the ship began to roll. When she awoke we watched the fog outside which was rather dense and the hooter was blowing periodically. The ship was travelling very slowly, we were then approaching Wellington harbour which has a narrow entrance and many passengers were anxiously watching our progress because it was at this spot that the other ferry, the Wahine, sunk in a hurricane a year ago. However, we proceeded safely and once in the harbour the fog cleared. Wellington is the capital city of New Zealand, yet only third in actual size, Auckland and Christchurch being larger. It was an impressive looking city, however, built on the slopes of hills with houses overhanging on stilts at the most precarious angles. The maritime frontage of the harbour covers four miles all round and the airport is built on an isthmus. If the aircraft land too soon they land in the sea and if they overshoot the runway they also land in the sea. We took a taxi to our hotel in the central part of the city called the Columbus Hotel. It was all very comfortable. After refreshing ourselves, we took a stroll around the town window shopping, and finding, on the whole, what good quality goods they have. We felt quite at home when we met a Scottish Pipe Band coming down the street. We found a restaurant which looked tempting, the sign said, 'special night - dine out for a dollar'. We went up the stairs and found a very classy dining room, candlelight and everyone in full evening dress. We were only in trousers and we felt like running away. Having made excuses for our state of dress, we enjoyed an excellent meal in tasteful surroundings, plus a pianist.

Tuesday we joined our coach tour 'Trans Tour' at 9am and began our four day trip to Auckland from Wellington. The driver's name is Trevor and the courier's name is Trevor. There are fifteen passengers including twelve Australians, one New Zealander and ourselves. We did a brief bus tour of Wellington covering the city, the Mount Victory look outs, the Harbour, the Houses of Parliament – the old one being the largest wooden building in the world. We then drove northwards through Levin where we enjoyed a smorgasbord lunch at the Kowhai Restaurant (Kowhai means 'nature flower') and then on to Wanganin where we spent the first night. There was nothing

Photo 24 – A Kiwi in New Zealand.

Photo 25 - The Harbour, Wellington, North Island, New Zealand.

particularly outstanding about the journey, we passed through rolling green fields (not literally, of course!) mainly used for dairy farming, through flax fields where the drying flax awaited processing for rope, etc. This greatly used by the Maori for their grass skirts. Sight-seeing around Wanganin showed us that the town is situated on the mouth of the river. We climbed up a lookout tower, 176 steps and had a panoramic view. The township itself was a fair size, we looked around the shops and had a quick look at the War Memorial and Art gallery. Visiting a rather unusual Children's Playground we were thrilled by the imagination used in building play projects. An igloo with large pipes in which the children can climb in and out, a dragon as a slide and an octopus with swings in each arched leg. Wanganin was the original site of native wars primarily over land transactions so it is important to New Zealand history.

We stayed at the Rutland Hotel, an old building being renovated, and we had a room with a shower and toilet. We have become friendly with a couple from Sydney, Don and Joan Smith who have five children, the youngest being sixteen years, and we usually share a meal table with them.

Wednesday dawned very wet, grey and disappointing and it remained like it all day. It was rather sad because we are going through volcanic country now. We passed the two largest volcanoes but did not see any of them. Anyway we arrived at Ractihi having passed many cattle on the way, one kind known as Galloways (black with a white band around the middle). They looked rather like a football team en mass! We also saw some deer. We were interested to hear that New Zealand have no native animals; all have been imported over the centuries. They do, however, have native birds by the thousand and, because they have no fear of death by animals on the ground, many of them used to live on the ground. This caused some species to lose the power of flight, a good example being the Kiwi. Since animals have reproduced these land birds have gradually become extinct and New Zealand is in danger now of losing her natural bird heritage. The rain poured down as we drove up the mountainous road to the 'Chateau', the central haven of skiers. A huge splendid mansion sitting at the foot of Mount Tongariro and therefore known as the Tongariro National Park. The Mount is a volcano and does smoke pretty continuously. The National Park contains a golf course, tennis courts, a cinema, shops, in fact, all was very luxurious. We had a smorgasbord luncheon which was positively superb. In fact, we had far too much and would have preferred a siesta instead of having to press on with our tour. We passed Mount Rhuapehu, which also continuously smokes and roars at times but saw nothing, also Ngauruhoe which is the noisiest one. The clouds obliterated everything but the foothills. Driving down the road it was interesting to see the preserved natural flora of the National Park, all brown hissock grass on the right and on the left reclaimed land fertile and green, having been treated with cobalt, which it lacked, to make it good farming land. We continued on our journey and saw the beginning of a massive hydro-electric power scheme by channelling various rivers and

Photo 26 - Mahuia Rapids & Mt Ngauruhoe, New Zealand.

streams via Turangi to Lake Taupo. By the lakeside of Taupo we found a great deal of pumice stone left by the excessive heat of the last volcano on the rocks and saved a piece as a souvenir. Taupo itself is a popular summer resort and has dozens of motels, a pretty boat harbour and is the beginning of the Thermal region which covers 100 miles. In various places on the hills steam can be seen rising from the ground in clouds. This is caused by underground volcanic actions. We visited a geothermal power station just outside Taupo, only the second of its kind in the world. They use this natural steam by separating the wet from the dry and using it to generate electricity. Scores of large chimneys are built over the vents and huge pipes channel the dry steam pressure to the station. The pipes are designed with a kink in them to allow for expansion. About 5pm we arrived at our lodging for the night, a luxurious Motel called 'de Brett'. We had a chalet to ourselves with bunk beds, radio and T.V., fire, shower, a cooking unit and a fridge. The Hotel owns thermal baths as well, these are filled with natural thermal springs, some of which are above boiling temperature. The water, containing minerals, has medicinal properties but it is advisable to only remain in them about fifteen minutes. We put on costumes and plunged in; they cool all the pools to body temperature all the time. It feels wonderful when you come out, we glowed with warmth for the whole evening and our skins were as soft as a baby. We sat in bed and watched T.V. while our costumes dried by the fire. We rose the next morning at 6.30am in order to have another swim intending to use the private baths so as not to wet our costumes again but we found them empty. Making sure nobody was around we jumped into the large open pool in our 'bathing suits' in true native fashion. The day was considerably brighter, we could even see the top of Mount Ngaurahoe which was smoking away happily.

We only had fifty miles to travel today but lots of visiting to do. Our first stop was at a place called Whakarei where we walked around a lot of crater holes, some containing boiling water and mud. The smell of sulphur was strong everywhere and there were yellow sulphur deposits. The mineral content in the water flow causes silica deposits which forms terraces of solidified rock over the years. As this process takes place the surface of the water looks fan shaped.

We then visited the Lady Knox Geyser which we saw spout up 400 feet at least. The Pohutu Geyser was also functioning very well. A geyser is formed when a column of water underground becomes boiling temperature, the steam is then flashed off and the water expelled. Then we saw lakes of boiling mud which really fascinated us even more. I went camera crazy and climbed as near as I could to get a good photo of one bubble popping. I nearly fell in my eagerness but I managed to get some pictures. We arrived at Rotorua, the central town in the thermal region, there seemed to be steam clouds spouting everywhere and plenty of strong sulphur fumes. It had begun to rain again by this time and although we took a launch trip to the Maori Island in Lake Rotorua we could not do much

Photo 27 - Geyser in Rotorua, North Island, New Zealand.

sightseeing. Then we visited a Maori village and saw around their beautifully carved buildings, especially the meeting hall. The Maoris have their own Christian Church called St Faith's in which they have a large window depicting the figure of a Maori Christ. The Church and window back onto Lake Rotorua so making Christ appear to be walking on the water. It is very effective. Elaine and the couple from Tasmania dressed in Maori costumes which caused a great laugh all round, especially as Elaine had hers over her anorak which made her look double the size. We had a group photo of the whole tour outside the Maori meeting house. Just as we were getting back into our seats we heard a familiar voice and who should we meet but Liz Pallin, the English Sister we worked with in Tasmania. She was also staying in Rotorua for the night so she came over to our travel lodge motel for an hour to catch up on all the news. It was great to see her again. We were fortunate to have lavish conditions overlooking Lake Rotorua with similar facilities as before. After dinner we were taken to a Maori Concert Party in their meeting house which we enjoyed tremendously. They are an extremely musical race, joyful and far more cultural than the Aborigines. Their voices were beautiful and the various 'action songs' very forcefully performed. They also did stick dances. The Poi beats were the best, these are raffia like balls on the end of string which they swing in time to music and bang the balls together. It is rather hard to give an adequate description but it is very clever when you see their superb motion and timing. They can swing

Photo 28 - The Canoi Poi Maori Dancers, North Island, New Zealand.

up to four Poi Pois together without getting the strings tangled and the beat wrong. The people of Rotorua have the thermal water piped to their homes for use, for example, for central heating and washing water, etc. Some people even cook over the steam vents in the ground.

Friday and the last day of our tour. The road took us through the large forests, the area covering 500 square miles. We visited the famous Waitomo Caves formed out of limestone. We were squashed like sardines in a small row boat and pulled quietly by ropes fitted in the cave deeper and deeper inside. It was essential that we made no noise at all. All over the walls and roofs of the grottos there were thousands of little glow worm lights, just like fairyland, absolutely spectacular.

We then drove through some of the richest dairy country that we have ever seen to Auckland, the largest city in New Zealand. It was very sprawling with sub-tropical hills all around. We left our coach crowd and found our way to Chris and Peggy's flat where we intend to stay for four days.

Saturday we had a lazy morning sleeping until 10am which was wonderful after so many early starts. The weather was beautiful and we had plenty to natter about to Chris and Peggy, especially me, as I had not seen Chris for so long. We took an afternoon tour around Auckland and were fortunate to have some tremendous panoramic views. Auckland has two harbours joined by a bridge, not unlike Sydney's. There is much preserved forest land around the city, sub-tropical and most attractive.

We then had a safe flight from Auckland to Sydney in a Boeing 707 B.O.A.C jet, a beautiful smooth ride. We stay in Sydney all day then tomorrow we leave for Hong Kong. The weather is very hot and humid here in Sydney after New Zealand. We are both well.

CALCUTTA, INDIA

Wednesday 7th May 1969

Our last day in Sydney was spent in the zoo and in the evening June and Ruth took us out to dinner in the King' Cross (à la Chelsea!) area of the city. A quaint old restaurant called Mother's Cellar, all full of old brass ornaments, etc. It was a grand evening. On Thursday morning June and Ruth took us to the Airport and waved us goodbye from the ground as we flew off Australian land once and for all. They gave us parting gifts and we were very mixed up about leaving. We have had no further problems with overnight luggage. We flew on a Boeing 707 K.L.M. line and it was a good flight, seven hours in all in the air, though we had to put our watches back on the way. We landed at Manila, the capital of the Philippine Islands at about 3pm. What a chaotic place, disorganised, noisy and scores of men trying to barter with you or organise you. It was very bewildering for a visitor and we were glad we had each other for moral support. We left our bags in charge of the customs so we had no problem with them. After much ado, we discovered that we were entitled to the use of a Hotel room and a free meal at the Airline's expense because of the time between connecting flights. We were therefore driven in the Tower Hotel bus to the large air-conditioned hotel where we refreshed ourselves before taking a quick tour of the city of Manila in a huge Dodge car. We went to a Museum and heard something of their history, about their revered rebel leader Raval who saved the Philippines from the Spaniards and was innocently executed. The Museum contained his possessions and a large number of writings. It is like a city within a city. We saw the oldest church in Manila, St Augustine's Roman Catholic Church, and it was all decorated for a wedding. We saw the Royal Palace which has a Spanish architecture with garden sculptures depicting liberty, forgiveness, etc. We watched the Changing of the Guard, saw the Garden of Remembrance to Raval and also to cholera victims. There was a large fountain in the middle with large trees giving much needed shade as it was very hot. There were many people around because it was Labour Day. They were a very friendly, happy-go-lucky people, the streets are pretty clean but poverty is rather prevalent especially in the Chinese zone. There were old war jeeps which had been renovated, painted in bright colours with bells and horns, etc. These were used as gay taxi runabouts. They appear to drive on the right hand side of the road and their highway code appears to be non-existent.

We had a shower to cool off on return to the Hotel and then had an evening meal before being driven out to the Airport once more. We drove along the sea shore, there were many large night clubs along the road, all different shapes and designs with novel names. At the Airport we found that our plane was delayed and so we had a long wait in very hot and stuffy conditions amidst crowds of people including American Missionaries returning home on furlough.

However, we survived and were quite relieved to sink into comfy aircraft seats with the coolness of air-conditioning. We flew Cathay Pacific Line and the flight took about two hours to Hong Kong, the aerial view of the lights of both Manila and Hong Kong were lovely to see on such a clear night. Taking a taxi to the Y.M.C.A., we eventually got to bed at 3am, this was on the mainland.

The following morning we found a Christian Welfare Tour run from the hostel and conducted by a Cornish lady. In this tour we were shown a real insight into the lives of the Chinese people, the rehousing projects, the old against the new blocks of flats. The huts housed one family in one room, very cramped but surprising clean and well organised. They often had to carry water up four flights of stairs. There was a welfare craft centre where employment was provided for women, knitting, sewing, smocking, etc. The work they turned out was really lovely. We visited a School of Technology, large classes of forty, etc., but the children are well disciplined and more than eager to learn. We saw classes of woodwork, homecraft and typewriting. Sad to think that, in spite of their enthusiasm, there is only a slender chance of them getting employment or anything worthwhile when they leave school.

We then did a tour of the Health centre and learned how Home Nursing Care is given. The streets look very gay as all the washing is hung out on the balconies or suspended on poles, the washing being remarkably clean under the circumstances. Babies are carried on their mother's backs and the children also carry them from a young age. The children are lovable, pretty and so happy. Goods are carried on the shoulder pole with a bucket suspended from either end or else balanced on the head. Hong Kong itself is very westernised, obviously under British influence and is well organised. It consists of two sections, Hong Kong Island and Kowloon which is joined to the mainland. The Y.M.C.A hostel was a lovely place for both men and women, had a swimming pool, a cafeteria restaurant, plus a garden café on the roof which overlooked the harbour and Hong Kong Island. In the afternoon we walked the shops and arcades and found some lovely goods, the native people were very crafty salesmen and you have to barter for most purchases, otherwise they cost you far more than the value. After a while you get sick of being badgered and just long to shop in peace.

On Saturday we took the ferry to Hong Kong Island, a twenty minute journey and then a bus to some Oriental gardens and Pagodas called Tiger Balm gardens. It was fascinating to see, we had to climb hundreds of steps to reach them but it was worth the effort. We then caught a bus to Aberdeen, a fishing town on the far end of the island. This was picturesque in itself, as hundreds of families live on the sea in boats of all shapes and sizes. These are anchored all over the place. The place was somewhat filthy and definitely overcrowded. We took a short ride around the boats in a San Pan. A woman worked the single revolving oar at the back of the boat and she steered us in and out with great skill. We ended up on one of the floating restaurants called the Tai Pak where we enjoyed a seven course meal with full waiter service. It was a fish dinner, very excellently prepared. Before they give you the menu they give you a glass of water and a clean wet cloth to wash your hands and feet, for perspiration, etc.

On returning to the centre of the Island we took the Vernacular Railway tram car up the hill, a very steep gradient, to enjoy a very lovely view of the Harbour looking across to Kowloon. We arrived back at the Hostel footsore and weary with blisters on our feet but we felt more than satisfied with our day's effort of coping with the local transport.

Early Sunday morning we left Hong Kong on Thai International Airways for Bangkok. This airline is known as the Royal Orchid Line and we were all given buttonholes of orchids which were really lovely but they did not last long in the heat. The flight to Bangkok took about two and a half hours and when we arrived we were knocked over with the heat and the humidity was so high it was misty. We were transported to a very posh hotel which was fully air-conditioned and was like sitting in heaven! We then phoned our missionary friends and arranged to meet

Photo 29 – Tai Pak Floating Restaurant, Hong Kong.

Photo 30 - Funicular Railway, Hong Kong Island.

them. After getting to know each other we took a taxi to their home where we were rooming in with Mary Levin, an English Missionary working with Christian Literature Crusade. The house was occupied with Mr and Mrs Syiblom and their children who are involved with the same Mission. They actually come from America and the home was simple and very comfortable. We found we had to take our shoes off at the door which was the custom and an afternoon siesta was usual when you actually undressed in order to rest. So we rested all the afternoon.

In the evening we went to a Protestant Christian Service held in the same Hotel where there were people from all nationalities present and it was interesting to hear of the different ways they had come to hear of the Gospel and their response to it. A Thai Evangelist took the service and his personal testimony was a wonderful miracle of God's grace. He shone with the presence and power of Christ and we learned something of the enormous task he has in this heathen land of spiritual darkness. There are approximately 99% Buddhists and less than 1% Christian.

On Monday we took a taxi to the Rama Hotel where we joined a tour. The open taxi is like a three-wheeled Honda vehicle with a canopy over the seat and is a little cheaper than an ordinary taxi. You have to barter for the price of the journey so we were fortunate in obtaining advice from our friends on an average price to pay. The tour consisted of a boat trip down the river to the floating market. This was 2½ hours on a motor launch going through the various waterways seeing how the people lived, actually in houses on stilts over the side of the river. They use the river water for everything and it is extremely fast flowing which is just as well. We saw young and old all taking their baths and cleaning their teeth. The floating market is just as its name suggests, all the goods being sold from little boats and floating wooden platforms on stilts. It really was very interesting indeed. Much of the foliage we passed was sub-tropical and, of course, the intense heat to go with it. On the return journey we visited the Buddhist Temple of the Dawn. Much of its superb decoration was taken down for cleaning but there was enough there to really make it impressive. We also saw the Palace, only from a distance, and visited the Royal Barges which are only used once a year.

After a few hours reviving ourselves in the cool of the Hotel, we took an afternoon trip to T.I.M. Land (Thailand in Miniature). This consists of twenty acres of ground developed for maintaining Thai culture and also to show the tourists a variety of aspects concerned with the work of the country. We saw the arts and crafts, weaving, pottery, umbrella making, ceramic paining, grinding and polishing rice which is grown in the paddy fields also represented there. Bullocks work in the rice fields turning over the water, etc. We saw displays of dancing from young children and older classical style, all done in national costume, singing and musical instruments. We saw cockfighting, Thai boxing and lumbering and watching the elephant being used to move the large logs. The man who owns

Photo 31 – The Emerald Buddha Temple, Bangkok, Thailand.

Photo 32 - Floating Fruit Market, Bangkok, Thailand.

Photo 33 - Children Thai Dancers, Thailand in Miniature Land, Bangkok, Thailand.

the place provides free education for children provided they learn one of the cultural native arts which is an excellent opportunity for the poor but gifted children.

After tea with our friends in their home, we bedded down for an hour or so. We caught the midnight Pan American flight to Calcutta arriving about 3am. It was so hot we were rather drained of energy. We hoped to go straight to the Salvation Army Hostel where we were staying but, instead, at 4am we were dumped in the lobby of the Grand Hotel and advised not to go out in the streets until daylight. We could vaguely see their point of view as coming along in the airport coach the pavements were covered with people sleeping but all the same we did need a bed. At 7am we arrived at the hostel and we could not find a soul with whom to book in. Eventually we got some breakfast and found we were sharing a room with two other girls, a tiny verandah with the sun pouring in. Elaine was passed caring, flopped on the bed and went fast asleep for two hours. Poor girl was very exhausted and, when awaking, felt ghastly still. I meanwhile had managed to make contact with a missionary friend, Shelia Masterton, and she was a real help and Heaven-sent I am sure. It was very hot. Elaine had a good shower on waking. Shelia came looking for us and took us off to her flat for a cool ice drink from the fridge and we began to feel human again. We spent the whole afternoon checking in for the Tour and arranging visas, etc. About 8pm we were contemplating bed when Shelia came round with another missionary, Joy, from the Baptist Mission. They dumped our cases in their car and brought us to the Baptist Mission Guest House. It was like walking into a palace and we could have wept. A huge old colonial house with large airy rooms and two beds sitting in the middle of the bedroom under the huge revolving fans. We only had a sheet to cover us. By 9pm we were fast asleep until 8am and we felt so wonderful. Even our ankles and feet, which had been so swollen, were almost normal again. We were originally going to stay here but the feeling towards English Missionaries is so bad that the Mission may have to go at any time so they were reluctant to take the chance. We were looked after so wonderfully well and we were grateful to God for His wonderful provision. To describe the state of living out here is difficult. They eat like animals off the pavements, wash in the streets from muddy water from pumps, use the roadways as toilets and throw all the rubbish anywhere. Hygiene is non-existent. It I unsafe to eat anywhere and to drink anything because of catching disease. So being at the Mission we were sure the water was boiled and safe, the food also. If we go out for a day they give us a packed lunch and drink to take with us. You have to wash all your clothes twice a day because of the heat and take salt and gastro enteric preventative pills also. Even with this protection the risk of infection is very high. Elaine and I are very fit at present though with the humid heat we feel we are in a sauna bath all the time. The results of malnutrition, beggars, cripples, are dreadful to see, many have no homes and just squat in shop alcoves. They prepare their food on hot charcoal on the pavement, most are unemployed, others drag cart loads on wagons so heavy a lorry would be taxed with power, just like slave gangs. There are rickshaws also which they pull along with passengers. I felt quite sorry when we both got in and he had to run a mile or so. Many of the Indians work with the black market, what a life, you virtually can trust no one.

We took a train from Howrah main station to Serampore, we got a 3rd class ticket and travelled in the Ladies' compartment where it is safer. They were all very intrigued with us as very few Europeans travel like this. We took a rickshaw from the station at Serampore to the Theological College founded by William Carey, an Englishman, and we passed along the banks of the Hoogley River and through the small village. The College was started in 1818 as a Theological College but is used for the arts and crafts and the sciences as well. Carey himself translated the Bible into thirty four Indian dialects. We saw many of these and were shown round the College with the Principal who together with his wife made us very welcome. It was all most interesting. We also saw the primary school and, on the way back to the station, we stopped at the Baptist Church. The Church was very old and falling down, the Pastor was away, but we met the Pastor's wife and children. I shall never forget her face, it shone with the love and joy of the Lord. They looked very poor in earthly things but were very rich in the Heavenly things. We took the train back to Calcutta and braved a train ride back to the Mission, you have to hang on to possessions very closely. The buses are even worse as there is

Photo 34 – Hindu Temple, Calcutta, India.

Photo 35 - Children outside a Timber Shop, Calcutta, India.

no limit to the number of passengers, they hang on to every window and ledge like leaches. The cows are sacred and wander everywhere at will which can be a nuisance at times. We joined three other people today and did a quick tour around, we did not have to refresh our minds of the squalor but we were interested to see some of the Hindu Temples. The sun was boiling and much of the place and surrounds were made of marble. On having to take shoes off at the bottom of the steps, we nearly lost the soles of our feet running up to the inside. The deafening ring of bells is continuous when a family is inside praying and paying homage. This is supposed to keep the evil spirits away. The cost of these temples when you see the squalor outside seems so wrong.

Tomorrow we leave at 7.30am on the overland coach for Nepal and the Himalayan mountains and we will not be disappointed in some ways, although I would have loved to have seen the Hospital. We met Christian Doctors who are very limited in what they can do as the Indians are in charge and they do not have the same compassion for their people at all. At the moment being hot and dry about 500 at least die every day from cholera. We attended a prayer meeting and Bible Study with Sheila and it was great to have fellowship with them all there in the Mission. We met many of the National Christians and some of them really love the Lord. The Pastor and his wife are wonderful and full of the Lord.

INDIA

Tuesday 20th – Wednesday 21st May 1969

We left Calcutta promptly at 7.30am with all passengers and baggage on board. My case was almost too big but, praise God, I managed to get it in. We had a large coach with good viewing windows but no air-conditioning which makes travelling rather sticky to say the least. We have covered 300 miles in all today and it took us most of the morning to get out of the slums and suburbs of Calcutta. For most of the day we travelled through farming land of small mud houses and well kept but very dry fields. It all looked a little more civilised than city life and the people appeared to be healthier on the whole too. We stopped for lunch at a wayside café where we ate our own picnic lunch which was safer. I know what it feels to be like an animal in the zoo now as everywhere we stopped scores of Indians stared at us. About 6.30pm we arrived at Bodh Gaya where we spent the first night. This is a tourist resting house rather like a motel in the making. There were a few rooms available but most of us slept on camp stretchers with sleeping bags provided by the coach in a large courtyard under the stars. Food was provided buffet style and we were well catered for.

In the morning we were up for 6am breakfast and then we took a walk around the town before leaving at 7.30am. We walked down to the village and visited the Temple near where Buddha first had his 'enlightenment' or vision under the Banyan Tree.

There are many large Buddhist Temples erected in memory and for the use of pilgrims. Not very inspiring inside and you have to leave your shoes at the gateway, in fact, we nearly lost them! Then into the coach again for another 285 miles of very hot travelling. You needed to wet your lips at least every half hour all day. Perspiration was pouring off us and there was hardly a whisper in the coach as everyone was trying to cope with survival.

We traversed the plains of Bengal, then a little further where rice fields were plentiful and the farmers were frantically preparing for the forthcoming Monsoon. We saw bullocks being used for ploughing and for grinding the rice and corn. Another major occupation was brick making from the plentiful clay. They are packed into a square shaped wood in the middle and clay around the edges, they are then fired until they are solid red and ready for use. The women work hard at this, too. We crossed the famous River Ganges, a large river bed at present rather dry. At the border of India and Nepal we had to wait hours whilst the Customs Authority was given for our entry and our Nepalese visas were passed. We stayed the night at the border town Birganj which was a pretty dead-end place. On our arrival we found that they only expected 28 people instead of our 48 people. Out came the camp beds and sleeping bags again, this time on the flat roof. There were only two showers and toilets for us all so you can imagine the chaos, plus the poor sanitation, so in spite of being so hot and sticky and smelly, most of us preferred to remain that way. The food was equally poor and the mosquitoes had a fine time feeding on us during the night. Still, we had a laugh and looked on the bright side.

The following day we were prepared to start at 7am for our journey to Kathmandu, the capital of Nepal. We had to leave our large coach behind as she was much too long for the winding mountainous trip and narrow roads. A local bus was provided with insufficient seats, so eleven of the party were flown by chartered plane – those who were older members of our party and those with upset stomachs. In the meantime, most of us climbed into the old bus, rather like sardines, but all the windows were open wide which gave us a very welcome breeze. It was a lovely day driving through the Tiger Country, then making a gradual climb to 8,000 feet. The panoramic views were wonderful and the Nepalese farms fascinating. They were mainly on the mountain slopes in tiers to allow for drainage. The corn and rice fields were neatly arranged and looked like a patchwork quilt. They were all planted and harvested by hand and everywhere was beautifully neat and tidy. Men, women and children Sherpas can be seen walking along the roadside with a sturdy stride carrying enormous loads in baskets on their backs with a supporting strap around their foreheads. They move with amazing speed up and down the mountains and are very agile. The houses too have character, built mostly of solid carved wood, shutter doors downstairs with a thatched roof. We revelled in the coolness of the mountain air before we stopped for our picnic lunch at a place

Photo 36 – On Indian-Nepalese border.

Photo 37 - Street scene with mother and child, Kathmandu, Nepal.

called Daman, high on the peak of the Himalayan Ranges where at certain times Everest can be seen but low cloud made visibility poor.

After lunch we began the long descent to the Kathmandu Valley, half way down the gears failed, but fortunately the brakes were good. We freewheeled much of the way until the grating noise underneath was unbearable and then we stopped whilst repair work was carried out. They managed to give us two gears so we proceeded more safely. We hadn't gone very far when we hit a small rock part of which became lodged between the tyres on one side. We had a Sikh on board who was a great help and he managed to get us clear at last. How we had not fallen over the edge of the road on many occasions was a wonder because there is hardly room or space to overtake. We got to the stage where we did not look over the edge. In Kathmandu we stayed at a large first class hotel, which we all appreciated, called 'The Shankar'. Here we had a cleaning up session of self, hair and clothes. After a really good night's sleep we were refreshed to explore the city. A sprawling city beneath the foothills of the Himalayas, the shops were surprisingly well stocked and reasonably set out after Indian standards. Markets and bazaars are everywhere with plenty of Hindu and Buddhist temples. The ornamental wood carvings are outstanding.

We visited the Temple of the Living Goddess where they keep a young girl from about 4 years until puberty and they worship her as their little goddess. She is chosen from pure Buddhist stock from a goldsmith's family. She is chosen for her beauty, purity and courage. She is kept shut away in the Palace and educated in splendid isolation. When she reaches puberty she is returned to her family. The great problem is that men are frightened to marry her as superstition has it that whoever marries the goddess will die. We drove up an overlooking hill to Bodhnath, the oldest shrine (Buddhist) with four eyes facing out in all directions – the all-seeing eyes of Buddha. We visited a Tibetan Refugee Camp and watched them skilfully make their handicrafts, carpets, jumpers, shoes. jewellery, etc. In the afternoon we looked round the shops and then early to bed. Tuesday we arose at 3.30am (which nearly killed us) and climbed into a convoy of jeeps which took us eighteen miles up the mountainside to a place called Nagrakot. It was a really rough ride which kept us awake. We went to see the sunrise over the mountains, particularly Mount Everest, which were so beautiful with the snow peaks. However, Mount Everest was not in evidence once again. We returned in time for breakfast and then spent the morning in bed. In the afternoon we caught a taxi to the Nepal United Mission Hospital which is supported by twelve countries and all denominations. England, for instance, had just supplied a modern X-ray machine. We were shown around the Hospital and wards by an American Hostess Missionary. The Hospital itself is an old palace which they have converted very well. The concubine quarters opposite have readily been adapted into Nurses' Accommodation. Most of the trained staff were from Western civilisation but it was encouraging to see the national Nepalese nurses being trained. While we were waiting for a bus back to the city a very large blue car came by, plus flag and chauffeur. It stopped and the British gentleman inside offered us a lift. He turned out to be a doctor who was the Director of the World Health Organisation in Nepal and he was most interesting to listen to as he had been in the service for twenty years.

Wednesday we got on the old rickety bus that took us back across the mountains to Birganj. The low clouds did clear long enough for us to see some of the snow covered peaks. From the first class hotel of Kathmandu we returned to the primitive set up once again. Still, it was cooler there and I slept well apart from mosquito bites.

Thursday we climbed into our own coach again and drove back across the border into India returning over the River Ganges to Patna. The heat was overbearing, 110 degrees all day inside the coach and it was difficult to maintain any kind of hydration in spite of drinking water, we were perpetually dry. At 11am the coach acquired a puncture which gave us a two hour delay. We found what shade we could under some Bamboo trees and had an early lunch consisting mainly of fruit and drink. A few were lying prostrate with exhaustion. We found some irrigation channels with fast flowing clean water in so we spent the time paddling in it to cool off. By the time we reached Patna and the Republic Hotel we were 'all in'. Elaine and I shared a cold beer between us which wonderfully quenched our thirst, we felt almost human again. Patna revealed a fair bit of ye old British colonial influence with British type buildings, houses, churches and parks, but still was very Indian in atmosphere. There was a large dome shaped building built by the British to house grain at a time of famine but it is not used anymore.

On Friday we drove 175 miles, with temperatures of 108 degrees, to Benares. We stopped for lunch at Sasaram where we looked around Sher Shah's Tomb which was surrounded by a lake. Sher Shah was a great scholar and leader of his time and was much revered, hence the huge tomb given him.

At Benares we stayed at a lovely hotel called 'De Paris' with verandas and overhanging trees and gardens all around. We were situated on the ground floor and there were numerous servants all around so we did not have to lift a finger. Our first thought on arrival, as usual, was an air-conditioned room and drinks, preferably water nice and cold. About an hour later everyone had sufficient strength to get to their bedrooms. The food was excellent, well served and appetising. On Saturday we arose at 5am and took a boat trip on the famous River Ganges which was extremely interesting. The far side of the river is absolutely bare, no houses or signs of life and it is known as Hell to the Hindu. The side where we and all the people are is known as Heaven. The Ganges is used for everything and is very holy to them. It is used for cleansing, curing, worshipping, burying the dead and washing the clothes, etc. The Ghats are stone steps leading down to the water's edge. They are divided up into sections and depending on your Caste or class you visit the appropriate one. The women are separate from the men.

Photo 38 - Holy Man meditates under the umbrella, Benares, India.

Photo 39 - Me on a rickshaw, Benares, India.

The Hindus take daily baths here, worship and are blessed by a Brahmin sitting under an umbrella afterwards. The Hindu then has to perform an act of charity and this is where the beggars earn their money. People from all over India make pilgrimages here before they die, like Muslims like to go to Mecca. If you have the good fortune to actually die by the Ganges you are supposed to go straight to Heaven. There are various Ghats, bathing ones for men, others for women, laundry Ghats and funeral Ghats where they burn the bodies on bonfires as near to the water's edge as possible. The ashes are then strewn on the river. For all Holy Men, boys under five years, leprosy victims or smallpox sufferers, they are not allowed to be burned. Instead their bodies are weighted and sunk to the bottom of the river. There were quite a few burning as we went along, rather a morbid sight.

In the morning we wandered around the streets and went into a real Indian silk shop, taking off our shoes according to custom and sat on the floor while we were proudly shown their marvellous display of wares. We drove back to the hotel in a rickshaw. That evening Elaine developed diarrhoea and vomiting which persisted all night and by the morning she was rather weak. Fortunately the coach seat rotation placed us on the back seat and she was able to lay flat with her head lying on my lap. Temperatures were still 100 degrees in the coach but somehow she reached the destination of Khajuraho and I must say I was pleased to get out of the coach as the sun had been pouring down on me through the back window. The Indian proprietor gave Elaine on our arrival a raw lemon with salt to suck and it worked wonders. Elaine decided to take an air-conditioned room and we shared it. She rested for the rest of the day and the following day also, while I went sightseeing with the others.

I went on a trip round the archaeological find of the Chandella Temples and the wonderful sculptures made on them. They were mostly built about the 12th century and discovered fairly recently. The carvings are rather crude and were used mostly as sex education guides. One of the boys particularly found it embarrassing and was glad to get out.

By the evening Elaine was fit again and we had a good journey on Tuesday to Agra through some very dry barren plains. Again we had a beautiful hotel owned by a British woman and on finding a swimming pool, we fell in for a cool dip after downing at least four glasses of water. The service at the hotel was excellent, a real joy to be there and we had all drinks served with ice. The days and nights were so hot Elaine rose at 5am each morning and had a swim in the pool. Gone are the days of using a towel after showering, the heat just evaporates the water in minutes.

We went to see the Taj Mahal, of course, and it was beautiful and it would make any other building seem very plain. The temple is made out of pure white marble, 300 years old and all the stone was carried by oxen cart 150 miles from Jaipur and it took 22 years to build. The marble is inlaid with perfectly symmetrical design of precious stones such as agates, jasper, jade and amethyst. There is black marble lettering inscribed around the entrance to the temple. It all looks equal in size in spite of the height as the higher it goes the deeper the inlay. The builder responsible was Emperor Shah Jehan who built it as an eternal tomb for his beloved queen. He intended to build one of black marble for himself joining the two with a bridge signifying they would always be joined even in eternity. This proved too expensive and, as his son imprisoned him for the last seven years of his life, the dream never had a chance of being fulfilled so he was buried in the Taj Mahal with his queen. We also visited the fort where he was imprisoned and much of the jewelled inlay was there too. We walked miles it seemed around the fort, up and down stairs, seeing the various quarters for the concubines, public and private audience chambers and various places of worship. Before entering the holy area we had to leave our shoes at the door and walk around the boiling hot floors with bare feet. You can imagine the colour of them afterwards!

Then we left Agra to drive to Jaipur, the pink city. On the way we stopped at another fort named Fatehpur Sikri, the first of the three planned cities of India. All the forts were built by Shah Jehan's father Akbar the Great. He built this one in the 16th century in red sandstone but it was deserted within 20 years by the Royal Court because of the lack of water. It was built as a new city to commemorate the birth of a long wanted son to Akbar. It was a thanksgiving as the Holy Man whose prophesy came true came from the hills of Sikri. Within the city were

Photo 40 – Taj Mahal, Agra, India.

Photo 41 - Riding on an elephant down the hill with Indian music, Amber, India.

harem quarters for Buddhists, Moslems and Christians and larger quarters for the Hindus as it was a Hindu who gave him a son.

The journey to Jaipur was very hot and we had dust storms for most of the way. By the time we arrived at the hotel we were parched and smothered with dust. We had four beds to a room and only one fan so, other than sitting under the shower all night, no one could sleep very well. You could not open the windows as monkeys roam free and wild and they could come in and be a nuisance. Jaipur is rather fascinating, made of stone and covered with pink substance. It is situated in a gorge with high fortress walls all around with gates at either end. The atmosphere is one of crumbling buildings, dilapidated places, yet the atmosphere of the Maharajah remains. This was the great city of the Rajputs, the great Indian warriors and is now the capital of the state of Rajasthan. In spite of the heat of 110 degrees we managed to stagger down the road to investigate the sight of the general architecture, the Palace and the Hall of Winds.

We were away promptly at 7am the following morning which mattered little as we had all had a pretty sleepless night and the 195 miles to Delhi was a nightmare. Many felt ill in the intense heat and we did not have enough space to lay everyone down. The heat was 110 degrees in the coach itself but we stopped for an hour at 8am to see the Amber Fort situated on top of a hill. We had an Elephant ride to the top which was great fun and we were accompanied by an Indian piper playing

– a real wailing in our ears. Halfway to Delhi the coach cooling system in the engine failed which caused us a little delay while the driver made a temporary repair with string. We were thankful to reach the Renjit Hotel with its air-conditioned reception room and lounge. Our room was cooled by fans so we took cold showers and went to bed wet, repeating as needed during the night depending on how hot we were. The following day we walked to the Mosque which was impressive outside but rather nondescript inside. It was terribly hot so we remained in the cool of the hotel for the rest of the day. In the evening we attended the Son et Lumiere performance at the Red Fort. This was very outstanding giving us a vivid picture of India's history over the last few hundred years. After Britain had occupied India independence came. They played their National Anthem and they all rose with tremendous gusto.

On Sunday we attended a service at the Indian International Centre where they have some lovely gardens, green grass and fountains. The service was interdenominational, very formal and boring, and mostly Americans present. We enjoyed a lovely cup of coffee or soft drinks afterwards. It was then I got talking to a national Christian who was very mixed up about his faith and it proved a profitable conversation. We went to the Ashoker Hotel, very posh with a beautiful swimming pool and shopping centre where we could enjoy all the amenities for a very small fee. The water was beautifully cool and a deep turquoise with umbrellas dotted around the garden to lounge under. There we stayed. I became rather burned as the sun and wind were scorching.

We were due to leave Delhi on the Monday but we were held up because the coach had to have new shock absorbers flown in from Germany. So on Monday four of us hired a taxi and a Sikh driver for the morning to explore New Delhi. We were shown a brightly painted new Mosque, very original. We climbed up the Victory Tower overlooking New Delhi, watched the Indian craftsmen at work with their designing on brass and lacquer work. We were shown the new Government Housing programmes where tenants are housed for 10% of their pay. We then visited Parliament House, a circular building built by the British and went under the large arch which is a memorial to the dead in the war. We saw many Government buildings and embassies. A well planned city with all the shops situated in a circuit and the official buildings altogether in another area. Trees lined the streets and the general standard of the Indians you met was of a much higher caste than we had seen previously. In the afternoon we went into the swimming pool again, a real treat.

On Tuesday we left at 5am to avoid some of the heat of the day. The drive was quite different travelling through the Punjab. The land was mostly owned and farmed by Sikhs, much more organised, education and intelligence seemed higher. Their farms were well mechanised, irrigated with large man-made canals and their crops much richer. They have the most important wheat growing area in that part of the world and we saw many markets where grain was being sold and sacked. We arrived at Amritsar where the Sikh religious centre is and we saw their Golden Temple and were able to go in and look around. Shoes have to come off as usual, then you wash your feet before going in. Unfortunately, in order to cross to the Temple your feet were scorched by the hot marble ground so we made a dash for it. It was all much more reverent, a more holy atmosphere inside and the decorations were very ornate. Their religion is very much a cross between Christianity and Islam and its mode of behaviour is founded on good works.

We spent a pleasant night in a Guest House in Amritsar complete with a small swimming pool and we had dinner served outside in the garden.

We have only travelled 150 miles today but it took us three hours to get through the Customs and red tape of the Indian-Pakistan border. We are now in Lahore, west Pakistan, where we shall stay for two days before going to Afghanistan.

AFGHANISTAN

Monday 2nd June 1969

The first evening four of us were escorted out by a Pakistan gentleman who proudly showed us some illuminated gardens and walked us miles ending up at a very intercontinental hotel for drinks and to hear music playing softly from the orchestra.

Photo 42 – Sikh wheat grinders, the greatest wheat producers in India, near Amritsar, India.

Photo 43 - Entrance to the Golden Temple, Amritsar, India.

275

We had something to eat and joined some friends of his for coffee sitting at a table under the trees by the swimming pool. I was asked for a dance at one point, so I agreed as the others were not at all keen. At 11.30pm we managed to excuse ourselves. The following day I had a raging fever of 102 degrees and across my chest and back I had come out in water blisters, the result of the sun in Delhi I think. I also had diarrhoea and vomiting which must have been associated with the sun as well. The temperature was 113 degrees outside so it was difficult to lower the fever. Elaine made me as comfortable as she could then went off to explore around the city with the other two girls, Doreen and Margaret. It was a public holiday to celebrate Mohammed's birthday so only a few shops were open and there was much jollification and festivities in the streets. They went to the fort in Lahore which was a red building on the outskirts of the city with wall decorations depicting elephant and camel fights. There was a beautiful Hall of Mirrors still standing and large areas of vivid green grass and flowers. From the fort you can view the Monument of Independence and the Badshai Mosque. The Pakistanis never left them alone and they got rather tired of them pestering them. They had many offers of dates for the evening which they refused. The place, on the whole, was much cleaner than India and much more westernised. They managed to acquire plenty of medicine against gastro-enteritis sickness so that we may be well supplied as we pushed on. After coffee and ice creams in the cool of a café, as the heat was intense, they returned to find me no better. I had just remained in quiet, dozing and comfortable enough in the circumstances. They dosed me up as best they could and by the following morning my temperature had descended to normal. I felt rather weak, however, as we were bundled into the coach. Then we had a very hot drive to Peshawar, the gun making town. Here the management of the hotel took pity on us and gave us air-conditioning free. We had a comfortable room for four and, apart from eating at the restaurant next door and worrying to find a money changer to change Pakistani money into Afghan money, we did not have the energy to explore the town any further, though we could see something of the street stalls and bazaars in abundance.

The following day was one of the most exciting from the point of view of travelling we had done when we drove from Pakistan through the famous Khyber Pass into Afghanistan. The tribesmen inhabit the Pass, warrior like nomads who live in the mountains and used to be known as the Khyber Rifles. Since British rule left and we are not 'loved' over there, Pakistan has taken over much of the control of this area. They are left much to themselves which avoids bloodshed. These people are very poor and short of employment so they resort to raiding, pilfering and smuggling in black market items. The Pass is very mountainous and is only open from dawn to dusk, heavily guarded all the time by Pakistani soldiers at forts situated at strategic points all the way through. Everyone carries a gun and the Afghans particularly look fierce. I liked their intense straight look, strong jaw and dark appearance. No photographs are supposed to be taken en route and the coach cannot stop but if you do they can land on you extremely quickly apparently. The Khyber Pass remains of strategic importance being the gateway from Central Asia to the Far East. All the great conquerors have passed this way at some time or other and the place is full of reminders of bitter wars. The construction of it is an engineering top achievement because of the sheer rock faces, steep gradients, etc. There are, however, three ways of travelling provided: a good but very windy road which the British built, also rail and the old caravan camel route where camel and donkey caravan traders can pass through. This main trading route is also known as the Silk Way leading from the Mediterranean to China.

We, at last, arrived in Kabul, the capital city of Afghanistan, in the afternoon. It's 6,000 feet above sea level surrounded by snow covered ranges of the Hindukush and Spin Ghar. We had passed through very spectacular gorges to reach it with fast flowing mountain rivers running down near the road. The hotel was pretty central and overlooking the Central Park. While we waited in the bus for Hotel and Room Allocation a student demonstration came by with their placards and their voices raised in angry protest. Apparently there had been an injustice performed against some students which had had drastic consequences and caused this reaction. It seemed a justifiable complaint; it reminded us a little of the dear Western World. I must say we liked the Afghan people on the whole but they are

Photo 44 – Kabul Reservoir in Afghanistan.

very poor and primitive in their outlook and behaviour. The climate is fresh and sunny, very bracing, cold at night and 80 degrees in the day. We even saw the odd goose pimple and had to have a sheet over us at night.

After a shower we walked across the square to the Khyber restaurant, a really up-to-date clean place with a wonderful selection of self-service food and then we felt much better. Afterwards we looked around for a church for Sunday next day. We walked miles in badly lit streets, falling in and out of holes, right round the Embassy block and Palace without avail. After a good night's sleep we took a taxi to the Christian Community Church situated out of town opposite the Soviet Union Embassy. It was a beautiful service with a good message but half way through the Communion Service there was a great thunderstorm and dust storm. We realised we were in the best place as afterwards we saw the wrecks of fences, etc., and some of our bus crowd were wet through. Doreen even had her sunglasses blown away.

After the service we introduced ourselves to Dr Christie Wilson, the Pastor and Missionary-in-Charge, a man much loved and respected by the Afghan people. We had already made contact with him by letter. Being a Muslim country missionaries cannot be admitted as such but they come in on Professional and Official capacities. He had himself been a teacher here for fifteen years.

In the afternoon we wandered around the bazaars, fur shops and jewellery stores which show the famous blue stone. We then decided to have an early night as we had to be up by 5am so we prepared for bed at 9.30pm. No sooner had we got into bed that a knock came to the door with a telephone message. Doreen and Margaret had been involved in a car crash and our Courier had gone out for dinner so he was not available. After much difficulty I managed to make the Reception understand that I wanted Dr Wilson and they phoned him for me. He came straight over and drove us to the Hospital which was quite a way on the other side of town. It was very providential that he was there as he spoke fluent Afghan and nobody in Afghanistan speaks English. It appeared that Doreen and Margaret had gone out with two chaps to have a drink and they had a crash on the way back as the driver had had a little too much vodka. Doreen was shocked and bruised but she was able to leave the Hospital, but Margaret had a badly lacerated skull, had lost a fair amount of blood, so she had to have a blood transfusion. I have never seen a more primitive I.V. fluid arrangement but it worked alright. After leaving we had to go to the Police Station with Doreen to sort out statements. Dr Wilson was wonderful and we all owed him very much. We eventually reached the hotel to find we were locked out but in the end we managed to knock someone up and crawled into bed at 2am. Breakfast and 5am came all too quickly. We left Doreen behind in Kabul to wait for Margaret's discharge from Hospital. They hope to catch us up by air later on.

Monday we left Kabul and drove a few miles outside town to watch for a couple of hours the filming of Anthony Quinn's latest movie 'The Horseman'. Once a year the Afghan's play a game called Buzkashi on the King's birthday, but, on this occasion, it was performed especially for the film. It is an equestrian sport displaying the remarkable horsemanship of opposing teams of Afghan riders. A carcass of a calf is placed in a circle with the riders all around and on a given signal the contestants on horseback rush to pick up the carcass from the ground, carry it to the end of the field and back to the goal. Much speed is needed and rough snatching is involved.

For the rest of the day we drove across barren desert land, rather uninteresting, to Kandahar for the night and the following day was similar driving to Herat. The road was Russian built and very good for travelling long distances fast. We are now driving on the right hand side of the road and we noted that the Russians had also built several hotels along the way. It was at one of these we spent the night at Herat, modern and quite comfortable, although electricity and water went off at 11pm. We have said goodbye to toilets as such and now have holes in the ground! Bush stops are preferable.

The next day was a long one. We had a short drive to the Afghan border where Custom formalities took five hours to complete. They insisted we untied all our baggage in case we were carrying fire arms, but actually, they only gave each case a very cursory glance and a poke. We learned afterwards that an important official had been visiting which had made them very pompous and fussy. Moving on to the Iranian border we had to pass through the Quarantine Barrier where you are usually

Photo 45 – The Mosque, Mashed, Iran.

given four pills to swallow against cholera but they had run out so we missed that pleasure. The Customs in Iran only took three hours but in all we had sat by the roadside for eight hours just getting out of Afghanistan and into Persia. We had a bit of trouble with the coach because of dirty diesel fuel and we had to keep stopping to flush the pipe through but we arrived safely about 8pm at Mashed.

Mashed is one of Persia's holiest cities, famed for its beautiful Golden Mosque and Gardens, fountains and roundabouts. All the Persian towns have illuminated archways, ready in case the Shah should visit, a way of showing their loyalty. We wandered around the city but the people follow you, pester you, touch you and even kick you, so it can be a bit trying some of the time. We visited the Museums situated in the Holy Compound and to do this we had to wear the Muslim Chudda robe over our head and shoulders. We had quite a game putting it on and many women were watching us and laughing at our efforts. We were not allowed to see any further into the Compound as the Mashed Mosque is supposed to be the place where Mohammed is supposed to reappear one day.

The following day we drove to Gorgan near to the Caspian Sea. It was a long drive, 350 miles, on all dirt gravel roads and it was our lot to sit in the back seat where the dust came in the back door and absolutely covered us so we became grey haired and absolutely filthy. As a shock absorber had broken, the bumps were pretty rough but we travelled through very varied countryside, desert, rich fertile land, rice fields, tobacco fields and two miles of most beautiful forest preserved as Crown Property, all kinds of trees richly green and refreshing. The extra long days travelling made up for the day we lost at Delhi on coach repairs so we are still up to schedule.

The three hundred mile drive on Saturday was nice too. We spent an hour at Babolsar, the centre of the world's caviar production, where we enjoyed a swim in the Caspian Sea. At this point we were very near the Russian border. Then we drove across the Elburtz Mountains to a height of six thousand feet to Teheran the capital. It was a fantastic drive as the mountain slopes were sheer with loose soil resulting every year in many landslides. In some parts the soil had blocked the road and in others the road had subsided into the river bed. Recent flooding had caused the road to be closed until the day before so we were fortunate to get through at all. it was quite a drive through tunnels, round bends and detours where the road was non-existent. We had a good view of the volcanic mountain, 1900 feet, called Mount Damavand. We saw shepherds moving their flocks of sheep with brown and black goats, also nomads with their makeshift tents called 'Kuchis' or 'Manus'. We then descended to a fertile plateau and to the cosmopolitan city of Teheran at four thousand feet. Here the typical Persia was engulfed in a rather nondescript and very modern capital city. There were insufficient rooms at the hotel so ten of us moved off to find accommodation elsewhere. It was much cheaper where we went and seemed clean enough.

The next day we travelled 250 miles through rather dull desert plateau country. Elaine had a good sleep while I dreamed the miles away. The weather was rather hot again but not as exhausting as India. We are now staying in a lovely large town for the night called Isfahan which is in transit to Shiraz.

PERSIA

Thursday 12th June 1969

We travelled to Shiraz and the sun became hotter – about 90 degrees. The journey down was through rather dry and barren country with very little vegetation, bare hills, a few nomads, some villages with mud huts and shepherds herding goats and sheep. About 35 miles outside Shiraz we stopped a while at Nagsh-e-Rustan, a spectacular series of cliff tombs, very enormous, where Darius I and II, Cyrus and Xerxes were buried. All very fascinating Biblical history. How they managed to place them so high is a wonder and the carvings above them and around them are very distinct and well preserved by the sand as some date back to the 3rd century B.C. The reliefs in the rock depict such things as the investiture of Shapur by Ardeshir, Shapur on horseback, various Persian kings at war and peace. There are some stone pillars visible which were used as fire altars. The city of Shiraz itself is most attractive with gardens, roses and tall cypress trees – the home of Persia's finest poets. It is the centre of the province of Fars, the national language, ringed by a sentinel of mountains and situated in a rich fertile valley ideal for vineyards and wine production.

The following morning we were taken out by coach to view the ancient town of Persepolis. It was very hot indeed which made it a little hard to concentrate on historical values and beauty but we absorbed as much as we could. Persepolis was founded in 518 B.C. by Darius I as a sacred national shrine dedicated to serve as a specific and beautiful setting for the Spring Festival together with esteeming the power of the Achaemenid Kings. It was only ever occupied on special occasions. It took 150 years to build and was destroyed by Alexander the Great in a drunken stupor, by fire, in revenge for the Persian destruction of Athens. The fact that the roofs of the great palaces were of mud and sand meant that the fire burned away any cedar wood pillars so the roof fell in the sand covering and thus preserving much of the beautiful carvings. Such places as the grand staircase, main courtyard and throne room, hall of 100 mirrors and the hall of 99 pillars can be outlined by the layout of the ruins and the various tall pillars left standing. The themes of the carvings are mostly servants paying homage, offering gifts and loyalty, all indicating imperial power. Behind Persepolis is the Mountain of Mercy with two more rock face tombs of Artaxerxes II and III. We climbed up the top and had a good view and overall picture of this great plantation where Persepolis stands even though it is in the process of excavation and therefore all in pieces. The rest of the day we had at leisure. On Wednesday we drove back across the plains to Isfahan where we spent three nights of rest and sightseeing. A traditional dish of food is Kebab. Some restaurants sell this only so you have had it if you do not like it especially in the villages. A Kebab consists of meat barbecued on an iron stick with a plate of rice followed by yoghurt and Persian bread which looks like an overdone pancake. The faith of the country is Muslim but there are Jews and Moravians as well as a smattering of Christians. The Muslim women are very underprivileged, very much the property of their husbands and used to the fullest extent! They start child bearing about 11 years and have an average of 18 pregnancies. The husband can have several wives and will only acknowledge that he has sons even if he has daughters. The women wear their veiled robes, not being allowed to show their faces and consider us Westerners naked with our bare legs and arms. The Persian men, on the whole, are well groomed. Their faith compels them to pray wherever they may be five times a day with seven parts of their body touching the floor – 2 feet, 2 knees, 2 arms and a forehead resting on the prayer stone which is round and made of clay from such sacred places as Mecca. Friday is their day of worship when they attend the Mosque. Once in a lifetime a good Muslim will make a long journey to Mecca. Only the rich actually do as there is little place for poverty in the Muslim faith.

This morning we had a varied tour of Isfahan which is rich in Islamic temples. We drove first to the famous centre of the city called the 'Maidan-I Shah' or the 'Shah Mosque' created by Shah Abbas in 1612. It is known as the famous Blue Mosque as the dome minarets and arches are a blaze of blue glazed tiles decorated with gold and silver geometrical designs, together with floral designs and giant lettering of the Koran – partly tiled in mosaic and partly in tile frescoes. It was enormous inside, partly used for public worship and also as a theological college. We then visited the Carpet Factory. It takes five years to make a full sized Persian carpet. We went into this room where there are children 5-12 years old, all girls, making the carpets by hand. They only have a graph pattern to guide them. Their little fingers are very nifty and they are taught and supervised well, but it is really slave labour as they only earn a mere pittance. They sit on trestles level with the carpet strung up vertically. Each strand is put in singly, all very fine work.

We saw the Friday Mosque (Jameh Masjed) afterwards which was relatively plain after the blue one but it had a beautiful carving done in plaster egg white and camel's milk which looked like stone from a distance. Walking through the bazaar we saw the bread making and were taken to see the underground linseed works. In a dark cellar a camel walks around and round pulling a four ton crushing wheel to crush the linseed. Once crushed it is mixed with a little water to form a pancake and then about 24 pancakes are placed one on top of another. A huge tree trunk of plain wood, 700 years old, is released on top of the pile and the pressure squeezes the linseed oil out into a container below.

Photo 46 - Children making Persian carpets, Isfahan, Iran.

Photo 47 - Women & Children, Isfahan, Iran.

We visited the 'Shaking Minarets' which are twin spired but when a man sits on the minaret and shakes it the other one shakes too. Quite a tourist confidence trick I feel. I wouldn't like to say how long they will stay standing. There are two different bridges spanning the river that runs by Isfahan. One has 33 archways which during the dry season in the old days used to have shops in each arch. The second is built on three levels. The bottom level of channels is to let the water through like a weir, the middle you can walk through and is used on Fridays for the Muslim worship and the top one is used for cars. Suspended between the top and middle channels is a large decorative room used by the kings and the harems when they wished to view the water.

The next day we have done almost nothing making full use of the day of rest from travelling and sightseeing. I called in with one of the Australian boys to the C.M.S., very famous in Isfahan, as he was having trouble with his eyes. The Outpatients was full of mostly women and they were very busy. I had been advised to look up some medical people here doing Mission work and in fact we did catch up with some. We had tea and a lovely chat about the Lord which intrigued my Aussie friend. He seemed very interested. The Doctor was very busy and couldn't come as he was about to do an emergency caesarean. The Aussie was advised, however, to leave for home and see a Specialist which he decided to do. We were very sorry to see him go.

We had quite a tiring drive to Teheran once again. It was very hot and humid. On arrival at the hotel in Teheran we had a note from one of my friends, Mary, who had done Midwifery training with me at Southmead. She picked us up at 6.30pm and we went and stayed with her family in their home. Because it was so hot we slept out on the balcony and it was really lovely. The Rahimian family were very friendly and kind even though they could not speak English and we really enjoyed being with them. Mary's brother and sister are both at present in England studying. They are a very devout Muslim family which has made it hard for Mary as she has been drawn to the Christian faith while in England. She has a very nice new car so we went for a drive out of town up the mountainside where the air was cool and refreshing. Alongside the car a fast mountain stream flowed and as we climbed higher up towards the snow-capped Mount Damavand there were many posh restaurants all lit up with various coloured lights. The Mount is 1860 feet and a volcano and if you energetically climb to the top you can see the Caspian Sea. On the way down we stopped at an open air restaurant with fountains playing, had a chicken kebab meal which was very tasty. We were taken on a tour of Teheran and the International Airport by night light which really was very enjoyable. It was very modern and progressive. It was about midnight when we arrived back so we went to bed. After a lovely cool night's sleep on the terrace Mary went off to work in the morning and we were left in the capable hands of another sister, Mona, who is 17 years old and learning

English at night school. Armed with Persian-English dictionaries she took us round the Archaeological Museum where we saw more ancient relics of Persepolis plus other relics dating back to 4,000 B.C. – pottery, carpets, jewellery, paintings and carvings, etc. We had a rest in the afternoon at her home and played some records, then we went to see the Persian Crown Jewels. Noted to be the finest collection of gold and jewels in the world, they are stored in the basement of the Bank of Melli with security +++, television eyes and doors feet thick. It was all truly magnificent, the blue stones, pearls, enormous rubies and emeralds, a map globe of the world in pure gold with jewels of different colours to show the different nations, the Shah's Coronation Crown and the peacock jewelled Coronation Chair. Not to mention the jewel boxes, swords, ornated shields, coronets, etc. There is a good Anglican Church which we tried to find for Service today but we failed to find it. The coach is now fitted with new shock absorbers once again. We trust these will take us through to Ostend without fault. Tomorrow we have a long day ahead, 400 miles on uncertain roads where there have been many landslides. Our last night in Persia before going into Turkey.

TURKEY

Wednesday 18th June 1969

We are now in Turkey. The weather is cooler as we are high in the mountains but it has revitalised us tremendously even though the cold hits much harder after the extreme heat. Our ride from Teheran was long and interesting. Much of the road was gravel but well graded, firstly over flat plateau land moderately green and fertile. We passed through Kasuin, the 11th century stronghold of powerful Assassins, a band of murderers who killed their victims whilst under the influence of Hashish. Apparently this was where the drug got its name. Very little of this old historical capital remains, just a monumental gateway with people living in mud houses dug out of the ground. From then on we began to traverse undulating hills, then we climbed to 6,000 feet above sea level. Whilst waiting for a hotel room allocation the men, women and children thronged round the coach and just stared at us. It was actually difficult to get through them to the hotel. In the evening we joined a young married couple and together we braved the streets to find a restaurant for a meal. We were thronged, nevertheless, having a man with us did help. Few women were around but hundreds of men, a mixture of Persians, Turks and many French speaking. After a meal we found a nice clean pastry shop so went in and had a freshly cooked cake. Elaine has almost acquired a taste for tea now, which is truly remarkable. She prefers it Turkish style with no milk or sugar and fairly weak. Travelling through hilly country the following day we saw plenty of colourful wild flowers. Throughout the day we were surrounded by snow-capped mountains. We had our first real rain storm and had to wear cardigans. On the Turkish border we were able to see Mount Ararat which is 17,000 feet high and has a smaller volcanic mountain next door which was clearly visible, all snowy white. Ararat itself is also volcanic and last erupted in the 19th century. We could not actually see the peak as it was so cloudy. The mountain is mentioned in Genesis as the final resting place of Noah's Ark and there is a desire to investigate but as it is situated so close to Russia that's as far as it goes.

The Customs and Border formalities for getting out of Persia and into Turkey were very efficient, only a couple of hours. We just had time for a meal and changing our money. Our passports are getting full of stamps, visas all interesting markings. The rest of the day we continued through green hilly country, such a change after the dry barren countryside we had known. We stopped at Agri for the night, a really small Turkish village. A rather shabby place, we were on the fifth floor of the hotel and the sheets looked as if they had been slept in many times – just a few fleas jumping on the pillow! When we walked down the street we were followed by a mob of men who jeered and mobbed us slightly and even threw stones at us. They were all peasants and obviously uneducated and unused to Western people. The one thing that really pleased us was the Turkish food, much more civilised and edible. The restaurants were called 'Lokantse' and it literally means 'Look and see'. You pass round the dishes of food on the hotplates and select what you want. Vegetables have now come back into our lives and chipped potatoes. Proper brown bread now replaces the previous papyrus paper in Iran. After eating a thunderstorm came and we did not feel like battling any further with the inquisitive crowd, so we retired to our luxury accommodation for a game of Scrabble and then sleep. We were asleep by 8.30pm but it was really 10pm as we had put our watches back one and a half hours. We are now only two hours behind London time.

In spite of the conditions we slept well and had a good breakfast, fresh loaf, honey, butter, etc. Turkish coffee is thick, black, almost pure coffee grounds – a little too strong to cope with so early in the morning, so we both stuck to tea. Today we had a ride of 120 miles and very beautiful. The hills were carpeted with flowers with plenty of poppies to add some bright colouring. We stopped frequently for photos and then at a mountain village in the north east corner of Turkey where certain nomadic people have settled. They are known as the Kurds. These people are hardly acknowledged by the rest of Turkey but we wandered around their village and they were most friendly. Their homes were made of mud brick and the women looked very gay in colourful clothes carrying water and washing, etc. The children were delightful and very well nourished apart from persistent sores probably due to lack of

Photo 48 – Kurdish women & children in a hill village near Erzurum, Turkey.

Photo 49 - Poppies & wild flowers near Erzurum, Turkey.

vitamins. They were very anxious to know where we came from. The people get rather confused as our coach is German with Klinger Wurzeburg all over the side (Wurzle for short) so they naturally assumed we came from there. The Turkish people are very mixed in facial features – a mix of Persian, Russian and European. We arrived in Erzurum about lunch time and had the rest of the day free. It is very quaint with horse and buggy for taxis. The shoe shine boys are busy in the streets with their brilliant bronze shoe stands. We could not take too many photos as the citadel and a few other historic buildings were under military control. In fact, the soldiers are very much in evidence throughout, especially along the Russian-Turkish border. We walked around the town with a long entourage of children behind us. We stayed at a brand new hotel for a change, but we had no hot water so washing goes by the board once again.

Thursday we had a long day's travelling all across the mountains on winding roads with tributaries of the Euphrates running through. From 4,000 feet we climbed to the highest point of 7,800 feet then down to 4,000 feet for a dinner stop. Up again to 6,000 feet and then a long gradual descent to sea level. Some of the scenery looked very Swiss with the green slopes and hillside houses with slanting roofs. Rich farming land with many miles of corn planted. The women in brightly coloured costumes till the land while most of the men can be found in the villages drinking tea. Poor old 'Wurzle' had quite a struggle with such a load plus steep gradients and she did not pull too well with a failing generator. We arrived safely at Trabzon on the Black Sea and today Friday we have a free day. A rather pretty seaside town with cobbled streets, old tiled houses, mosques with their tall towering minarets, mountains all around, a fishing port with gaily painted boats and nets dyed all colours too. We walked all morning through narrow winding streets seeing how the people live and we saw the remains of the old fortress, went inside the Mosque which was richly carpeted and had a beautifully carved wooden pulpit. This had been painted over which ruined it.

Just out of the town we visited the Church of St Sophia standing on a hill overlooking the Black Sea. It was formerly a Christian church, probably from the Byzantine Period, but is now converted to a Mosque in appearance and used as a Museum. There are some exquisite mural paintings depicting scenes of the New Testament. The ones on the ceiling have been particularly well preserved as they are out of reach of destructive hands. Sightseeing completed, we planned to have a swim but a thunderstorm came over and put paid to our intentions so we had a lazy time in our hotel.

Then on Saturday we drove to Sansum, a very pretty drive winding round by the sea all the way. Most of the beach is black sand and shingle and the colour of the sea itself varied from deep clear blue to turquoise when the rocks were below and muddy where the rivers flowed in. We went up and down many hills and through thick hazelnut forests which is one of their chief industries. During the dinner break we had a quick swim and unfortunately we had to choose a rather dirty area. The generator on the bus is now completely burned out so we even have no air blowers for ventilation now. The bus does get pretty stuffy but it is not too hot today. We will have to wait for a new generator to be flown out from Germany before they will be functioning again. They will probably catch us at Ankara.

Soon after we arrived at Sansum the weather broke and we had a thunderstorm. It is good to see some rain after our hot trek through India. Sansum is an ordinary seaside resort, a fishing port, with a fair selection of varied shops and bazaars, material and shoe shops were particularly plentiful. It was interesting to note that at set intervals all along the Black Sea the Americans have radar bases, all very hush-hush, but presumably to keep their watchful eye on the Russian front. The American forces are not allowed to mix with the Turks at all, it is complete segregation. They have all their food and provisions sent in by the U.S.A.

We left Sansum at early morning and drove all day arriving at the capital Ankara at 5.30pm. This place has been an important caravan stop on the trade route to Persia for centuries. Driving across the plateau we did make one detour to see if we could inspect some excavations of ruins originally built by the Hittites, mentioned in the Old Testament, $16^{th} - 14^{th}$ century B.C. Little is known about them except that they spoke with a European language. 'Wurzle', the coach, would not reach to the ruins but we could see quite well from the road. We did go into one area and saw some carvings and reliefs found on some of the stones which showed the style of dress of that period. We had rather an overcast drive from Ankara to Urgup but later in the afternoon the day brightened for some sunny photography. We were able to visit the Mausoleum of Turkey's first great President Ataturk. Through him Turkey has really come onto her feet and has been much more prosperous. They worship him very much and there are statues and gardens around showing much of what he has done for the country.

We spent the afternoon exploring the Gôreme Valley originally occupied by Christians in the fourth century. It is a volcanic region and one can see the various levels and colours of the lava. The soil is very fertile and many orchards and vineyards thrive very well. The area became a monastic sanctuary because they found that by digging into the rock face making rooms, chapels, etc. they were safe from any caving in of rock and they were very well hidden from any enemies. The volcanic pinnacles and cones are honeycombed with cells and painted churches almost like fairyland! Hundreds of small pigeon holes were along the walls, used to keep pigeons for sending inter-communications. By climbing through tunnels, up and down stairs, we found little churches hidden in the high cliffs. There were frescoes of New Testament pictures painted on the ceilings and walls. They were done in the 8th century and only the high ones have been preserved as gross vandalism has defaced the lower ones. There were some kitchens, dining rooms and store houses and one six storeyed building to house the Nuns and a four storeyed building for the Monks. The churches had odd names such as 'Church of the Apple', 'Church of the Sandal', 'The Dark Church', etc. The peace and quaintness of the surroundings lends itself to a sanctuary away from the hustle and bustle of the world.

We spent the night at Urgup, a few miles further on, a small township also situated in the hillside. We perused the shops and had an enjoyable evening looking at Persian carpets and fine copper ware. We finished off with a display of folk lore dancing in the cellar of our hotel. The music was not melodious as we know it, rather more like a noise on the drums and the dancing steps altered very little. The men were all dressed in national costume and some of us were invited to join in. I had a go, very exhausting but great fun. After having a meal they return your change to you with a toothpick!

To go into more detail about the centre of Ankara to where we then returned. The Ataturk Mausoleum was known as the Quirt Kahir. It stands on a hill and was built between 1944 and 1953. At the entrance are two halls, one of independence, one of liberty, and these have open windows overlooking old and new Ankara. Outside there are statues of three men, a soldier, an ordinary man and a countryman. All have played their part in the independence of Turkey. Opposite them there are statues of three women weeping in sadness over the death of Ataturk. An Avenue of Meditation and Peace leads to the main Hall of Honour. Steps lead up to the Tomb with a sculptured relief on the walls. The ceiling of the Tomb is gold mosaic. Ataturk was most admired and respected for his reforms in Turkey during the early 20th century, e.g. surnames compulsory, Western laws, Western way of dress, votes for women and the veil removed from them. The country was no longer Muslim only. We then looked at the Citadel, some ruins, an excavation of a Roman bath, the Temple of Augustus built on the site of a temple built in the 2nd century B.C. in the Corinthian style with the Hari Bayram Mosque built next door. We had our last Asian meal in a modern restaurant and looked around a modern shopping centre. This was before we left Asia to cross to Europe for three days in Istanbul. We crossed the Bosphorus on a bright day but it is gradually getting colder at this point singing 'Now is the hour to say goodbye to Asia'. The scenery was lovely on our way to the sea passing through pine forests, Lake Sapanca and the Sea of Mormora. We still have no generator for the bus and suddenly we had a hot day and cooked wisely! One of the highlights was a lunch stop on the top of a hill overlooking a huge valley and our first encounter with a snack bar that sold Western food. Hamburger and chips was on the menu – certainly a change and very enjoyable. We very much enjoyed our stay in Istanbul and we had two free days to explore a really lovely city, full of character, charm and history. The people too were really much more friendly toward us. In the morning we went to the Bazaar, world famous for the sale of leather and suede suits, at such prices as twenty dollars for a leather jacket, 33 dollars for a suede suit. We had great fun trying them on but we could not manage to buy unfortunately. The things did not fit as well as they could which helped in resisting the temptation to buy. Many of the tour did purchase quite a few things, goodness knows how they will ever get through the customs. We were fascinated by all the stalls, carpets, jewellery, etc. Unlike all the other bazaars we had seen, this was very orderly and clean. After dinner of typical Turkish food of stuffed tomatoes known as dolmars, we began to explore further. We walked all through the Palace of Topkapi, formerly used by the Sultans and situated in the same peaceful gardens overlooking the Bosphorus Sea and the Asian port of Istanbul. The actual edifice was not particularly striking with its four courtyards but the contents of the rooms were fine quality. The royal kitchens were massive with great iron cauldrons for cooking and a little row of fireplaces over which to cook, hundreds of pieces of crockery of all shapes, sizes and colours hanging all over the walls and cabinets full of fine silverware. There were rooms displaying different items, one has the costumes and robes of the Sultan through the ages, another had jewellery in the form of sabres, coronets, ornate boxes, etc. There were two splendid thrones of low design and large enough to be sat on cross legged. One cabinet had a large diamond set in black velvet surrounded by grey drapes with a spot of light on the centre of the jewel. There was a room of miniatures where books, paintings and manuscripts were displayed with the fine painting of letters, etc. The rest of the rooms had a religious bearing with various things connected with the prophet Mohammed, his cloak, chair, books, etc. After

Photo 50 - Sultan Ahmet's mosque, Istanbul, Turkey.

this we were rather weary and every seat we came to one of our number were sitting!

Once out of the Palace, however, we mustered enough energy and enthusiasm to visit the Sultan Ahmet Mosque or Blue Mosque. It is very famous, possessing all of six minarets and inside all the walls above window and the ceiling were tiled blue. It was beautiful and had a reverent atmosphere about it and a wonderful peace unlike any others we had been in. We met an educated Turk inside who was delighted to tell us how much the Turks thought of Florence Nightingale. They had much more knowledge about her than we did and, in fact, celebrate her birthday every year.

The following day dawned wet but the air was fresh and, although it was pretty muddy paddling through the cobbled streets, it was not enough to keep us in. We walked up to the Sutayuran Mosque which stands in all its grandeur on a hill overlooking the harbour. We had to wind our way around tiny cobbled streets and through market stalls to reach it but it was worth the effort and the climb. The rain looked as if it had set in for the afternoon but we decided to proceed with our plan to take a boat trip up the Bosphorus. We left Istanbul at 1.30pm returning again about 7pm having travelled up as far as the Black Sea. It was a ferry boat and we therefore stopped about every quarter of an hour to drop or collect passengers. It was too hazy to take photographs but we enjoyed what we saw – the various homes, old wooden ones which tilted a little on the water's edge, large ones, almost Queen Ann types, tall thin

ones with overhanging shutters like the Dutch. There were a
few castles and some modern properties with swimming pools
and boat ramps. You can only swim in selected parts of the sea
because of conflicting currents. We saw plenty of fishing
vessels and on reaching the farthest point we were allowed
ashore for one hour. We found ourselves in a small fishing
village and the coloured nets were draped all along the streets
with the boats pulled up high onto the shore because of the
rain storm. It was quite picturesque. We sheltered from the
rain in a café jutting out over the sea. We had a wonderful meal
of fried fish, our first fish for a couple of months. We sat there
until the boat set of again on its return trip.

The coach still lacked its generator but the following day we left
for Greece. It was uneventful getting through the Turkish and
Greek borders. The weather was overcast but comfortable for
travelling. We stayed in a very pleasant hotel overlooking the
beach at Alexandrapolis. We had new double units which
opened out onto the beach. We had a good swim in the Aegean
Sea and a nice view of the islands directly off shore.

GREECE

Sunday 29th June 1969

We left Alexandroupolis today but we would have liked to have
remained to sunbathe and swim in the beautiful clear calm
water. We had a splendid scenic run along the coast passing

many bays with little islands close to the shore, with others farther out all misty and mysterious. We stopped for a couple of hours at Kavalla which used to be called Neapolis. This is a very historic port dominated by ramparts of a Byzantine Fortress and a well preserved Roman aqueduct stretching right across town with little houses built underneath. There are two harbours full of fishing fleets, obviously a large industry, also they export their local grown tobacco. It was here that St Paul landed on his second missionary journey from Troas to Asia Minor by ship.

We then travelled overland to Philippi. It was named after Alexander the Great's father and, of course, it is mentioned in the New Testament, one of the new early Christian churches started there. A great battle was fought here between Brutus, Cassius and army against Mark Anthony and Octavius in 42B.C. to decide the heir to the Roman Empire after Caesar had been brutally murdered. Octavius and Mark Anthony won and they made Philippi very prosperous by settling military and civilian communities there. Brutus and Cassius on finding defeat committed suicide. Among the ruins of various temples and old buildings is the site of St Paul's prison cell. It was here that the first European, Lydia, was christened. Little is heard of Philippi after the 11th century but all along the road are things to remind you of the past history. The Castle and Fortress built by the Crusaders in the eleventh century beneath Mount Olympus, the Lion Monument supposed to be over the tomb of Posidius, a Spartan General killed when trying to capture the

Photo 51 – Ruins of a 5th century A.D. chapel on the site of the Prison of St Paul, Philippi, Greece.

area from the Athenians. At intervals along the road are little altars built by the Greek Orthodox Church to give encouragement to the travellers.

We arrived in the evening at Thessalonica founded in 315B.C. and named after the wife of a general who was sister to Alexandra the Great. It is the capital of Macedonia and northern Greece and has Demetrius as its patron saint. A very busy sea front and port with many ships, a very modern city with some lovely shops and also a dirty industrial area. An obviously progressive town also attractive to tourists with its large promenades and many open-air restaurants. We did a little sightseeing but not too much as evening was drawing in. Along the sea front is a tower called 'The White Tower'. Built in 1430 it once ended the sea front and was a prison. In the gardens surrounding the Tower a brass band was playing some beautiful music. At the end of the programme they played the Greek National Anthem and all the traffic stopped, people walking stood still and people sitting stood up. Quite a change from Britain where many show little respect for the Monarchy. We decided to visit one Greek church and choosing the Church of Sofia we found that a wedding was about to take place. We sneaked in by the side door to se what was going on. The Bride was, of course, , beautifully dressed in white, all the guests were ringed around her with the Groom all talking at once regardless of the fact that the Priest was actually going through the service. Just now and again you could catch some mumbled words coming forth from him. Some of the guests climbed all over the pulpit, in fact on anything handy, in order to have a better view. We saw the church all aglow with chandeliers alight which gave the frescoes a strange appearance. Very colourful but we left before the end. The general impressions of Greece and the Greeks have been good. They seem clean and well mannered after the Asian people. It makes a change not to be stared at wherever you go, to have crowds around you even if you stop for a breather and to feel at ease in the streets. The people are very friendly and helpful, many speak French and German, so in one way or another you can make yourself understood. One thing that makes a difference is the fact that we are more or less out of Muslim countries where women are dirt and men are 'it'. Here the women are respected and treated as normal human beings. They are well dressed and well groomed.

Monday 30th June 1969

After leaving Thessalonica at 8am and managing to find a snack bar for breakfast we travelled on. Elaine had her first glass of milk which she lapped up like a cat with cream. Our next destination was Delphi about 240 miles away. The first part of the journey was on a fast motorway so we made good time through pleasant country via Katerini. We passed by the foothills of Mount Olympus which were blue and too hazy for photographs, though Olympus itself was snow-capped. Of course, many legends of Greek Mythology are connected with it. Passing through the valley of Tempo, the springs of Daphne, Diana and Venus, the river being spanned by a swing bridge, we climbed into the mountainous country again. As we wound higher and higher we looked back at the town called Lauria which was once an important port but the Gulf waters have receded and it now lies quite a few miles from the sea. It was easy enough to imagine though. A great deal of road construction was on the way but we continued to cross the range of mountains, through the colourful villages, through olive groves, almost down to sea level again at the Bay of Corinth. Then up high we climbed to Delphi. A very picturesque town, not much bigger than a village, perched on the rocky slopes of Mount Parnassus with the River Pleistos winding its way through the valley to the Gulf. Created as a perfect setting for mystery and religious prophecy. Here Apollo spoke through a medium of a Priestess called Pythia. People came from all over the world to ask questions. Pythia used to go into a trance in the inner shrine of Apollo's temple chewing bay leaves and swooning over the fumes of a hemp fire. Then in a kind of fit she uttered strange words which were later translated by Prophets and other Holy Men. The Temple grew rich and was subsequently plundered and, with the advent of Christianity, paganism was outlawed by Theodosius in 381. Our first impressions were one of delight. Little whitewashed homes connected by the main street by large steps suitable for donkeys and mules as well as humans. Flower boxes neatly arranged on either side of the steps rather like Clovelly. The whole town overlooked a big valley with the Gulf of Corinth always in view. Our hotel had a restaurant balcony overlooking all this. We wish we could have spent a week there with the beauty and the peace. The shops were gaily decorated with national goods of woven materials, furs, stone craft, metal ware, etc. On the first evening we simply wandered around the streets breathing the fresh clean air, enjoying the beauty and meeting the people.

Tuesday 1st July 1969

We decided to do our tour of the Delphi ruin early before the heat of the day. They are situated on the mountain slopes. We passed through the Roman Agora, the remains of various offering quarters, the treasury houses, one standing in almost perfect condition, the treasury of the Athenians. Gradually climbing up the steps you come to the remains of the tall pillars of the Temple of Apollo. Overlooking the Temple is the Theatre and above that way up, hidden amongst the trees, is a huge stadium. This was in excellent condition complete with starting line. One could imagine the great athletes competing with crowds sitting on the stone steps and seats cheering them on. It was here the Pythian Games were held, second in importance to the Olympic ones. Returning down the hill we saw a waterfall and the Castalian Spring which is supposed to be sacred water said to echo the inspired voices of Apollo's muses. We were rather hot and thirsty so we had a drink but I cannot say we were really inspired. Farther down in the valley were further archaeological discoveries, the Gymnasium and the circular Temple of the Marmaria. A quick browse around the Museum and the morning was gone. It was time for dinner and then we left Delphi at 1pm.

We had an afternoon drive to Athens across the mountains. Athens, of course, being the capital is very large with old and new areas. Our hotel was reasonably central which was an advantage for sightseeing all around. Food was very expensive with a good percentage service charge even for serving a cake. Making our way to the Square of Ommonia there were coloured fountains playing. Then we took a taxi to the top of the hill on which the famous Acropolis stands. We watched a lovely 'Son et Lumiere' here in the evening. It showed the history of the Acropolis and Greek mythology. The lighting effects were most impressive and certainly captured the atmosphere, the dialogue was good. We mustered up the energy and walked back to the hotel calling in at a café en route for a drink. With the illuminated Acropolis towering over us it was a splendid sight.

Wednesday 2nd July 1969

We had a good roam around Athens all in one day. There was so much to see we didn't know where to start. We began by walking through the main streets via Ommonia Square, down by the open market stalls to the foot of the Acropolis. We then meandered through a lot of winding streets where we found many interesting old shops selling everything you could possibly think of; the materials and antiques were nice. We visited the Greek Orthodox Cathedral which had lovely frescoes on the wall above the main portal. The inside was very ornate, rather heavy decoration similar to the Roman Catholics. In the shadows of the Cathedral is a tiny little church called St Elifthemos, possibly the oldest in Athens and at one time the Cathedral, the smallest in the world. Another church we saw was one of the Apostles called the Kapinkarea Church, again small and ornate and very old but well cared for. We then climbed the hill to the Acropolis on the way seeing two of the ancient theatres: 1. The Theatre of Herod Atticus; 2. The Theatre of Dronysis. They were both built in the slopes of the massive rock on which the Acropolis stands. The theatres were well preserved with their semi-circular stone seats. One has to be modernised and is used for Athenian drama production. The Acropolis is the ancient citadel of Athens built about 447B.C. under the inspiration of Pericles to the glory of their protecting goddess who had brought them victory over the Medes and Persians two generations before. She was supposed to be responsible for placing Greece on top of the world victorious. Entered by the Beula Gate one climbs high shiny well-trodden steps and we met hundreds of tourists. This was our first real encounter with lots of tourists as most of the other countries were out of the holiday season. The mass of people all climbing and talking rather took the atmosphere away, yet it was an impressive sight, nevertheless. There was once a statue of Athena with a sword in her hand directly opposite the entrance. Various pillars remain indicating various rooms, etc. but the main one is the Parthenon which is a gigantic temple built for Athena seventeen columns on either side of the building, eight columns top and bottom, each column 35 feet high. Little wonder it was so impressive against the skyline. During the centuries the Parthenon has been used as a Christian chapel, a harem, Pasha's Palace and a Turkish Arsenal. It remained complete until Doge Morosini of Venice fired a cannon ball in 1687 in order to try and capture Athens. The sun beat down upon us so we were thankful for the Museum to go around in the cool. It mainly contained pieces of sculpture and utensils found amongst the ruins. One part of the area which has remained reasonably intact is the Caryatids which are six pillars sculptured in female form. These are situated on the side of the Erechtheion, a group of porticoes dedicated to the god of Erechtheus. From the Acropolis we had a magnificent view over old and new Athens stretching out to sea. A heat haze limited the taking of photography. We could distinguish the Gardens, the Parliament House, a view of the remaining pillars of the Temple of Zeus and also over an area known as Agora. This was in fact the market area where we had previously walked, literally it means where people bargain and talk. This is where Socrates did his teaching of philosophy. By this time a cold drink of beer and some chips was the order of the day as it was too hot to think. Revived we walked back to street level

Photo 52 - The Parthenon, Athens, Greece.

under the Arch of Hades by the stadium where the first Olympic Games were held, by the Royal Palace which is guarded by soldiers in national costume, white pleated skirts, white stockings, black garters and pointed shoes with large pom poms on them. We then had a picnic lunch in the gardens before walking back to the hotel via the main shopping area, past the Museum and University where they have some fine sculptured figures outside of learned men. About 3pm we arrived back to our rooms where Elaine promptly fell asleep for two hours while I rested.

In the evening we caught the underground train to the foot of the Acropolis, walked up the hill to the theatre where we saw a magnificent display of Greek Folk Dancing. Performed in all different costumes from various parts of Greece, the Islands, Macedonia, and the Black Sea area. It was surprising how varied they were, some had a Russian and Turkish flavour. At one stage there were 64 dancers on the stage vividly dressed under the spotlights in the cool night air. Most impressive and enjoyable but we were glad to get to sleep being rather footsore and weary. On leaving the theatre I caught my little toe on someone's shoe and bent it backwards. It was very painful but I managed to walk back alright.

Thursday 3rd July 1969

Well, off we go again and it is very hot. The generator is now mended in 'Wurzle' but the air blowers do not do much for us in the heat. We drove by some beautiful beaches, calm, cool, clean water. We would have loved to stop and have a swim but we had to get going as we had 300 miles to cover. Leaving Athens at 8am we drove on the main motorway which stretches pretty well the whole length of Greece along the coast. Sometimes we were at the water's edge, sometimes in the mountains, otherwise in the valleys – an attractive drive. Some of the resorts looked so peaceful it tempted us to return for a holiday sometime. Walking on my foot is not easy just now and my toe is very bruised and swollen.

We arrived in Thessalonica at 5pm and stayed at the same hotel as before so we feel quite at home. Then we were leaving Greece which made us sad, we had loved every minute and been very relaxed. Crossing the border was no bother. In fact, we were out of Greece and into Yugoslavia in three quarters of an hour, quite a record. We had to fill out the usual identity cards which we have done about fifty times before.

We had a pleasant drive through vivid green farming land and hills. There are flags everywhere hanging from windows and in all the buildings. Without really knowing the background you can sense immediately that this has been an oppressed country for years having been in the hands of the Turks, Romans, Germans, who left various symbolic things behind them in the buildings but little else. We noticed that the highways were excellent, more soldiers were in evidence. On approaching Skopje, one of the biggest towns in Yugoslavia, we were shown the new area where all the buildings are uniform, mass produced flats all rather monotonous, as opposed to the old part with its ancient citadel and a Turkish Mosque with its pointed minaret and many old houses, the River Vardar running between the old and the new. We were interested to see the effects of the 1963 earthquake. There are cracks down the new buildings, some older ones toppled over at an angle. The old station clock has been left at 4.20am when the earthquake took place.

We met a very nice young man who helped us order our dinner from a modern restaurant and afterwards he walked around town with us. He was a Primary School Teacher on holiday. He has taught himself English in one year by the Linguaphone method and he is waiting for a work permit to come to England to work in the Shaftesbury Handicapped Children's Home. He seemed to enjoy the talk with us trying his English out and learning as much as he could about living in England. We, in turn, learned much about how the Yugoslav's think – e.g. nothing about the Turks is good – that, on the whole, they are a solemn, deep thinking people. He said that he had been told that when he gets to England never to mention where he is from because of political differences – presumably the communism. There is no doubt about it you can feel the undercurrent of communistic control. By the way, we now have to pay when visiting public toilets so we have all voted to return to 'Bush Stops!' We then drove to Nis where we stayed for the two nights. A horrible town full of dark grey square blocks of flats, most unattractive. We have not bothered to do too much walking around and anyway my small toe was very bruised and swollen still. We had a thunderstorm on arrival which cleared the air. Outside the bedroom window was a shrubbery of trees which looked so green and fresh after the rain. Historically speaking I think Nis has been the centre of many conflicts as there are Museums full of cultural and historical displays, a Concentration Camp and also a Tower of Skulls which were fitted into the rock. We decided not to go in as we felt it was rather horrible, obviously the ends of a massacre of types. In fact, the native Serbians rebelled against the Turks, they were far outnumbered and killed, 900 of them were beheaded and all the skulls are cemented into the concrete as a warning to others not to contemplate rebelling. From Nis we travelled via Belgrade to our next night's stop at Zagreb. It was a pleasantly warm day for driving. We had a fleeting look at Belgrade as in the old part no coaches are allowed to park within the city radius. You can park outside and walk in but our time was too short. Originally Belgrade meant 'White City' but although it was interesting in parts, especially the old buildings, the same dull concrete buildings seemed to predominate again which is not too surprising as it had been destroyed 28 times. As you cross the River Sava over a large span bridge it is possible to see where it enters the River Danube. In the middle of the old city stands the huge Citadel of Kalemegdan on a 200 foot cliff, the only historical reminder of the city that once was. It is flanked by huge walls, a strange mixture of architecture in the citadel can be seen even from a

Photo 53 - A farmer with bullock drawn cart, Nis, Yugoslavia.

distance, different periods and countries of occupation at the time have added more. On the far side of the river a new city is being built consisting of rows of tall white blocks of flats, also large Government buildings are growing to replace the somewhat drab edifices of the old town. We paused in the new town at a cafeteria for coffee.

At Zagreb we found ourselves just outside the city at a beautiful motel. Elaine and I were allocated to a two bed chalet and there was camping accommodation also, but Carol, Sue, Marie and Claire found they were in a six bed chalet so we moved in with them. It was 'A' plan and there were four beds on the floor and two in the loft and also the beam supporting the loft floor was almost cracked through. When Sue turned over there were loud creaks but no major calamities. The facilities otherwise were excellent with constant running hot water for showers, etc. On arrival Sue, Carol and I went for a walk whilst Elaine joined the others in partaking in a swim in the lake by the camping ground. They all shared a bottle of wine with a good steak dinner eaten sitting out in the open. We began to feel like tourists again as there were cars from many different countries parked at the motel. We kept meeting them along the road too, almost building up queues again. The next day which was Sunday 6th July we crossed the border into Italy with very little problem. They did not even stamp our passports on the Italian side, they just came into the coach to make sure we were each holding one. We drove through pleasant undulating country and some forest to the coast and Trieste for dinner. A bright seaside town with a harbour full of ships of all shapes and sizes, cargo cruisers, sailing and rowing boats. The main buildings of Government, etc. were in a square opposite the sea front which was colourfully decorated with flags guarding the entrance and pigeons sitting all over the cobbled paving stones in the centre. We then had a bite to eat in a restaurant off the square and were horrified with the price of the bill for what we had; a bowl of soup at 250 lira and service charge at 250 lira with a charge on use of cutlery, cloth, etc. 50 lira. We decided after that that we would be slimming drastically in Italy! We consoled ourselves by buying off a barrow an ice cream which was full of fruits and nuts, a real Italian ice cream. We climbed high above Trieste in the coach on the way to Venice and had some beautiful views of the Adriatic Bays and holiday resorts, some of the homes were really lovely.

About 4pm we found ourselves crossing the bridge and crossing the railway, the only way to Venice. We left the coach at the coach station and carrying our luggage went down a tiny passage and found ourselves crossing a bridge and the first of the canals. I had been there before and, although there were changes, the place still had a charm for me and Elaine fell in love with it too. We crossed about three bridges before we reached the hotel area. The hotel booked by the tour was rather expensive so, together with about 50% of the passengers, we elected to find our own. Whilst Elaine collected the post, etc. Carol, Sue and I went hunting returning very quickly having found a suitable place. Down a lane beside the hotel we had found two double rooms beautifully clean with a bath at less than half the hotel price. We quickly refreshed ourselves as we were eager to explore some more. Many people don't like Venice because it is so touristy, rather old and dilapidated and the canals smell sometimes but somehow it was insignificant to the lovely atmosphere of the place, after all tourism is their livelihood. The city itself is gradually sinking below the water and the foundations are crumbling and the general expectancy of its survival is about fifty years. It is difficult to express on paper the charming atmosphere, colours and beauty. There is one main canal running through the centre, wide and flanked by large impressive buildings. Off the canal there are lots of smaller ones, like secondary roads, where the houses are very close in apposition and then even smaller ones wide enough for only one gondola. The houses are in various states of dilapidation but it does not seem to matter, flowers bloom brightly from their window boxes. Everything moves by canal. If you want to catch a bus it is a boat and the same with the police, ambulance, freight, taxis, etc. In between the canals there are lanes where all the shops and restaurants are, only wide enough for pedestrians. It is a joy not to have to worry about traffic and it is so peaceful without it. Elaine and I wandered around, got quite lost, but found ourselves by a quaint back street restaurant overlooking the canal. There we quietly enjoyed our evening meal. Re-fuelled, we then found our way back but it was still such a lovely clear night that we decided to walk in the opposite direction. We walked to the

Rialto Bridge and from the top we stood gazing at the canal, all dark except for the odd lantern. Then round the corner came three gondolas with little lights bobbing in front. One of the gondoliers was singing in his deep rich voice and it sounded just wonderful. Returning to our room we fell into bed tired and happy.

The following day dawned bright and we enjoyed hot expresso coffee and a ham roll for breakfast before setting forth on our day of sightseeing. This was our last free day of the tour and it was hard to believe. We took the Express Boat Service to the Rialto Bridge but could not see anything en route as it was packed out with the daily commuters. At the Rialto Bridge we wandered through the very colourful market stalls which sold absolutely everything, great bunches of colourful scarves and hats, the most enormous peaches I have almost never seen, not to mention the leather and shoe shops. From the Bridge we wandered through the magnificent narrow lanes fascinated by the beautiful clothing shops on either side and spectacular displays of Venetian glass ware. We found ourselves in St Mark's Square which was full of pigeons, people feeding them and tourists wandering everywhere in various modes of dress. Elaine went into St Mark's Cathedral. I had been there previously and in order for her to cover her shoulders she used the only scarf we had. It is very dark inside, so she said, but there were plenty of candles and lights burning to show up the most important parts, the carvings, the stained glass windows and the frescoes on the ceiling. Afterwards we went to a small glass factory and watched a specimen vase made by glass blowing over a hot furnace and then we wandered around fascinated by the magnificent pieces for sale of all shapes and sizes but all rather expensive. The main part of the glass making is performed on the Island of Murano easily visible from the sea front.

In one corner of St Mark's square adjacent to the water's edge is the Doge's Palace adjoining the Basilica of San Marco, a very ornate building from the outside. Inside it is obviously well built, solid in appearance, thick stone staircases and walls with overlying wood carved panelling on some parts and some of the walls and ceilings in the great halls have some magnificent frescoes recalling the proud days of the Republic. The Armoury had a fine display of armour and weapons together with several portraits of famous Italian leaders all adorned in full ceremonial and battle dress. From the window of the Palace there are some picturesque views. The windows are all large casements with stone seats in front and it would not be difficult to imagine the occupants of the Palace sitting and pondering over Venice here. Scenes across the closely adjacent red tiled roof tops looking down on the narrow canal running under the Bridge of Sighs or out to the Gulf of Venice with the ever changing moods of the sea and the gondolas being tossed unrhythmically by the waves. On to San Marco Square which I should imagine has always been a hive of activity now full of tourists, umbrellas, dining tables, of orchestras playing romantic and classical favourites, so much in keeping with the whole atmosphere of

Venice. After finishing the tour of the cultural beauty we were brought back to reality as we descended the winding stone steps into the Dungeons. We followed the steps of the prisoners who as they crossed the bridge used to sigh as they knew they would never retrace their steps but end their lives in the cold dark prisons on the other side. Thus the Bridge of Sighs was named. Nearby is a tall tower which we ascended by elevator, the Campanillo Tower. From the top we had a clear view over all the square and surrounding buildings as well as out to sea with all the little islands. The Campanillo is a bell tower and unusually stands apart from the churches. After a quick snack meal we took a ferry boat across the Gulf of Venice to the Lido. This is so different since I saw it some years ago. It is very expensive and very commercialised. There are roads and cars here as opposed to the city itself. The very typical Italian restaurants line the streets and look very gay. We walked the width of the Lido to the Marino side where swimming is allowed on the open sea but all the beaches were roped off and too expensive so we left it. For a whole day it would be fine but for a couple of hours we decided against it. We decided to have a drink and both of us had our hair trimmed. Our return to Venice was delightful. We took a slow ferry that stopped at all the landing stages up the Grand Canal and we had plenty of time to fully appreciate the beauty of the houses all bedecked with window boxes of geraniums. The fact is the houses have sunk on their foundations, the people are in fact living on the second floor instead of the ground and first floors. How busy the canals are with traders, of how comparatively clear the water was considering how littered the streets become. In the evening we were joined by Carol and Sue for dinner with wine and perhaps the last chance to really relax and recall the most outstanding parts of the journey. A pleasant evening was enjoyed by all though afterwards slightly dampened by Cherry being taken by canal boat ambulance to Hospital with appendicitis or ovarian cyst. We had been through so much together as a party with cold once again after our heat that it was like losing part of the family.

Taking our cases back over the little bridges we found our 'Wurzle' (coach) waiting for us. Leaving the city of waterways behind us we travelled across the north of Italy, everywhere looked green and fresh and we found ourselves climbing slowly up into the mountains. Panoramic views are all around us of mountains, villages and lakes with beautiful reflections. It was so nice not to have to absorb historical facts but just sit back and enjoy the simplicity of nature and God's creation. As we climbed higher up the Alps the weather got more and more overcast but somehow we did not mind. Rain began to fall. We stopped at an Italian ski resort for dinner and found everyone clad in trousers, anoraks and thick boots. Climbing out of 'Wurzle' in our summer clothes and thongs we realised how sensible they were but there was little we could do as we had not been able to have our suitcases out for seven days. Making the most of feeling cold once again after our tour in temperatures of 115 degrees, never to complain again we began a brisk walk around the town. Those who were flushed with money went to the nearest restaurant whilst the majority of us found a local grocers and pooling our resources bought rolls, cheese, salami and chocolate. We sat in the archway of the Post Office devouring lunch wishing we had enough Italian lira for a cup of coffee. It was obviously a very popular resort as there were plenty of hotels and smaller places to stay, also an Olympic ski jump and skating rink.

We then descended a little in altitude as we sped towards the Austrian border and the Brenner Pass. It was not long before we found ourselves surrounded by the great towering snow covered peaks of the Alps. There was a general feeling of excitement as in some places snow could be seen falling on the mountainside. The Brenner Pass is the pass through the Alps most frequented as it is the lowest one to go through at the height of 4,495 feet. Originally it was called the 'Valley of the Trent Route'. It is known as the Gateway to Italy and has been traversed by various peoples since as far back as 800B.C. Today right from the border of Austria massive roadworks are under construction making the pass an Autobahn all through as far as Innsbruck at the other end. In some places large fly-overs have been constructed and, although travelling along straight roads for long distances is monstrous, from our height we had impressive views of the villages below and the meandering road of the Brenner pass. As we approached Innsbruck the rain was pouring down and we could no longer see the mountain tops and the town looked grey and rather miserable. We did

Photo 54 – The village of Gries near Innsbruck, Austria.

not stay in the hotel but joined Carol and Sue in finding a more typical Austrian abode. We found a small tourist Gasthof in the quaint old part of the town with a few rooms at the back of the café. For a third of the price of the hotel we had a huge six bedded room, spotlessly clean, true to Austrian style, with hot water, etc. and the comfort of huge eiderdowns.

It was too wet and fresh to bother about sightseeing but we enjoyed the friendly atmosphere of the place. We found a hotel in the old part where we had dinner of Weiner Schnitzel followed by Apple Strudel. Having eaten far too much we snuggled into bed. 'Into' being the word as it was practically the first time we had slept covered up. Setting our alarm for 5am was the only way of getting up in time to have a look around the town but before taking the final plunge we put our heads out of the window to see if the weather warranted an early rise. Pleasantly surprised by the dry fresh clear morning we watched the sunrise over the snow capped mountains. We saw the people busily rushing around with milk cans and opening up the shops. We found a little tiny back street dairy where we enjoyed rich fresh milky coffee and a cheese roll for breakfast. The girl who served us had a lovely face, clear skin, fresh cheeks and such smiling eyes. It all fitted together to give us a really fresh happy start to the day.

We were soon tucked up in the coach at 7.30am for a long day's drive to Heidelberg. We were on the motorways throughout with few stops at all. The countryside was enjoyable, though the persistent rain did spoil a little of the beauty of the Bavarian forests and mountains. It was interesting to travel through the Austrian skiing resorts like Worgl and Oberan and see them without snow. Elaine remembers them from her skiing holiday in 1960. Most people in the coach were hurriedly trying to finish the last chapter of their borrowed books. It was 6pm before we reached Heidelberg and we were looking forward to stretching our legs, sightseeing, followed by a farewell dinner for the whole party. Our plans were dashed as on arrival we found that there was no accommodation available at the hotel. Some of the party found beds in nearby Gasthofs but seventeen of us were left without anywhere. The only solution was to go out of town which meant that we would have to forget the dinner, sightseeing, etc. and that was Heidelberg as far as we were concerned. We were escorted by our coach driver, Mike, to a little village about six miles from Heidelberg along the river. We soon made ourselves comfortable in our little Pensione and I do not think the village knew what had hit them because we were determined to have a good time in spite of the disappointment. We found a little hotel and commandeered a corner of the dining room and there we sat until 11pm filling our hungry stomachs with good food and tasting the German beer. We talked and played games and sang and a good time was had by all. The landlady had a tremendous sense of humour and fully entered into the spirit of things getting us all organised with spooning out the soup, etc. with second helpings on the house.

At 7.30am the following day we were on the road again, having collected the rest of our party from the other part of town. Another day was spent on motorways, how monotonous they are. The scenery was flat and mostly farmland and there was plenty of traffic on the road. We stopped at Koln for dinner and a quick look around the cathedral which was partly hidden by scaffolding and massive road projects all round. The day in the coach was spent exchanging addresses, finding out plans and destinations of various people, drawing maps of guidance, a general return of books to owners, together with a mass clearance of luggage racks which were full of purchases and thermos flasks. The weather remained wet and depressing and all the Australians could say, plus a few English returning home, was, "Well, what do you expect in this part of the world? After all, England never has any sun!" About six we arrived in Brussels to find yet again no accommodation at the hotel we had booked at. Someone had apparently said that our tour was a day behind schedule and the bookings were cancelled. However, accommodation was eventually secured and we began the task of going through our luggage squeezing in extra purchases as unobtrusively as possible in case of customs queries. With four people squashed into rooms made for two, plus luggage and unpacking, you can imagine the mess. After the luggage it was a case of hair washing and general clean up session. Many of us did not sleep well, we were all too excited. We were up at 6am for 7am departure and I do not think any of us have been more ready to go. We bade farewell to Afra and

Photo 55 – The white cliffs of Dover seen from the English Channel.

Lennie who were catching the train from Brussels to their homes in Holland. We had our last ride in 'Wurzle' who we had become very attached to. It took about one and a half hours to reach Ostend and still the skies were black and the rain kept falling. All the cases were taken from the coach and piled together on the porters' trolleys. We thanked Mike, our driver for all his care and said goodbye to Margaret, the Courier's fiancé. 'Wurzle' was to be driven back to his home town Wurzburg near Heidelberg. The rest of us joined the 9.30am ferry from Ostend to Dover. We had a really calm crossing and as we progressed across the Channel the weather improved so that we reached the white cliffs of Dover in bright sunshine. After everyone's sarcastic comments about England she really turned up trumps. We had no difficulty in getting through Customs as our Courier got us through without anyone being stopped. Elaine and I were met by our mothers who were very excited to see their long lost daughters again. Angela, Pamela and Sue were also met at Dover while the rest of the group boarded a coach and made for their final destination in London.

I can honestly say that we have had a full and exciting time with plenty of troubles and joys. God has never failed us. We have proved His faithfulness in all circumstances and we are stronger in Him.

Patricia E. Sandys.

Appendix One

Penn Tour No 351

Name	Occupation	Home
Mike	Driver	Hereford, U.K.
Travers Cox	Courier	Brisbane, Australia
Margaret	Courier's Fiancé	Germany
Colin Sale	Geography Teacher	Australia
Maxine Sale	Biology Teacher	
Lawrence Stack	Ex Forester	U.S.A.
Maureen Stack	Retired	
Stan Reed	Botanist (World authority)	New Zealand
Jean Reed	Educationalist	
Mrs Walker	Social Teacher	Adelaide, Australia
Barbara	Hotel Receptionist	
Miss Daly	Cook	Melbourne, Australia
Diana	Secretary	
June Miller	Secretary	U.S.A.
Miss Thomas	Ex Teacher	U.S.A.
Eric Short	Psychiatrist	U.K.
Sharon	English Teacher	Canada
John (tall)	Pharmacist	Australia
John (ginger)	Lay Preacher	Australia
Angela	Radiologist	U.K.
Pamela Warren	Lab Technician	U.K.
Afra	Lab Technician	Holland
Lennie	Lab Technician	Holland
Doreen	Occupational Therapists	U.K.
Margaret	Occupational Therapists	U.K.
Tricia	Secretary	Melbourne, Australia
Mary	Secretary	Melbourne, Australia
Jenny	Nurse	New Guinea

Anna	Lab Technician	Scotland, U.K.
Lyn	Food Analysis	U.K.
Hazel	Factory Work	U.K.
Helen	Degree in French	New Zealand
Carol	Optometrist	U.K.
Sue Black	Nurse	U.K.
Jenny Crabb	Nurse	Scotland, U.K.
Frances	Touring Asia	U.S.A.
Carol	Pharmacist	U.K.
Barry	Accountant	Australia
Chris	Anything!	Switzerland
Conrad	Electrician	German
Jim	Radiologist	Canada
Marie Hancock	Nurse	Australia
Claire O'Dea	Nurse	Australia
Jean Allen	Left tour in India	U.K.
Mike Allen	Left tour in India	U.K.
Elaine Barton	Nurse	U.K.
Pat Sandys	Nurse	U.K.

Appendix Two

List of Photographs

Photo 1 – Elaine, David & Rosemary and me by a pyramid in Egypt.
Photo 2 – The flat in Adelaide.
Photo 3 – Donna, the car, second-hand but sturdy and strong.
Photo 4 – Robe Sands, South Australia.
Photo 5 – A Kookaburra bird.
Photo 6 – Elaine at the entrance to the cave at Talia.
Photo 7 – A boxing match with a kangaroo at the Fauna Animal Reserve in South Australia. They are very strong!
Photo 8 – Elaine on the 'Wave Rock' at Hyden Rock.
Photo 9 – Me on the Jaws of Death in the Grampian Mountains
Photo 10 – The McKenzie Falls in the Grampian Mountains.
Photo 11 - Staff at Alexandra District Hospital, Victoria, Australia. Irene Turnbull, Matron, John Macdonald, Surgeon, Norma Price, Nurse and Raymond Young, Anaesthetist. The doctors were from the UK.
Photo 12 – The Fairy Penguins landing at dusk on Phillip Island, Victoria.
Photo 13 – Sydney Harbour with the Bridge and Opera House.
Photo 14 – The Billy Graham Crusade in Sydney where Elaine and I sang in the Crusade Choir.
Photo 15 – Elaine with Donna in the snow on Mount Buller.
Photo 16 – Feeding the dolphins.
Photo 17 – Feeding the birds at the Bird Sanctuary on the Gold Coast.
Photo 18 – Butterfly Fish on the Great Barrier Reef, Green Island, Queensland.

Photo 19 – Me with some Aborigine children at the Lutheran Mission.

Photo 20 – Ayers Rock in the Northern territory.

Photo 21 - Nursing in North East Soldiers' Memorial Hospital, Scottsdale, Tasmania. Back Row Left to Right: Myself, Carol Jay, Jean Borman, Joan Chugs, Elaine, Ann Chibbett. Front Row Left to Right: Liz Pullin, Matron Smith, Ann Winter.

Photo 22 – Christchurch, South Island, New Zealand.

Photo 23 - Lake Pukaki & Mount Cook, South Island, New Zealand.

Photo 24 – A Kiwi in New Zealand.

Photo 25 - The Harbour, Wellington, North Island, New Zealand.

Photo 26 - Mahuia Rapids & Mt Ngauruhoe, New Zealand.

Photo 27 - Geyser in Rotorua, North Island, New Zealand.

Photo 28 - The Canoi Poi Maori Dancers, North Island, New Zealand.

Photo 29 – Tai Pak Floating Restaurant, Hong Kong.

Photo 30 - Funicular Railway, Hong Kong Island.

Photo 31 – The Emerald Buddha Temple, Bangkok, Thailand.

Photo 32 - Floating Fruit Market, Bangkok, Thailand.

Photo 33 - Children Thai Dancers, Thailand in Miniature Land, Bangkok, Thailand.

Photo 34 – Hindu Temple, Calcutta, India.

Photo 35 - Children outside a Timber Shop, Calcutta, India.

Photo 36 – On Indian-Nepalese border.

Photo 37 - Street scene with mother and child, Kathmandu, Nepal.

Photo 38 - Holy Man meditates under the umbrella, Benares, India.

Photo 39 - Me on a rickshaw, Benares, India.

Photo 40 – Taj Mahal, Agra, India.

Photo 41 - Riding on an elephant down the hill with Indian music, Amber, India.

Photo 42 – Sikh wheat grinders, the greatest wheat producers in India, near Amritsar, India.

Photo 43 - Entrance to the Golden Temple, Amritsar, India.

Photo 44 – Kabul Reservoir in Afghanistan.

Photo 45 – The Mosque, Mashed, Iran.

Photo 46 - Children making Persian carpets, Isfahan, Iran.

Photo 47 - Women & Children, Isfahan, Iran.

Photo 48 – Kurdish women & children in a hill village
near Erzurum, Turkey.

Photo 49 - Poppies & wild flowers near Erzurum, Turkey.

Photo 50 - Sultan Ahmet's mosque, Istanbul, Turkey.

Photo 51 – Ruins of a 5th century A.D. chapel on the site of the Prison of St Paul, Philippi, Greece.

Photo 52 - The Parthenon, Athens, Greece.

Photo 53 - A farmer with bullock drawn cart, Nis, Yugoslavia.

Photo 54 – The village of Gries near Innsbruck, Austria.

Photo 55 – The white cliffs of Dover seen from the English Channel.